THE EUROPEAN IN INDIA
OR
Anglo-Indian's Vade-Mecum

THE EUROPEAN IN INDIA

OR

Anglo-Indian's Vade-Mecum

A HANDBOOK OF USEFUL AND PRACTICAL INFORMATION FOR THOSE PROCEEDING TO OR RESIDING IN THE EAST INDIES, RELATING TO

Outfits, Routes, Time for Departure, Indian Climate and Seasons, Housekeeping, Servants, etc., Etc.

Also an Account of
Anglo-Indian Social Customs and Native Character

EDMUND C. P. HULL

TO WHICH IS ADDED A
MEDICAL GUIDE
FOR
ANGLO-INDIANS

R. S. MAIR

THIRD EDITION WITH ADDITIONS

GYAN

Published by

GYAN

Gyan Publishing House
5, Ansari Road
Daryaganj, New Delhi-110002
Phone: 011-47034999, 9811692060
E-mail: books@gyanbooks.com

Distribution Network
gyanbooks.com
India, USA, Canada, UK, Australia, France

ISBN : 978-81-212-3369-9 (PB)
First Published, London, 1878

2nd Impression 2020

Printed at: Gyan Press, Delhi.

The
European in India
Authors: E. C. P. Hull & R. S. Mair

THE EUROPEAN IN INDIA;

OR,

Anglo-Indian's Vade-Mecum.

A HANDBOOK OF USEFUL AND PRACTICAL INFORMATION FOR THOSE PROCEEDING TO OR RESIDING IN THE EAST INDIES, RELATING TO

Outfits, Routes, Time for Departure, Indian Climate and Seasons, Housekeeping, Servants, etc., etc.;

ALSO AN ACCOUNT OF

ANGLO-INDIAN SOCIAL CUSTOMS AND NATIVE CHARACTER.

BY

EDMUND C. P. HULL,

Author of "Coffee, its Physiology, History, and Cultivation."

TO WHICH IS ADDED A

MEDICAL GUIDE FOR ANGLO-INDIANS,

BEING A COMPENDIUM OF ADVICE TO EUROPEANS IN INDIA, RELATING TO THE PRESERVATION AND REGULATION OF THEIR HEALTH. GIVING ALSO PLAIN AND COMPLETE INSTRUCTIONS FOR THE TREATMENT OF THE MORE PREVALENT, SUDDEN, AND DANGEROUS INDIAN DISEASES, FOR THE USE OF THOSE BEYOND THE REACH OF MEDICAL ADVICE, AND OF OTHERS IN CASE OF EMERGENCY UNTIL MEDICAL ADVICE CAN ARRIVE. TO WHICH IS ADDED A SUPPLEMENT ON THE MANAGEMENT OF CHILDREN IN INDIA DURING INFANCY AND CHILDHOOD.

BY

R. S. MAIR, M.D., F.R.C.S.E.,

Late Deputy Coroner of Madras.

THIRD EDITION, WITH ADDITIONS.

LONDON:

C. KEGAN PAUL & CO., 1, PATERNOSTER SQUARE.

1878.

TO

HIS GRACE THE DUKE OF ARGYLL, K.T., P.C.,

ETC., ETC.,

(LATE) HER MAJESTY'S SECRETARY OF STATE FOR INDIA;

THIS VOLUME IS,

By Permission,

MOST RESPECTFULLY DEDICATED.

PREFACE TO THE FIRST EDITION.

AMONG the first persons I met upon returning home last summer, from a residence of fifteen years in Ceylon and different parts of India, were two near relatives, themselves about to go out to India. It was, therefore, natural that there should prove to be many subjects upon which I found myself in a position to give them information and advice; and such were the circumstances which suggested to me the idea, at a time when I was temporarily released from the harness of regular occupation, of writing a work, to serve as a compendium of practical hints relating to daily life in India, for the use of that important class who year by year go out to swell the ranks of the Anglo-Indian community.

The young European, on receiving an Indian appointment, is in the majority of cases beset by a variety of doubts and anxieties, which it is not easy to set at rest. He feels himself about to set out on a pilgrimage, regarding which he is necessarily very ignorant, and naturally feels impelled to look round for information, (1) as to the outfit he should provide himself with; (2) as to the route he should take; (3) the time to set out; or, if unable to regulate the time, (4) the season he is likely to meet with in India, when he gets there; and so on almost *ad infinitum*. Probably he comes across people who have had some experience of Indian life, and picks up a little information from one and another ; but owing to the looseness of these scraps, and the divergence sure to be met with in the hastily expressed opinions of a number of different persons, he finds himself as much bewildered as ever, if not more so.

At this period, too, Indian life assumes for him an interest, which (although if *obliged* to do so, he might wait for an experimental knowledge) he will be glad to satisfy at once, on an opportunity being presented. And even after he arrives in India, every European finds himself surrounded by a state of things probably quite different from the picture formed in his imagination, and in every respect strange and new ; and at once sees, that there are numberless details in matters of everyday life, with regard to which judicious advice, explanation, or warning, would impart to him confidence and protection.

As far as I am aware, there is no book yet published which assumes to fill the void created by this state of things. "The English-woman in India," published some years ago, though containing many useful hints to ladies, is somewhat curt and limited in scope ; while the ordinary hand-books, though interesting as guides to places, and diffuse in descriptions of locality, do not pretend to take the place with regard to everyday life, which is the object of the present work.

All these considerations I have kept carefully in view throughout, having recalled to memory my own feelings when I first went out to the East in 1855.

Commencing with the subject of outfits, the following pages will be found to treat of routes, first impressions on landing, climate, servants, housekeeping, travelling and a variety of other subjects.

Some space is devoted to a description of native

character and manners, under the conviction, that a knowledge on these points is indispensable to all who would cultivate the natives' esteem and confidence, an object of special importance to probably the majority of Anglo-Indians.

It was suggested to me, that such a work should be terse and concise, so as to consist merely of a set of dry practical rules and facts under different headings, to which (without looking through it as a whole) the Anglo-Indian might refer for casual information from time to time, as immediately necessary. My own view, however, has been that this could easily be carried too far, and that there is a class of readers at home to whom the present volume might be made interesting—their tastes and position being also borne in mind: persons who though not themselves going out to the East, are yet interested in India through having friends and relatives there; or who consider the fact of its being a part of the queen's dominions, containing about six times the population of Great Britain, a sufficient plea for such interest.

I must now refer to what is certainly not the least valuable part of this volume—that written by my friend Dr. Mair. In designing the scope of the work, it became obvious to me, that it would be incomplete without the fullest instructions for the means of preserving health, and for the treatment of the more common forms of disease. And here a difficulty presented itself; for, though I had had considerable amateur experience, while abroad, in the treatment of some of the most prevalent climatic disorders, I did not feel warranted (not being a professional man) in putting forward for public acceptance my own views upon such subjects.

I then wrote to Dr. Mair (an old friend, who had been

my medical adviser in Madras, and who returned home only two months later than myself), and proposed to write down what occurred to me in this direction, if he would revise and correct my remarks. He thereupon most generously and kindly offered, to take in hand that part of the book *himself;* an offer which I of course gratefully accepted, and for which I here take the opportunity of recording my obligation.

The chapters by Dr. Mair on Individual Hygiene will be found most valuable; not alone on account of their writer's wide experience during an Indian practice of sixteen years, but also from the fact, that large numbers of Europeans in India live miles away from the nearest resident medical man; and may any day find themselves placed in such a position, that a rudimentary knowledge of the treatment of the more common forms of disease, or of the action of a few simple remedies, would prove of invaluable service, in relieving suffering, averting dangerous illness, or in actually saving life. In some parts of India, one may travel over large tracts of country without ever being in the neighbourhood of another *white man*—much less of a medical man, and such isolation is the permanent experience of hundreds of our fellow countrymen in the East; so that it must be evident, even should they escape casualty themselves, there will constantly be cases occurring, where persons dependent upon them are suddenly stricken down by fever, sunstroke, or cholera, in each of which immediate attention and remedies are called for.

How great, then, the advantage, of each intelligent person so situated being able to put his hand on medical instructions! On the other hand, how often are maladies, not originally serious, made so by ignorant meddling with medicine by unguided amateurs, which a few plain and practical instructions taken down from the book-shelf would have obviated.

I myself lived for years more than fifteen miles from any medical man; who, if sent for suddenly, might often chance to be visiting patients twenty miles distant in the opposite direction. Twenty-four or forty-eight hours would often, therefore, necessarily elapse before he could answer a summons; and such may also, not improbably, be the case with many of those who read these pages. For their case, Dr. Mair's chapters will prove invaluable, while his advice on Individual Hygiene will be of the utmost use, in teaching every one so to regulate his daily life as to produce the minimum of physical deterioration in a climate by nature (to a certain extent) inimical to the European constitution.

CONTENTS.

CHAPTER V.

INCOMES AND OUTLAY.

CHAPTER VI.

HOUSEKEEPING.

CHAPTER VII.

SERVANTS.

CHAPTER VIII.

SERVANTS.

CHAPTER IX.

CHILDREN.

CHAPTER X.

TRAVELLING.

CHAPTER XI.

HORSES AND DOGS.

CHAPTER XII.

SOCIAL CUSTOMS.

CHAPTER XIII.

CHAPTER XIV.

CONCLUSION.

MEDICAL GUIDE.

THE EUROPEAN IN INDIA.

CHAPTER I.

OUTFITS.—*Advantage of taking a complete outfit.—High prices of Indian shop goods.—Outfit to be adapted to the future life.—Importance of wearing wool.—Waterproof clothing necessary.—Sketch of outfit for mofussil life.—For town life.—Ladies' outfits.—Instructions regarding packing.—The voyage.—Cabin accessories.—Sea-sickness.—Amusement on board ship.*

IT is impossible to lay down an exact specification of the clothing, etc., required by every intending sojourner in India. Much must depend on the means, tastes, and prospective calling of each person; and I shall, therefore, merely confine myself to such suggestions, in connection with the subject, as appear capable of general application.

At first sight, it may appear superfluous for a person on the eve of departure for India to lay in an "outfit" at all. There are plenty of large cities there, each containing a European population, which for the most part supplies its wants on the spot; and it might, therefore, be inferred, that those of the traveller could also be supplied from time to time after arrival, without all the trouble at present taken in preparation before leaving home.

This conclusion, however, would not, for many reasons, be a wise one. True, there are cases in which, owing to a necessarily hurried departure, persons find it impossible to make due provision beforehand; and they, of course, have to make amends for the deficiency as best they can, by supplying their wants after reaching India; but it does not thence follow, that it is desirable to dispense with special outfits as a general rule.

It is said that Sir Charles Napier, on being suddenly ordered out to India to take a military command, under circumstances of great exigency, started *next morning*, with only a carpet-bag; but it can hardly be supposed that the gallant general's comfort was greatly increased by the fact of his having so slender a supply of conveniences.

If there be any disadvantage in having an ample outfit—provided, of course, it is a suitable one—it is the trouble of having a quantity of baggage to look after *en route*. But this difficulty—if one at all—is comparatively trifling, and of short duration. Indeed, it is a question, whether there is more trouble in looking after the transit of a dozen packages than of two—oı even one, if that one is too large to be carried by the owner himself; and if every package is clearly and correctly addressed, with the *owner's name*, *destination*, *conveyance*, and *route*, there is little risk of miscarriage.

There are, on the other hand, many advantages. Of course, there are plenty of shops in places like Calcutta, Bombay, and Madras, where most of the articles in use by Europeans can be bought; but it cannot be supposed, that such articles are there sold at anything like home prices. The Indian shopkeeper obtains his European goods, in many cases, from retail dealers at home; at any rate he has to import them from Europe, paying exchange, freight, insurance, and a variety of other charges—and in addition, incurring risks from damage, etc., against which no insurance will provide; as well as that of having even those goods which reach him in a sound condition left on his hands for an indefinite time.

In India, as elsewhere, the objects probably aimed at by the tradesman are—ready sales, fair profits, and quick returns. But, to make ready sales, there must be a large community of buyers, in proportion to the number of shops competing for custom. Where this is wanting, sales on a large scale are impossible; while in proportion to their insignificance, a larger profit is required to afford the shopkeeper his support. It unfortunately happens that there are comparatively few customers in India; and this is, therefore, another reason why shop prices there are invariably high. Then, Anglo-Indians object to high prices, which drives the shopkeeper into the expedient, too often, of supplying inferior goods at an *apparently* moderate price; the result being, that Indian shop goods in general have come to be looked upon as necessarily inferior to similar articles obtained direct from England by private individuals at a much lower cost; and many persons systematically supply themselves in consequence, year after year, with nearly everything they require, direct from home.

Again, the Indian shopkeeper's great difficulty being paucity of customers, he is driven into giving long and often indiscriminate credit, which not unfrequently leads to bad debts, from which he derives some of his heaviest losses—and this also tends to necessitate high prices.

Altogether, it will thus be seen, the position of the Indian shopkeeper is a difficult one: to make a living in the face of limited sales, heavy expenses, and other drawbacks, requiring no ordinary ingenuity.

Another cause of constant and heavy loss which he has to encounter, is the liability of nearly every kind of goods to become damaged, owing to the nature of the climate. Some articles will hardly keep undeteriorated for the shortest period; and consequently "unsold" soon becomes a synonym for "unsaleable." Silks are mildewed; woollens perforated by a minute insect; gloves spotted; leather or wood-work gets eaten by white ants, or falls to pieces; while cutlery becomes speedily injured by rust. What wonder, then, that from six to eight shillings are asked for a pair of gloves, seeing that whole cases full, a few weeks ago new and sound, have now to be thrown aside as worthless?

While, however, admitting that high prices in Indian shops are unavoidable, it is obviously the interest of persons having a regard for economy, to render themselves as far as possible independent of the circumstance; and this alone is a sufficiently strong argument in favour of a complete outfit.

But it is not the only one. The Anglo-Indian starting in life will probably be somewhat limited as to income at the outset; and as he will, moreover, have many heavy expenses to meet shortly after his arrival in India, it is evident that the fewer articles of clothing he has to provide himself with, for a year or two, the better.

And not only would I advise the provision of a stock of clothing to last some time, but I would also recommend every reader going out to India, to make arrangements before leaving England, to have clothing, etc., sent out from home by friends or agents, as required, during the whole term of residence abroad. With this view, directions for self-measurement should be obtained. The saving in cost, to say nothing of the superior workmanship and material, which may be looked for as the result of adopting this plan, will amply repay any extra trouble which it may involve. English made clothes will always surpass in comfort, durability, and appearance, anything that can be got in India at the same cost.

Old Indians, on returning to England, generally find their garments more or less *outré*, and calculated to draw attention, however particular they may have been in choosing their tailors while abroad. Before leaving India myself, I ordered amongst other things, from a well-known European tailor, an overcoat; and, being perhaps rather out of date in the matter of "fashion," was well enough satisfied with it. On arriving in London, however, it occurred to me that a little alteration was required, and I therefore took the coat to a tailor. The latter confidentially informed me, that the unfortunate garment was "altogether a seedy affair,"—taking the opportunity of politely observing that there was "no sit whatever" about any of my clothes. Probably this expression of opinion was not altogether unbiassed, but I was conscious of its containing sufficient truth to prevent my being altogether impervious to it.

The other day, I met a friend lately returned from India, who told me that when he reached home, he at once saw there was something different in his appearance from that of other people, and that he had to spend £40 at a tailor's before he felt himself fit to appear in public, without attracting notice as "a gentleman from foreign parts."

In selecting an outfit, it is of course important to keep in view the probable conditions of the future life in India. For instance, a young man going out to join the Forest Department, or as a coffee planter, would require many things which would be useless to a civilian or mercantile clerk; for the simple reason, that in the former case the life in prospect would be mostly out of doors, involving much exposure, in localities where society is sparse and ceremony scant; game would often be met with, while there might be encounters to be provided for with animals more formidable.

The civilian's or merchant's occupation, on the other hand, would be principally within doors, in some large town; more sedentary than active; and except during the annual trip to the hills, or on an occasional day's snipe-shooting, he might never walk through an acre of jungle, or see a head of game—except such as had previously made its appearance in the market stall.

In fact, the difference between the one life and the other

would correspond to that between the life of the farmer or of the field geologist and of the city man, in England; only that while in England, the city man must to a certain extent be provided against exposure, there is hardly the same necessity in the case of the Indian man of business; who need never go out of doors (except in the cool of the day, and in fine weather) but in a carriage.

Before proceeding further with regard to the selection of outfit, I wish to enforce the following point. Flannel should *always* be worn next the skin; and this applies to Anglo-Indians of both sexes, and under all circumstances.

It is the best safeguard against fever, dysentery, and other disorders that carry off so many victims in the tropics. When the body is heated a profuse perspiration moistens the clothing; evaporation follows, checking the perspiration and causing a chill, and hence illness in numberless cases.

An Indian doctor, whose name I do not know, but who must have been a sort of Abernethy in his way, once said, he "would not throw good medicine away upon any one who could be such a fool as not to wear flannel."

Chills are the authors of most complaints in India, and should be more carefully guarded against than the heat itself. In their wake come fevers, diarrhœa, dysentery, and even cholera. That they should follow evaporation from damp clothing is not to be wondered at, seeing it is a common practice to cool beverages (in places where ice is not procurable) by the same process.*

Evaporation takes place more rapidly from cotton and linen than from wool; and they are, therefore, to be eschewed as much as possible for under-clothing—especially linen. Neither does wool absorb moisture so readily as cotton. Take a piece of flannel, and stretch it over a

* Thus; bottles or other vessels containing the liquid to be cooled, are wrapped round with damp cloths, and exposed to the sun and wind, when in a very short time the contents are found to be admirably cooled.

glass of water, just so close that the ends of the fibres touch the water; then do the same with a piece of calico or linen; and it will be found, that the woollen fibres have hardly sucked up more water than they were in contact with; while the moisture will have penetrated to the upper surface of the calico or linen. This explains the fact of chills more quickly arising from cotton and linen clothing. Perspiration penetrates at once to the external surface, and is acted on by the atmosphere; while with a woollen garment, it is retained within, or absorbed so gradually as to produce no bad effects.

Wool, again, is a non-conductor of heat. Put a woollen sock on a warm foot in winter, and the foot will keep warm much longer than if covered only with a cotton one. For the same reason, a woollen shirt will keep its wearer *cooler, in an atmosphere above blood heat*, than a linen one. This can be proved as follows:—

Place two beds beside each other in a room, in India, open to the hot land-winds. Cover one, in the cool of the morning, with sheets and a couple of woollen blankets; but, on the other, instead of blankets, put over the sheets the same weight and thickness of cotton counterpanes, etc. In the afternoon, when the heat of the day has reached its climax, test with a thermometer the temperatures of the two beds, under the clothes; and it will be found that that upon which the blankets were laid is several degrees cooler than the other.

All this goes to prove, that an object covered with wool is less susceptible to changes of temperature than one clothed with cotton; and in the degree that cotton is inferior in this respect to wool, linen is inferior to cotton. This might have been concluded, from the fact that wool is the natural clothing of animals, and would therefore, of course, possess the properties best calculated to protect them from atmospheric influences.

If the climate of the tropics is warmer than that of

temperate latitudes, it is also more characterised by rapid and violent changes, which render comparatively warm or *non-conducting* clothing essential to health. In some parts of India, and at certain seasons, for example, the thermometer which stood at 5 a.m. at 55°, will by 1 or 2 p.m., or perhaps earlier, have risen to 90°, and by 8 p.m. have again fallen to 60°. It was this peculiarity in the climate of Abyssinia which produced so much sickness among our troops in 1868; the variation of the thermometer during the twenty-four hours being often 40 degrees.

While making a morning call in the hot season, the Anglo-Indian in the course of a few minutes may experience a change nearly as great; for, while in his carriage the heat may possibly be 110°, the tattied, shaded drawing-room, with its gently-swinging punkahs and thermantidote, into which he is ushered, will have been cooled down to 80°; and as it is not possible to adopt a change of dress to suit every change of temperature, the object should be to adapt one's clothing to serve as nearly as possible equally well, whether the temperature be 30 degrees higher or lower—an object which can be best attained by wearing light woollen garments.

A woollen coat has the merit, not often thought of, of protecting the *back* from the sun; linen, silk, and cotton coats may "look nice and cool," but they afford no protection in this respect.

While, however, giving due regard to the necessity of adopting such clothing in India as will afford protection from the sun and heat, it is equally needful to be provided to a certain extent against influences of an opposite character. All who have to encounter an out-of-door life in the hills, are liable to be exposed to cold and wet; and every Anglo-Indian must be prepared for an occasional trip to the hills, and for the weather he must there sometimes experience.

I should, therefore, advise all, to provide themselves with waterproof clothing. A loose, light Mackintosh cloak, to come down as far as the knees, and leggings of the same material reaching to the thighs, will render the wearer impervious to rain. Black india-rubber waterproofing should be avoided, as not at all adapted to a hot climate. The heat causes the preparation on the cloth to melt; and a cape of this material, if laid by for any length of time, will most probably be found, when taken out for use, stuck together in a solid mass as folded; and when once opened out, after having been in this condition, it is rendered quite useless. The light-coloured Mackintosh is not affected in this manner.

One of the pests of the Indian forests and jungles is leeches, which fasten on the legs and ankles of the unwary pedestrian in moist situations. The bites are not painful, but are apt to fester, and a number of them involves a considerable loss of blood. Leech-gaiters, or stockings made of some cotton material, should, therefore, where these pests prevail, be worn over the ordinary socks, inside the boot but coming up over the trowsers to the knees, and there drawn tight and fastened. A dozen pairs of these gaiters may be included in the forester's or planter's outfit. They will also be found useful by sportsmen, when plunging through wet paddy fields in pursuit of snipe.

The following is somewhat the style of outfit I would recommend for a bachelor having before him a rough out-of-door life in the mofussil;* of course, it is capable of modification according to individual tastes.

Bedding.—A portable cork mattress; bed curtains of strong, rather close, coloured, musquito-netting, to fit a single cot: dark-green is the best colour; by having coloured netting the necessity for washing is obviated. Two or three good warm single blankets—one coloured, say red or blue; and a railway rug or wrapper. A Mackintosh waterproof sheet is also a valuable article, and where there is any possibility of camp-life, it should be

* *Mofussil* means, up-country, provincial.

provided without fail, being suitable for use either as a tent, or as bed-covering. A feather pillow.

If the cabin has to be furnished for the voyage, the washing-stand, toilet set, lamp, swinging tray, etc., should be retained and taken ashore, as they will without doubt prove useful. I say this, as it is a common practice with passengers to bestow these articles, at the end of the voyage, upon the stewards. The mattress, pillow, and blankets, above mentioned, may be used during the passage out, if necessary, otherwise they can be packed up and put away in the hold.

A supply of small, strong light sheets and pillowcases (the latter may be either of cotton or linen) may be taken.

For the Field.—A good double-barrelled, breech-loading, fowling-piece of medium bore, in portable leather case, with appurtenances complete. A hunting knife, blade eight or ten inches long, with sheath and waist-belt attached. A strong, moderately light, hogskin hunting saddle (by some good maker), with bridle and girths complete; the saddle should have plated or brass loops in front, for passing straps through, so that a waterproof or anything in that way may, if desired, be carried on the pommel. A pair of spurs. An Ellwood's patent ventilating helmet; and a couple of ordinary stiff felt hats, of any shape preferred. Two or three pairs of strong walking boots, not too thick or heavy; a pair of long riding boots, without tops; one or two pairs of leather gaiters; a pair of cord riding trowsers, and a pair of cord breeches.

The General Clothing should be mainly of light tweeds, or of mixed wool and cotton; but some warm suits will not be amiss, among which should be included a comfortable "reefing jacket," and one or two short double-breasted coats (to be worn buttoned, without waistcoat) of blue serge or some similar light, warm, lasting material. There should be a good supply (say a dozen) of what are known as Crimean shirts, made either of wool or of a mixture of silk and wool, of neat check or striped patterns: grey or blue are the best colours; mauves and magentas being useless, as the first week's wear and a washing carry away the dye. Printed flannels should be avoided, as soon getting shabby; and care should be taken that the material has been thoroughly well shrunk before it is made up.

American drill trousers are very useful for all Anglo-Indians, during the hot weather, and a dozen pairs will not be too many, as each pair in the towns can only be worn one day. Linen materials should not be used for trouserings, as being very apt to give colds.

A suit of white flannels for boating or cricket will probably be found useful.

As every one in India sleeps in loose drawers, or "pyjamas," a supply of these will be required. They may be made of any light cotton material or, for the hills, of wool; striped prints are much in use, and silk, or silk and wool pyjamas are very comfortable, but more expensive. A loose jacket is generally worn with the pyjamas, made of the same material, and the two articles are called a sleeping suit.

For Anglo-Indians who have a sedentary town life in prospect, I need hardly lay down any particular rules as to dress. That found most suitable for summer use in England will, for the most part, suit India well enough; and indeed the foregoing instructions under the heading "general clothing" will be almost as applicable to the banker's clerk as to the coffee-planter, when due allowance is made for the difference of life and climate, as previously explained. A greater number of linen, and fewer flannel shirts will be required; fine light woollen or angola jerseys taking the place of the latter. Tweed suits, American drill trousers, and cotton, wool, or silk pyjamas will be required in all cases.

Where there is less walking or riding expected, less provision need be made for those exercises; nor will a camp equipage be required by those who live in towns. Every one, I imagine, will be glad to have such articles by him as a gun and a good saddle, and will probably find them useful sooner or later.

All gentlemen going to India should get their black evening suits made of the lightest material, especially those much in favour of dancing. A large supply of collars, cuffs, and neckties may be taken, those articles being expensive on the spot.

I must not leave this subject without giving a few hints applicable to the requirements of lady readers, so many of whom now annually take wing for the East. The time was, when the advent of ladies to British India was "strictly prohibited" by our old-fashioned ancestors of the Honourable Company, unless they should previously have obtained a special passport from the directors in London, which was no easy matter. Indeed, so decided, for some reason or other, was the old Company's government in its misogyny, that one lady was actually reshipped to England, on having arrived at Calcutta without a permit. But all this is happily changed now.

The following remarks are necessarily of the most general character, but will, I trust, be found of special value, having been kindly contributed, for the most part, by a lady who has herself lately returned home, after a residence of some years in India.

It is a matter of no small importance to a lady about to enter upon life in India, to know as far as possible, the best articles to provide herself with in the way of outfit. Much after-regret may thus be saved, and much comfort ensured.

If the Indian home is to be on the plains, too much care cannot be taken to provide the lightest and coolest clothing, but in saying this, let me at the same time remark, that the wearing of woollen under-clothing (upon which so much has been already said) is a rule which should never be departed from. An inner garment of fine Welsh flannel, instead of adding to the sufferings caused by the heat, will diminish them, and prevent those sudden chills caused by punkahs, draughts, etc., to which in the tropics one is so liable.

The under-linen should be of fine, light long-cloth, and, in some of the hottest parts of India, even nainsook will probably be found the best material. In most cases, in the plains, tight nightdresses with long sleeves are found absolutely unbearable, unless made of the lightest fabric. These garments should, therefore, be made low at the neck, and very loose, with loose, open sleeves.

Plain thread stockings will be found the best kind, as being cooler than cotton ones, and open pattern stockings, as commonly worn at home in summer, greatly facilitating the attacks of the musquitoes when on the plains, and of the fleas when on the hills.

Muslin dresses will, as a general rule, be found best adapted for ordinary wear. Even when silk skirts (which by the bye will be found also very useful) are worn, bodies of the same material are unendurable in hot weather, and if worn are speedily soiled by excessive perspiration. Such being the case, white muslin bodies are universally worn, and too large a supply of them cannot be taken out.

For those who contemplate going out much in the evening, a good supply of evening dresses will of course be provided; but, as in all countries, "full dress" is much alike, no particular instructions on this point are necessary: silks, moirés, and other materials worn on similar occasions in England and elsewhere, will be found quite suitable.

Most ladies spend a part of every year on the hills, and a supply of warm clothing to be worn on these occasions will be required. For the evening drive also, dresses of some thicker texture than muslin are desirable, the temperature undergoing a sudden change after sunset, and becoming often damp and raw, owing to heavy dew-fall.

Silks and mohairs will now be in requisition; bareges, however, should be avoided in India, owing to their tendency to catch in the screen-doors, etc., and to get constantly torn.

Ladies, who can afford the luxury, usually keep a riding horse, and provision for equestrianism should therefore be made. If morning rides only are contemplated, brown holland, grey linsey, or drab piqué riding-habits are preferable to the stereotyped black cloth garment. Those, however, who have it in view to disport themselves on horseback at the evening band-stand or other fashionable promenade, will require the usual black hat, cloth habit, etc., as worn in Hyde Park or elsewhere. If practicable, therefore, it will be better to have a habit of black cloth, and one of some lighter material, which can be used in common and in the hot weather also.

Strong walking boots will be required for the hills, and a supply of light kid or prunella boots for the plains; and the prices of all such articles being in India about double what they are at home, it is well to be liberally provided in these particulars.

Except for the hills, where it is the common practice to walk or ride at all hours of the day, no provision is necessary for the protection of the head; ladies never elsewhere venturing out in the daytime but in close carriages, and generally only emerging from their seclusion when the sun is nearing the horizon; the ordinary hat or bonnet being all that is needed on the latter occasions, a small number of both will of course be taken out. Pith hats or "suntopees," can always be procured at the shops for hill excursionists.

Gloves being extravagantly priced in India, supplies should be obtained direct from England, either in single pairs by post, or, which is the better plan, in sufficient quantity to last a season, carefully wrapped in flannel while thoroughly dry, and packed in a wide-mouthed bottle.

In packing up the outfit, a distinction must be made between articles that will be required during the voyage, and those that are not to be used until after arrival in India. The packages containing the former (which should be as few and moderately sized as can be made compatible with comfort) ought to be marked "Cabin," or "Required on voyage," when arrangements will be made by the ship authorities for stowing them so as to be accessible accordingly. One portmanteau three feet long and fifteen inches wide and deep, is as large as can be pushed under a cabin berth, and will be found to contain enough changes till Suez is reached, when lighter clothing will be required; and should be taken out of another portmanteau, which has till then been kept in the hold. The rest of the outfit should be put in cases lined with tin or zinc, carefully soldered down, and put away in the hold till the end of the journey.

These packing cases should not be too large or heavy, nor too deep; the principal dimensions being in length and width, as their contents will thus be more easily got at. In fact, the ordinary "sea-chest" is as large as any trunk or case should be; and the weight, when full packed, ought to be under 100 pounds. The lid should have hinges and locks, so that the cases can be opened at the end of the journey without being broken to pieces, and so be useful again; and these lids may be *screwed* down without affecting this result. A list of the contents of every package, whether trunk, portmanteau, or case, should be pasted inside the lid; every one should also be numbered, and a list, giving the number and contents of each, kept by the owner in a memorandum book in addition.

For the voyage, besides mere clothing, linen, etc., many other articles will be required: above all, a comfortable folding chair for use upon deck. This should be of wood, very strong, and as light and portable as possible, so that it may be easily moved about without being broken, in cleaning decks or in rough weather. Sailors and ship's officers have a strong dislike to clumsy, heavy, passengers' chairs; to which, when in the way, no mercy is shown—especially at night or early in the morning, when the owners are below.

Every passenger should take also a bag containing screws, brass hooks, and brass-headed nails of sizes; tacks, a hammer, one or two gimlets, a screwdriver, and a chisel. Also twine, cord of different thickness, scissors, thread and needles, and an assortment of buttons—in fact, all sorts of sundries are sure to be found useful, either on the voyage or during residence in India. A cake of marine soap will be handy if it is desired to wash in sea water, which gentlemen very frequently do. A long pocket for fastening along the cabin-side, about nine inches deep and three feet long, divided by stitched bands into many compartments of different size, each having a flap to button down, will be found most useful as a receptacle for hair-brushes, slippers, books, and, in fact, for everything that, while constantly in use, is yet apt to get in the way.

In case of probable sea-sickness—that most depressing of all disorders—or other indisposition, several little comforts, not always easily procurable on board ship, should be kept at hand. I recommend the following supply:—A pound or two of really good strong-flavoured tea; one or two tins of biscuits and gingerbread nuts; also of chocolate; and one or two of favourite jams or marmalade.

For sea-sickness there is no general specific, though some remedies are occasionally found very efficacious. Champagne, Moselle, or sparkling hock, are often found to have an excellent effect in settling the stomach; and a small case of pint or half-pint bottles of either, would probably, therefore, be found a valuable acquisition. A bottle or two of really good port or sherry would not be amiss in cases of subsequent prostration. All effervescing drinks are good in sea-sickness. In most well-found steamers, however, all these can be purchased at moderate prices, and passengers are not allowed to take on board wines, spirits, or other liquors, for use during the voyage.

For persons much upset, and who find it impossible to take ordinary food or even delicacies, the following hint will prove invaluable. Take a fresh egg (of which every good passenger vessel will have an ample supply) and break it into a wine glass; add a few drops of vinegar, and a little black pepper from the cruet, and gulp down as in eating an oyster. This will be found wonderfully sustaining.

Every kind of amusement for which one has a leaning on shore, becomes doubly attractive during the tedium of a sea-voyage; and provision for passing the monotonous hours agreeably should, therefore, be made. Those fond of fishing may take a few lines and hooks; those who prefer shooting, a fowling-piece, for practice at sea-birds. Light reading will pass much time easily; improving reading, much time profitably. Those fond of the games should certainly have with them the appliances for chess, drafts, backgammon, whist, cribbage, bézique, etc.

CHAPTER II.

ROUTES AND BEST TIME OF YEAR FOR DEPARTURE.—*Former routes.—Euphrates.—Cape.—Egyptian route: Southampton, Marseilles, Brindisi routes.—Future route.—To Bombay, Madras, Calcutta.—Suez Canal.—Long sea voyage for "homeward bounders."—Baggage insurance.—Season to arrive in India.—Red Sea heat.*

BEFORE considering which is the best route to India, it may be interesting to look back for a moment upon a period when the subject could not be so easily disposed of as now; and when a journey to the East involved real difficulties and dangers.

At one time, the way lay through Tripoli in Asiatic Turkey, *viâ* the Euphrates and Tigris, to the Persian Gulf, and thence into the Indian Ocean. But difficult and arduous as such a route must have been (and there were, no doubt, at that period dangers to be encountered that now hardly exist), it was probably preferable, in point of time, and in other respects, to the sea-voyage round the Cape.

The Cape was first doubled in 1497 by the Portuguese, who obtained a footing in India some five or six years later; but in 1528 our countrymen were still attempting to reach India by the north-west passage—attempts which were unsuccessfully persevered in for many years; and the English were finally compelled to adopt the highway opened for them by their nautical rivals of that date, despatching their first fleet round the Cape in 1601. For the 225 years following, the Cape route to India continued to be principally made use of for general traffic, notwithstanding that the voyage either way lasted from six to eight months, a year and a half sometimes elapsing between despatch of a letter to India, and the receipt of a reply.

In the beginning of this century, steam was first applied successfully to marine propulsion; but it was not till 1825 that a steam voyage was made to India, by the *Enterprise;* while it was later still before the "overland route" and steam navigation were combined, to bring Europe and the East into communication with each other.*

For many years since that time, however, the "overland route" (so called because it crossed Egypt) enjoyed almost the entire monopoly of the passenger traffic outwards. And naturally; for, of course, persons obliged to reach India by any particular time of year, and at the same time wishing to see as much as possible of their family and friends before leaving home, selected the shortest and quickest route. But the opening of the Suez Canal, and the gradual improvement, which has been obvious to the public, in the class of steamers placed on that line by other shipowners, combined with lower rates of passage money, and, in some cases, equal punctuality and speed, have induced many to select that route, thereby avoiding the change from one steamer to another as well as the railway journey through Egypt.

The steamers of the Peninsular and Oriental Company take their departure from Southampton; formerly they started only once a month, afterwards once a fortnight, and at present they leave every Thursday morning for Bombay, *viâ* the Suez Canal; every alternate Thursday for Ceylon, Madras, Calcutta, Penang, Singapore, Hong Kong, Shanghai, and Yokohama; and every fourth Thursday for King George's Sound, Adelaide, Melbourne, and Sydney. To those, however, whom business or inclination induces to prolong their stay to the latest possible time, the route *viâ* Brindisi offers the advantageous alternative of deferring

* Probably this took place about 1839 or 1840. The Peninsular and Oriental Company obtained their charter in the latter year.

their departure for a week after the steamer has left Southampton, when by proceeding through France and Italy to Brindisi, they will be in time to leave that port by another line of the same company's steamers for Alexandria, from whence they cross the desert by railway to Suez, reaching that place in time to proceed by the steamers provided for the continuance of the voyage to Bombay, Calcutta, or elsewhere.

Until the Franco-Prussian war, Marseilles was the point of departure for this second line of steamers; but when communication through France with that port was interrupted, a change became necessary, and the rising port of Brindisi in Southern Italy is now reaping the advantage. Brindisi had been for some time an alternative route to the East, it having been used as the European terminus of a line of steamers owned by an Italian Company, and the possibility of its being used in the same way by the P. and O Company had been for some time before the public mind. The European terminus of the line is Venice, leaving which port, the steamers call at Ancona and thence proceed to Brindisi to take in the mails, so that passengers may embark at either of these three places; but the longest time in Europe and the shortest sea voyage, are secured by joining the steamer at Brindisi.

The Brindisi route has the advantage of being the shortest and quickest; the whole distance from Calais to Brindisi, probably some 1300 miles, being performed by railway; leaving a distance of only about 800 miles to be accomplished by sea, to Alexandria, in place of a voyage of some 3000 miles from Southampton to Port Said, at the homeward end of the Suez Canal.

To outward passengers who wish to prolong their stay at home, and to homeward passengers who wish to reach home with the least possible delay, the week saved by the Brindisi route will be considered no small advantage; while the great curtailment of the water journey which it affords, will be an important recommendation in the eyes of bad sailors.

It is possible, however, that the time may come, and that before the lapse of many years, when even a more direct and expeditious route than any of the foregoing will have been opened up,—literally "overland," nearly the whole way to India. Soon, it is expected, there will be uninterrupted railway communication between Calais and Constantinople; while later, there will be a connected series of lines running eastward, as far as our Indian empire—from Constantinople through Asia Minor, down the valley of the Euphrates to the head of the Persian Gulf (at about Bassorah), and thence through Persia and Beloochistan into the Indian province of Sinde. Utopian as such a scheme may appear, and gigantic as it undoubtedly is, it has been discussed for the last thirty years; it being indeed a favourite idea with the Ottoman Government, that the capital of the empire should become the grand central junction of the European and Asiatic railway lines. Once this had been effected, Turkish politicians clearly see, it would more than ever become the interest of England to withstand the Russian solution of what is called "the Eastern question." And there are not wanting thoughtful Englishmen who firmly believe that this will, sooner or later, become *the* route to India; a route which would make from London to Calcutta little more than a seven or eight days' journey.

Passengers by the P. and O. Company's vessels, leaving Southampton for Bombay, Ceylon, Madras, Calcutta, Singapore, China, Japan, or Australia, on Thursdays, arrive at Gibraltar about the fifth day; and after staying there a few hours, proceed to Malta, where they remain about twelve hours; they then leave for Port Said, usually arriving there on the fourteenth day from Southampton, and, after a short stoppage, proceed through the Canal to Suez. Here the Canal passengers meet with those who, after performing the voyage from Venice or Brindisi to Alexandria, have come from thence to Suez by railway—a distance of 224 miles, occupying ten hours.

The weekly steamers leaving Southampton to go through the Suez Canal start for Bombay and Calcutta on alternate Thursdays, but when a Calcutta-bound steamer arrives at Suez, the Company provide another one at that port to receive the passengers for Bombay. Thus there is a weekly passenger service to Bombay, and fortnightly to the other Eastern ports. At Suez, therefore, the passengers either all go on towards Bombay or, dividing, some proceed thither, and the others to Point de Galle (Ceylon). Having arrived here, the passengers and mails for Penang, Singapore, China, and Japan, are transferred to another steamer which goes as far as Hong Kong; those to Australia (every fourth week only) to another, and that which has carried all from Suez then proceeds onward with her remaining complement of passengers, to Madras and Calcutta.

The journey from Southampton occupies, under ordinary circumstances, twenty-eight days to Bombay, thirty-four days to Madras, and thirty-eight days to Calcutta. The passenger steamers for Bombay leave Suez once a week; but those for Ceylon and all other Eastern ports, only once a fortnight; passengers *viâ* Point de Galle for Madras and Calcutta, therefore, can only leave Southampton every alternate Thursday.

When *time* is the principal object with passengers for Calcutta, their best route, eastward of Suez, lies through Bombay; and thence by railway to Calcutta, "the City of Palaces." The following information regarding this railway, extracted from the *Madras Mail*, will prove of value to this class of travellers.

"The most important event connected with Indian railways last year,* was the junction of the East Indian with the Great Indian Peninsular Railway at Jubbulpore, by

* 1870.

which communication was established between Calcutta and Bombay. The distance between the eastern and western capitals is 1470 miles. The journey occupies about seventy hours, * and costs to first-class passengers about £14, to second £7, and to third £2 13*s.* The journey will be shortened by about seventy miles, when the cord line from Luckeserai to Calcutta is opened. Mr. Danvers reminds us, that by the opening of the line between Bombay and Calcutta, a saving of three or four days has been made in the journey between the latter city and England, and adds, 'No greater time is now occupied in reaching Calcutta from London than it took, twenty years ago, to get from one end of India to another.' We should think not, indeed! Why, plenty of old Indians must be still living, who remember the journey from Calcutta to Delhi as a three months' job."

Since the first edition of this book was published, the railway extensions connecting Bombay and Madras, constructed by the Madras and Great Indian Peninsula Railway Companies, have been completed up to the intended junction at Raichore; and the route *viâ* Bombay now forms the quickest and most convenient route to Madras also. The length of the journey is about forty-five hours. Under these circumstances, and taking the quickest route on the European side also—that *viâ* Brindisi—it is possible to perform the journey from England, to each of the three Indian Presidencies, in the following spaces of time:—

To Bombay in 21 days;
To Madras in 23 days;
To Calcutta in 24 days,

Or thereabouts; something depending upon the time of day at which the steamers reach Bombay, with reference to the hours fixed for the departure of trains.

Of course, war complications on the Continent would render a journey lying through its greater length, a matter

* It has since been reduced to sixty hours.

of doubtful prudence; while the many changes of conveyance necessary on the most expeditious routes, would prove a drawback to many—especially to those travelling with ladies or children.

But, whatever may be the route selected on the European side of Alexandria, that city will be a point in the journey hereafter aimed at by a large proportion of the travellers to India, who will thence proceed *viâ* Suez and the Red Sea. The alternative course is the Suez Canal route, which is now chosen by many who prefer to avoid the land journey through Egypt, and the consequent necessity of changing steamers.

Formerly, there was some slight saving in expense to be effected by going round the Cape, in preference to taking the Overland route; but even this recommendation has now to be withdrawn, in view of the reduced fares for which the various companies running steamers through the Suez Canal and Red Sea are working; and it is not too much to say that there is now no passenger traffic with India by the Cape of Good Hope.

Previous to the 18th November, 1869, when the Suez Canal was formally opened to traffic, there were but two or three regular lines of steamers running between India and Europe *viâ* the Red Sea; now, the number is much increased, and first-class steamers are taking passengers between England and Calcutta for 50 guineas, in place of the old charge of something over £100. The P. and O. Company, not to be behindhand, have made a heavy reduction in their fares, following in this respect the example set by the Messageries Impériales or French packets line.

This latter Company, which, previous to the Franco-Prussian war, ran steamers from Marseilles to Madras, Calcutta, China and Japan on alternate weeks with the P. and O. Company (making thus a weekly service to those places), had its operations circumscribed while communication through France was interrupted, but has now, under the new name of "Messageries Maritimes de France," resumed working, and despatches on alternate Sundays from Marseilles for Ceylon, Calcutta, Madras, Batavia, China, and Japan, *viâ* the Suez Canal, which restores the weekly communication with those places, with this difference, that the English steamers start from Venice and Brindisi, and the French from Marseilles.

But however much the P. and O. Company has been affected by the competition which the opening of the Suez Canal has brought to bear upon it, it still retains, and is likely to retain, a very large share of public favour and patronage. To this line belongs the credit of having so largely developed the trade and resources of India; and it has earned an honourable name by the perfection of all its arrangements, the speed and punctuality of its service, the equipment of its vessels, the skill and courtesy of its officers, and its uniform consideration for the comfort and convenience of passengers. The circumstance that it carries the English mails must always give it an advantage over competitors, as it is thus bound under penalties to perform its voyages under certain limits of time.

The first-class fares by P. and O. Company's steamer from Southampton are,—to Aden, £48; to Bombay, Ceylon, Madras, and Calcutta, £68. From Brindisi the fares are £8 less in each case. These rates are independent of the cost of railway transit through Egypt, for which through tickets are issued, price £3; but passengers through the Canal are not subject to any extra charge. A reduction is made for return passages within six or twelve months.

The fares by the French mail line (Messageries Maritimes) are,—from Marseilles to Aden, £40; Pondicherry, Madras, and Calcutta, £60.

In addition to the lines of steamers already mentioned, the following convey passengers at somewhat cheaper rates; but, as no mails are carried, the dates of sailing are not at regular intervals, and are in some cases liable to postponement.

Hall Line—Liverpool to Bombay.
Anchor Line— „ „ „
Star „ „ „ Calcutta.
City „ „ „ „
Ducal „ London to Colombo, Madras, and Calcutta.
British India Steam Navigation Co.—London to Colombo, Madras, Calcutta, and Kurrachee.

To attempt to enter into particulars regarding these lines of steamers, however, would be more likely to mislead than to guide, as it is impossible in a work of this kind to give trustworthy details of matters in which changes are so constantly occurring; and the best advice that can be offered to those who have occasion for precise information on the subject is, that they should apply to an East India agent, who will readily furnish all particulars that may be required.

In the days of the old East Indiamen, when the only passengers to India were the servants of the Honourable East India Company, and the voyage was of six months' duration, a journey to India was an undertaking not to be lightly thought of. Then the young cadets and writers took passage as though they left England for ever; and if they returned at all, it was only at the end of a long career, to die in the old country. The means of getting to India were proportionate to the need, and there was no difficulty about choice. As years rolled on, such vessels as the *St. Lawrence*, and *Hotspur*, the *Lord Warden*, and the *Nile* took the place of those of a preceding generation, and their reputation was well sustained to the last in the hands of the Messrs. Green and T. & W. Smith. But they, in their turn, have entirely given place to the steamers of the present day in the conveyance of passengers, while the bulk of our goods is no longer conveyed in sailing vessels *viâ* the Cape of Good Hope. The rapid growth of our trade with India demanded a more speedy and regular means of transit for mails and passengers, and this was first provided by the P. and O. Company, to whom the public interested in India owe a lasting debt of gratitude. Not less indebted is commerce to the spirited projector and constructor of the Suez Canal; and at a dinner given in 1871, by the Lord Mayor and corporation of London, to M. de Lesseps, at the Guildhall, the Lord Mayor justly observed, that by persevering labours during many years, and through evil and good report, M. de Lesseps had overcome difficulties long regarded as insuperable. Our great engineers had all condemned the project, but it was nevertheless a *fait accompli.* It would be an incalculable saving of life and time to England. In conclusion, his lordship characterized the canal as the greatest triumph of engineering skill in modern times.

M. de Lesseps, in reply, said, "It was a question of bringing into comparatively rapid communication, on the one hand, one hundred millions of human beings, skilled more or less in science, and engaged in commerce, navigation, and manufactures; and on the other, a population occupying a fertile territory, capable of furnishing the elementary products essential to the manufacturing enterprise of England. The canal would replace the long and tedious route by the Cape, and in that respect was replete with 'Good Hope,' indeed, for the future.

"The Lord Mayor had been pleased to allude to the perseverance with which the enterprise had been carried out, and to the advantage that was likely to accrue from it to England. He (M. de Lesseps) had observed, with much pleasure and satisfaction, from all the demonstrations which had been held in his honour since his arrival in England, that this country was convinced of the immense advantages likely to result to it from the facility of communication which had been established between the eastern and western hemispheres; and certainly if the great minister Lord Palmerston, whose memory he honoured, and who had opposed the enterprise in its political phase, believing that it would be injurious to the interests of England, had lived to witness its completion, he must have been convinced to the contrary, seeing that, out of the fifty steamships which passed through the canal in the month of June (1870), forty were English. To France, in fact, the world was indebted for the canal, but he relied mainly on England to maintain it."

Some of the steamers which passed through the canal during the first few months after it was opened were selected for this service without sufficient regard to ventilation below decks, the result being many casualties among the engineers and firemen, and much misery to the passengers. It will therefore be advisable, before deciding upon one's conveyance through the Red Sea by any other than a steamer belonging to some well-known line, to ascertain that there can be no grounds for complaint on this score; more particularly should it unfortunately happen, as must sometimes be the case, that the journey has been arranged for an unfavourable time of year. There are also one or two other points to be attended to, before fixing upon the first cheap steamer that offers:—first, is the vessel a full powered or auxiliary steamer? for, as an Indian paper* points out, none but full powered steamers can make headway against an adverse monsoon; and often have casualties occurred in the Indian Ocean, and steamers, at great peril, been swept far out of their course, owing to their inadequate steam power.

The public must not be misled by the "indicated" horse-power, which is the utmost the engines can be made to do with safety. The figures to be looked to are those showing the *nominal* horse-power, as compared with the registered tonnage; the former should be, say, one-fifth of the latter: thus, for a steamer of 1500 tons register, full powered engines would equal 300 horse-power, *nominal*. Unless

* The *Madras Mail*.

some attention is paid to this point, there can be no certainty as to the duration of the voyage. Again, some understanding should be come to, as to what arrangement would be made for forwarding passengers to destination, in the possible contingency of *a breakdown* during any part of the journey. Such a thing as a screw breaking in the Mediterranean, or elsewhere, might cause a month's delay; or fifty other accidents might happen, preventing the vessel's prosecuting the rest of the voyage. In the event of such a thing happening to a Messageries Maritimes or P. and O. steamer, the passengers are forwarded with the least possible delay, at the expense of the company; and passengers by new lines should therefore insist upon some agreement to the same effect, before engaging their places or paying their fares.

The foregoing remarks assume the abandonment of the long sea route, which indeed few outward-bound passengers are found willing to undertake. But to persons or families returning home from India, either for good or for a prolonged stay, especially those who are in impaired health, the voyage round the Cape, in a comfortable, well-found, capably commanded, and fast sailing ship, offers many very decided advantages. It is a means of restoration to health and strength, after long years of hard work in the tropics, which cannot be surpassed; it is also an opportunity, hardly likely to occur oftener than once in the life of a business man, of obtaining three or four months' mental and comparative physical rest, combined with the enjoyment of the invigorating sea-air; all of which is obtained, one may say, almost free of expense, seeing that there is no more to be paid for the passage than that by the short route. To military officers and others returning to England, on furlough or sick-leave, with their families, it is surely no small advantage, to be able to derive the above benefits, while some three months' allowances are accruing during the period occupied by the voyage; they and their party being in the meantime boarded and lodged, without any outlay other than they would at any rate have to pay for mere conveyance.

With regard to the benefit to be derived by persons in ill-health, from making the long sea-voyage home from India, I am entitled to speak with some emphasis, having myself experienced it. When I was obliged to revisit England, it was by the doctor's orders, and this route was insisted on. It was considered necessary that my departure should be immediate, and consequently, owing to the early sailing of that vessel, in five days I was at sea in the *Gosforth*, having embarked in a most precarious state of health, and while extremely weak. Before a fortnight had passed, all my unfavourable symptoms had subsided, my appetite began to return, and ultimately became absolutely voracious; so that, after a remarkably quick and most agreeable voyage, I arrived at home in excellent health, to the great surprise of my friends. I shall always connect my very rapid and remarkable recovery on this occasion, under Providence, with the *Gosforth*, and her amiable, excellent, and efficient commander—Captain H. P. Wight.

Before leaving the subject of passages, it may be well to make one very common-place suggestion, *i.e.*, that passengers should insure their baggage before embarking. Insurance does not at least *increase* the risk of loss; while those who are inclined to think it hardly "worth while," may remember that cases *have* been known of passengers losing all their effects at sea, and yet saving their lives and persons. The most prominent instance before my mind at the present time is that of the P. and O. steamer *Carnatic*, Capt. Jones, wrecked off the Island of Shadwân, in the Red Sea, in October, 1869. The surviving passengers lost their all in this sad catastrophe, and were subsequently landed at Bombay without a single change of clothes! On an application for compensation being made by these persons to the owners of the steamer, the directors of the P. and O.

Company, the reply was, that having neglected to take the precaution of insuring their baggage, for doing which every facility was afforded, the passengers were not entitled to prefer any claim.*

The cost of insurance is very trifling, not exceeding $1\frac{1}{2}$ or $1\frac{3}{4}$ per cent. on the amount covered, and it is prudent to insure for an amount exceeding the actual cost, or English value, of the property by forty or fifty per cent., so as to prevent pecuniary loss by the necessity, should it arise, of replacing what has been lost, in India, where all such articles will be found so much dearer than at home.

In deciding upon the best time of year to go out to India, the points to be considered are—firstly, the season in England at time of departure ; secondly, the best season in which to pass down the Red Sea, so as to avoid as much as possible the suffering consequent upon the heat during that part of the journey; and thirdly, the season upon arrival in India. The great object, of course, is to make the immediate change of climate to the traveller as inconsiderable as possible.

The Englishman leaving home in March, after a late and severe winter, to arrive in Calcutta or Madras near the 1st of May, the beginning of the hot season there, would naturally suffer more from the change of climate, than if he had left hot weather behind him. So also, would a person leaving England in mid-winter, and arriving in India a month later (though January is the height of the Indian cool season), suffer from the transition. Again, it would be unfortunate, should any one leaving England

* The matter came into court in London some months later, the jury awarding damages to the passengers ; but I would not advise others to accept this as a precedent, conclusive of the responsibility of shipowners for loss in all cases ; it being evidently the impression of the jury, that in the present one, the loss was due to error of judgment on the captain's part, in not taking an excellent opportunity which was afforded, of landing the mails and luggage upon the island, before the steamer sank.

arrange so as to reach India in the middle of the hot season, even although to do so he might be leaving hot weather at home; for the change would still be a violent one.

But if it could be so planned, that the traveller should be transferred from warm summer weather at home, into the Indian cool weather, it is obvious that the minimum of immediate change would be attained. This arrangement is not quite possible, but an approach to it may be arrived at by leaving home in the middle or end of September, which by the overland route would bring the traveller to India in the middle or end of October, the beginning of the cool season there. He will then have had the benefit of the whole English summer and half of the autumn, often as hot as summer, and have before him, after reaching his destination, the whole of the cool season, lasting until toward the end of March.

With regard to the seasons in India, and the real influences bearing on them in the different presidencies, I must refer the reader to another chapter, where the subject is treated of in detail.

And now for a few words about the Red Sea, which during the greater part of the year presents a trying ordeal to those who have to travel over it, whether eastward or westward bound. Indeed, this is generally looked upon as the worst part of the journey, and many a poor debilitated Anglo-Indian has found a last resting-place beneath its waters, ere he could reach the mother country in whose native air he had hoped to regain health and strength. Others, again, have sunk after having survived the actual duration of this part of the journey, in consequence of the increased debility it has brought about. Even hale men have been known to die in the berths, from apoplexy, caused by Red Sea heat; while the commanders of steamers sometimes have to back their vessels, with open stern ports, to create a current of air for the relief of gasping passengers and crew between decks, windsails and other ordinary appliances proving insufficient.

Nor is this much to be wondered at. A glance at the map will show the Red Sea to be situated within the parallels of twelve and thirty degrees of north latitude, the tropic of Cancer cutting its centre. Further, this elongated salt lake, which is hardly in any part more than 200 miles wide, is bounded on the one side by the burning, sandy deserts of Arabia, and by those of Africa on the other; and either receives from either side the breezes which must previously have become heated often to scorching, or is deprived of its own cooler currents of atmosphere by the conflicting attractions created on both sides, by the heat which is ascending from those sandy wastes.

During the summer months, from the 1st of May till the end of July, the heat is almost unendurable; but it begins to mitigate in September and October. March and April are also considered comparatively cool months; and though this period is unsuitable for departure to India, the fact is of importance to Anglo-Indians returning home, who should endeavour to time their arrival in England about the beginning of summer.

A medical friend, well acquainted with the Red Sea, writes to me on this subject:—"The Red Sea is hot all the year round, there being but little difference in the temperature in any one month. March and April are commonly reported to be the most favourable months; but there can be little doubt, that the best time for any person to leave England for either of the presidencies is September or October." He also adds:—"Any one going out to India for the first time will, as you know, feel the heat less than old stagers." This is an interesting and well-established fact, and affords a consolation for those who entertain gloomy misgivings on the subject.

The following extracts from the letter of a lady will probably prove interesting. The letter is dated, Aden, Oct. 21.

On board the P. and O. steamer, *Deccan*. "I had intended preparing a long letter to go from Aden; but, alas! the fourth day of Red Sea heat proved too much for flesh and blood, and I was obliged to succumb. I have now only the few moments before the post goes to tell you that thus far all is well, thank God. At ten we sail out finally from the Red Sea, without any serious consequence to any one, though many have suffered grievously. It is just a week this morning since we left Suez in this splendid vessel. Everything possible is done to alleviate the heat on board We have punkahs, windsails at our ports, and ices daily at tiffin; also salt-water baths, which, however, even at between five and six in the morning, are no longer cold."

On the other hand, Miss Carpenter tells us, that though she had heard a great deal about the heat in the Red Sea beforehand, she suffered little when actually passing over it, on her way to India, in September, 1866; and even looking back upon it, after her return home, she did "not remember having found this part of the voyage peculiarly unpleasant. Nor do I recollect," she says, "that those of our fellow-passengers, who had usually been on deck, found it so either. *The cabins* must have been extremely hot and oppressive, and we thankfully accepted the arrangement made for us by the captain, to separate off part of the deck for us ladies; that we, as well as the gentlemen, might pass the night there."

It is a common experience, that evils are greater in anticipation than in their fulfilment; and the heat in the Red Sea, such as it is, like many other disagreeables one must meet with through life, will be more easily endured if accepted in a cheerful spirit; the more so, that every appliance is usually brought into requisition on board the regular steamers which can mitigate it during the short passage, which seldom exceeds a week.

CHAPTER III.

FIRST IMPRESSIONS.—*Landing in India.—Indian house.—Naked natives.—The native dress, features, colour.—Complexion of different races and creeds.—Anglo-Indians.—The country.—Physical aspects.—Antique usage and modern civilization.—Historical reminiscences.—Political prospects.*

A VARIETY of new impressions must be awakened in the mind of the intelligent European, about to land in India for the first time. If he be bound for Madras or Calcutta, he might almost fancy himself in Fairyland, when after having but a few days since left the arid rock of Aden, black and treeless, the sight of the beautiful harbour of Galle with its splendid background of distant hills and its beautiful front view of waving palms on scores of little foam-encircled islets, bursts upon his delighted eyes. The funnily balanced boats, which presently swarm round the steamer, manned by long-haired effeminate-looking petticoated Cinghalese, all afford matters of astonishment, and on arriving at Madras, his wonder, on seeing men apparently steering upright on the top of waves, will not be diminished. When once landed, the passenger will probably be conveyed in a gharry* to one of the hotels, if not met by some friend who hurries him off to a more comfortable and genial asylum.

How pleasurable and exciting his emotions on finding himself once more on *terra firma*, after at least two or three weeks of tossing and rolling about at sea, surrounded by the annoyances inseparable from a steam voyage! How glad he is to be no more assailed by that peculiar odour, savouring of tar, boiling oil, and singeing hair, which one finds in every steamer; no longer to be galvanized by the

* "Gharry" is the term in general use in Calcutta and Bombay for conveyance; in Madras the synonym is "bandy."

never-ceasing, jarring vibration of the screw; no more to have to hold on to the hen-coop, or to some fellow-passenger's chair, when wishing to move, or when an unexpectedly boisterous lurch disturbs the even tenor of the walk on deck; no longer to have to duck one's head at the companion hatchway, when going to dinner or to bed; to find himself again surrounded with green trees, and grass, and flowers; to hear the crows cawing, the bees buzzing, the dogs barking, and the horses neighing! How pleasant to look upon busy streets, though of unwonted aspect; rows of handsome offices, funny-looking but picturesque bazaars; or pretty villas surrounded by trees yielding grateful shade, or others decked with gorgeous blossoms!

Let us suppose the new arrival driven up to the door of such a villa. He is struck by its un-English appearance: no oblong, rectangular, brick-coloured building, with stacks of smoking chimneys and rows of staring windows, is here; no closed doors and iron knockers. On the contrary, he probably finds a somewhat low, or at least only a two-storied, wide-spreading, irregular, flat-roofed block, with deep verandahs, white pillars, and open doors. A red-turbaned domestic, previously squatted on his hams at the top of the easy flight of steps, starts into life as the carriage draws near; the horsekeepers, previously running on either side (to invent a "bull") like pedestrian outriders, take the horses' heads, let down the steps, and open the carriage door; other domestics, turbaned and dusky, clean and solemn, appear from within; and the traveller enters a house open to every breeze, and apparently eager to welcome every visitor.

Shown into the drawing-room, the traveller finds a lofty, cool, and darkened apartment,—a swaying mass occupies its upper half, and this when accustomed to the light, he discovers to be a punkah. Doors are on all sides, those opening to the outside being darkened with venetians, those communicating with the rest of the house only half occupied with prettily papered screens. Instead of a carpet, the floor has for covering fine rush or cane matting; instead of a fireplace he finds a mirror, or a pier table with marble top; the other tables also, instead of being covered with embroidered cloths, having bare white marble tops, as being cooler.

The new arrival is next shown to his rooms. Entering his sleeping apartment, he finds the floor covered with cane mats, cool and shiny. A small cot without curtains occupies the centre, under the punkah, and with a wardrobe (or "almirah"), a couch, a table, and a few cane-bottomed chairs, completes its furniture. The next apartment is the dressing-room; here is more cane matting, a washing-stand, and toilet table, with more marble tops, all clean and cool and bright. Next door is his bathroom, with its great tub of clear, cold water.

Now enters the dressing-boy, or perhaps at this early stage, the butler or khansamah, to receive the "sahib's" orders. And here we leave our Anglo-Indian, in the meantime to make himself comfortable, prepare for tiffin, and to prosecute a variety of promiscuous inquiries as to manners and customs with which he is at present somewhat unfamiliar.

By-and-by, he begins to look more about him, and to study details connected with his new life; and the appearance of the natives must be one of the first subjects to attract notice. Nor will it be long before he makes the acquaintance of these fellow-men; indeed, he has already done so in some measure before setting his foot on shore. As soon as the anchor was dropped, a number of apparently naked savages swarmed on board the steamer, from the boats alongside, and but that he knew beforehand how peaceful were their intentions, and saw they were unarmed, the apparition might have given rise to horrible visions of cannibalism, or at the very least of scalping. The attire of these specimens of humanity is somewhat scanty, certainly, but as far as coolness goes, admirably suited to the climate. It may be described as consisting of a coloured handkerchief tied round the head, and a small piece of cotton cloth, or perhaps another handkerchief, round the loins.

Such is the garb in which some dozen muscular, well-formed, mustachioed men suddenly present themselves before the passengers of every newly arrived vessel, and the result is no doubt to produce in some cases a slight shock to the susceptibilities. But we soon get accustomed to this sort of thing in India: indeed so much accustomed, that ultimately most people fail to see anything at all capable of reform or improvement in this neglect of clothing, which at the least is hardly refined.

Probably the dark skin goes a great way towards weakening the effect, for the same degree of nudity in a white man would undoubtedly be far from reconcilable with average European ideas of propriety. But "use is second nature," and what causes native nakedness soon to cease attracting any attention, is its universality among the lower orders, manifestly without the least thought of impropriety.

It must not, however, be understood that the light and airy costume above described is common to the whole population, it being confined almost entirely to the labouring classes, coolies, boatmen, etc. Domestic servants of Europeans are always attired with neatness and propriety; and the middle and upper classes also, upon all public occasions. True, the latter are careless about attire in private life, and frequently in their homes—especially in the hot weather—divest themselves of all clothing but the waistcloth (or "dhotie"), of flowing muslin, which extends from the waist to the knees or lower; but in public these persons wear a turban and a shoulder-cloth in addition; and if educated or somewhat refined, a shirt and long coat, of white calico or cambric, or thicker material in cold weather. Hindoo women, as a general rule, wear a long roll of cloth, over a yard in width, passed two or three times round the lower part of the body, then carried across the breast and over the shoulder, something after the manner of a Scotch plaid and kilt in combination. Some wear small tight-fitting jackets in addition, as do all the Mussulmanees; on the Malabar coast, many even of the most respectable Hindoo females wear no covering above the waist, but in most other parts of the country such neglect is only found among those of the lowest and impoverished classes.

From the clothing of the natives, let us turn for a moment to their physiognomy and physical features.

It will at once be observed, that there are in India many different races, bearing little resemblance to each other. Some of the hill or jungle tribes actually possess characteristics of feature which one is accustomed to look for only in Africa—frizzled hair, thick lips, and flattened nose, in a modified degree. Others, again, are similar as to nose and lips, but have coarse, lank hair, not unlike that of the aborigines of Australia.

But the generality of the Hindoos have handsome, well-formed features, especially in youth. Here, is the open forehead, the aquiline nose, and well-cut lip; again, we come upon the Mongol type, with high cheekbones and wide nostrils; while on every side we may see features such as are most common in those parts of Europe where dark complexions prevail.

There is one peculiarity of feature which I have marked in different parts of India very commonly, and that is the thick, loose under lip, which gives a coarse and somewhat sensual appearance to the mouth. This is more noticeable in the old or middle-aged than in the young, which suggests the question, whether, instead of indicating any mental deficiency, it does not *arise* from indulgence of the physical rather than the mental appetites.

As to colour, we find every shade; from the swarthiness of an English gipsy, down to the dark brown of an old penny. The Hindoos or Mohammedans, however, are never black like the natives of Africa, though I have met with some approach to it, occasionally, among the coolies from Southern India.

To distinguish between races and creeds, the following hints will afford some assistance. The Parsee of Western India is at once distinguished by his peculiar tall shining black hat, long coat, light complexion, and closely cut whiskers. The Mussulman by his shaven head, flowing beard, large loose turban, and frequently by his wearing loose drawers and slippers. Most Hindoos shave the beard and whiskers, but grow the mustache; many shave part of the head; others, all but a lock on the top. One or two tribes and the Brahmins, shave the whole head, closely.

The Madras Hindoo is much stouter, generally darker, and of franker bearing than the small-boned slight-framed native of Bengal Proper; and more robust and masculine than the Malabar of the opposite coast. The latter is of light complexion, effeminate bearing, and closely shaven head and face, with the exception of a single lock which he allows to fall over his forehead. The Rajpoot of Central India is well built, tall, muscular, and noble-looking; the Chuttries, the warrior castes of Oudh, from whose ranks the great bulk of our native army used to be recruited, are of splendid physique and martial and aristocratic bearing; the Mahratta is small and lithe, with sharp intelligent features, and copper-coloured skin; the Sikh, tall, good-looking, and of independent bearing.

The passenger for Madras or Calcutta landing at Point de Galle (Ceylon) will find the Cinghalese a handsome but effeminate-looking race. They allow all the hirsute appendages to grow; men often having hair which would fall below the waist, were it not fastened by a comb at the back of the head, after the same fashion as is adopted by the women. As the attire of the latter is also very similar to that worn by the men, it is often difficult to distinguish females from boys of less than eighteen years of age.

Having thus tried to give some general idea of the externals of the natives of India, perhaps the reader will expect me to say a few words on the appearance of Anglo-Indians. The principal difference between Europeans at home and Europeans in India is that, of course, the latter adopt a lighter style of clothing. Tassa silk and alpaca in some measure usurp the place of the conventional broadcloth; and pith topees, or wide-awake hats, with more or less gorgeous turbans or puggrees (which, by the bye, are pretty generally worn at home now in summer), take the place of the black "chimneypot." People who go out to India in the cool season, and remain there only a few months, are apt to express satisfaction at the robust and healthy appearance of the European residents; and conclude straightway that what is said about the climate being inimical to the European constitution is "all nonsense." But after passing through the months of July, August, and September, either in Calcutta or Madras, the Anglo-Indian seldom looks or feels very vigorous. Of course, with those who are able to spend the hot months, from beginning to end, on the hills, and the cool weather only on the plains, it is a very different matter.

The sun and heat affect the complexion differently in different persons. Thus, dark persons become sallow and pale; but naturally florid complexions burn *red;* and the latter being ordinarily regarded as the hue of robust health, a new comer is apt to set down all fair complexioned people as strong and hearty, and all the brunettes as sickly and delicate.

When a man comes home from India, with a sallow complexion,—"Ah!" say his acquaintances, "poor fellow, his liver is gone." But when an unfortunate invalid, ordered home with a real liver complaint, arrives in England with a red face, his friends tell him he must have been mistaken, or his doctors and he must have been in collusion. A red-faced Anglo-Indian friend of mine, who suffered incessantly from his liver, used to deplore the above fallacy, as totally depriving him of all chance of sympathy in his ailments.

There is, however, a surer proof of the relaxing effects of long residence in the tropics, often to be found in the Anglo-Indian's languid listless gait, sometimes amounting to a positive slouch, as if it was too great an exertion to walk upright. The active, springy buoyancy, noticeable in Englishmen at home, is often wanting, something approaching a stern gravity taking its place, —duties being performed and gone through, not unwillingly, but evidently without the effort called forth being lost sight of.

Of the physical aspects of the country, it is difficult to convey a general idea in few words.

Along the western side of the peninsula, the eye generally ranges over wide expanses of cultivation, terraced ricefields, gardens of plantains and pepper, with now and then groves of mangoes, jack, and other trees, whose luxuriant foliage affords a grateful shelter to hamlets nestling beneath. Here are plantations of cocoa-nut, palmyra, and areca-nut palms, which, with their graceful, waving branches, lend a peculiar charm to the landscape. From twenty to fifty miles inland, a background is formed by the mountain range, known as the Western Ghauts, extending with little interruption from Surat to Cannanore. These mountains, closely covered with magnificent forests, dense and evergreen, reach an elevation at some points of some 8000 feet above the sea, the average elevation being probably about 4500; and sloping away towards the east, form the vast tablelands of the Deccan, Sattara, and Mysore.

On the eastern coast, a tamer and different view is presented. There are no great mountain ranges to catch the eye of the approaching navigator, and the land being extremely low and flat, is not seen till close at hand. Here we have long, low-lying, sandy expanses, varied with tracts of green but by no means luxuriant country. The view is characterised by much sameness, and is terminated inland by groves of palmyra and other palms, of cocoa-nut and plantains in Bengal, and of banian, mango, tamarind, and other shady trees in the Upper Provinces.

The newly-arrived European cannot fail to be struck with the manifest Orientalism of all around him, whether as to vegetation, buildings, or people. Waving palms, terraced roofs, antique-looking pagodas, brown-skinned semi-nude natives, are all in keeping with each other, and unlike anything seen in Europe.

One also notices strange inconsistencies; a grotesque jumble of ancient usage and modern ideas, primitive rudeness and advanced civilization. Here, for instance, is a group of native women with jewelled ears and noses, bare arms and feet, yet graceful withal, filling their vessels at the well; there, a European lady drives past in neatly appointed brougham; now, a rustic drives a wooden plough behind a yoke of buffaloes, while over his head pass the wires connecting India with London and Paris, from or to either of which capitals a winged message may at the very moment have flown.

Then when we get into the railway carriage, and are whirled away at thirty miles an hour, what an incongruity we ourselves become! Sped along by the iron horse, we pass villages of the fashion of 2000 years ago; huts and temples and cultivation, repeated from generation to generation. The Indian ryot who tends his flock or wades through his ricefield to-day, is as calmly satisfied with his mud-hut, his village-tank, his tamarind or banyan grove, his pagoda and the idols it contains, as ever were his ancestors. A few ceremonials he has been compelled to give up, such as widow-burning, self-immolation, and so on, at the arbitrary dictum (as he thinks) of the race which for the time being happens to be dominant; but in all other respects his life and manners, thoughts and feelings, are an exact representation or exact reproduction of those of his progenitors of fifty, or even a hundred, generations back.

Then, is it not a curious thought, that the jungle-covered hills round which we glide, and the forest-clad mountains which bound the view, are the home of the elephant and the bison; and that the engine's whistle may startle from their lair the tiger, the panther, or the bear?

Everything tends to remind us, that while the rest of the world has been undergoing ceaseless changes, India has indeed stood still for perhaps 3000 years. Not much longer than 1500 years ago, the people of Britain were painted savages; but at a period far more remote, the ryot was probably quite as civilised as he is to-day. Indeed, the Brahman religion is supposed to date back to about 1000 years B.C.; about 150 years after the siege of ancient Troy, or 200 years before the founding of Rome.

But neither will a crowd of thrilling historical associations be wanting to the Englishman. It will have been in connection with stirring episodes of modern English history, that he has received his earliest lessons regarding the "gorgeous East," as the scene of all that is rich and luxurious, as well as of much that is poetic. The narrative of Indian history from the time of the first English settlers is without parallel.

A handful of merchants land among a population alien by colour, language, and religion; and by dint of superior knowledge and force of character, at once take up a dominant position, which is maintained and continually strengthened in spite of all opposition. A considerable territory is conquered, and ever enlarged, until finally it has formed a prosperous empire, containing 150 millions of inhabitants.

This achievement was not accomplished without heroic self-sacrifice, and the annals of chivalry furnish no nobler list than that of the heroes whose names must be recalled by a sight of the shores of India. Clive, Warren Hastings, Munro, Cornwallis, Wellesley, Napier, Gough, furnish a roll not to be surpassed; but it does not end here: our own generation has seen the list extended. A crisis arrived in 1857, when all that had been fought and died for would have been irretrievably lost, had the race of British heroes become extinct with the Clives or the Wellesleys. This was the occasion that brought forward the Lawrences, Nicholson, Havelock, Campbell, Wheeler, Outram, Neill, Rose, Hodson, and others, whose names will have an honoured place in history, and will be gratefully remembered for generations to come by thousands whose ancestors participated in the fearful scenes of "THE MUTINY."

It is probably not too much to say, that the annihilation of the rebel armies of 1857, produced a conviction among the people of India of the irresistible sovereignty of Anglo-Saxonism over their country; and with such a conviction immense obstacles to the progress of European civilization must necessarily be removed. There now appears, as far as human foresight can discern, the promise of a long period of calm having dawned on the political horizon of India.

Never again, at least with present knowledge and resources, could any considerable part of the population contemplate the possibility of throwing off (without foreign intervention) the British yoke: a yoke, if such it can be called, destined ultimately to effect the regeneration of the different races now subjected to it.

So long as the British government in India keeps in view its moral as well as its physical responsibilities, and discharges them conscientiously, so long, it may safely be predicted, will it be firmly established.

CHAPTER IV.

CLIMATE AND SEASONS.—*Variety of different climates in India.—Latitudinal divisions.—Two summers annually within the tropics.—Climate affected by local circumstances.—Summer defined.—Delhi, Calcutta, Bombay, Madras, Colombo.—The monsoons.—Land-wind.—Temperature.—Hill sanitaria.—Rainfall.—The sun, and danger of sunstroke.*

THERE are no spring and autumn seasons in India; nor is the winter distinguished by those features with which the European mind is wont to clothe it. "Father Winter" is not there, as here, ushered in by the sear and falling leaves of autumn; nor is his immediate presence announced by moaning blasts, carrying on their wings the cheerless frosts and snow. There does not appear, within the tropics, to be any distinct interruption or suspension of the operations of nature throughout the year; nor is there any periodic decidence of foliage, except as the vegetable kingdom is affected by rains or drought.

A description of the Indian seasons is somewhat complicated by the immense latitudinal area of Hindostan—stretching over 27 degrees, or nearly 2000 miles, from north to south. Even in Great Britain, which extends over only some nine degrees, how much variation of climate is to be found in different parts; as for instance between Devonshire and the north of Scotland; it being not uncommon, toward the winter season, for heavy falls of snow to have taken place even in Cumberland, while no further south than London the season still continues mild and warm. How great then must be the difference at any stated period, between the climate prevailing at Delhi, and at Tuticorin, there being just the same difference of latitude between these two localities as exists between Morocco and St. Petersburgh, or between Malta and Archangel.

Under these circumstances, it is evidently impossible to speak of India as a whole in regard to climate and seasons; and I shall, therefore, divide it into latitudinal sections, as follows:—

Firstly; from Delhi, lat. 28° 40′, to Calcutta, lat. 22° 38′ N.
Secondly; from Calcutta to Bombay, lat. 19° 15′ N.
Thirdly; from Bombay to Madras, lat. 13° 10′ N.
Fourthly; from Madras to Colombo, lat. 7° N.

A considerable part of Northern India is not within the tropics; the tropic of Cancer running through Hindostan just one degree north of Calcutta. The Punjaub, Delhi, Nepaul, Rohilcund, Oude, Sinde, Rajpootana, Behar, and part of Bengal, all are north of this line: the Punjaub extending up as far as lat. 34° 40 N.

As a natural consequence, these countries, and especially the Punjaub, experience a considerable degree of cold during the winter months, which may be regarded as lasting from the 23rd of September to the 20th of March. The 21st of December, when the sun has become vertical at the southern tropic, being the shortest day throughout the whole of India, as with us; the most southerly point of the peninsula being several degrees north of the equator. Even Calcutta enjoys a cool and bracing climate at this period, fires being appreciated.

On the 20th of March, the sun has reached the equator in its apparent course northwards, and becomes vertical at Colombo about the 17th of April; at Cape Comorin about the 20th of April; at Madras about the 10th of May; at Bombay about the 3rd of June, and at Calcutta about the 17th of June. Eight days later, returning south, it is again vertical at Calcutta about the 25th of June; at Bombay on the 9th of July; at Madras about the 1st of August; at Cape Comorin on the 20th of August, and at Colombo in Ceylon about the 25th, arriving over the equator again on the 23rd September.

From this it will be seen, that these and all other

places within the tropical limits, have the benefit, such as it may be, of two midsummers every year; those of Calcutta being only a week apart, while as far south as Madras, the space between the two is nearly three months. At the equator, the sun never being more than about $23\frac{1}{2}°$ from the point of vertical incidence, summer is perpetual; midsummer occurring twice, at intervals of six months, on the 20th of March and the 23rd September.

Could one regard this question of the climate and seasons in India from a purely astronomical point of view, it would then follow invariably, that the nearer one got to the equator the less would be the degree of cold experienced during any period of the year. Thus, Colombo, in Ceylon, is *never* more than about 30° from the point of vertical incidence, while Madras is 36°, Bombay 42°, and Calcutta about 46°, when the sun is in Capricorn on the 21st December. Swat, in the north of the Punjaub, being at the same time of year removed from this point just 58° of latitude, which should give there, at this date, a climate similar to that of London at the end of February.

It will perhaps give a clearer idea of the subject, to compare the relation of different parts of India to the vertical incidence of the sun's rays, with that of different places more familiar. Thus, London, Leipsic, and Warsaw, all being in about lat. 57°30′ N., are in just the same relation to the sun's rays on the 20th of March, as are northern Sinde, Delhi, and Bareilly, on the 21st of December; while on the 21st of June, when the sun is in Cancer, the inhabitants of Madras are in the same relative position to its rays, as those of Beyrout in Syria, Candahar, or South Carolina on the same date, *i.e.*, about 10° of latitude.

But there are in every country *local circumstances*, which materially affect the climate during the different seasons. Thus, countries surrounded, like Great Britain and Ceylon, on all sides by the sea, are possessed of greater humidity, and consequently of a more temperate climate, than inland territories; while places on the sea-coast benefiting during a considerable portion of the year from the cooling ocean breezes, like Bombay and Madras, are more advantageously situated in regard to temperature than localities surrounded on all sides by large tracts of country, like Nagpore, Gwalior, and Allahabad.

Other districts,* situated near lofty ranges of snow-clad mountains, over which the breezes are drawn into the vacuum created by their own warmth, are cooler than comparatively endless plains. Then, there are prevailing winds, like the Indian monsoons (to which I shall refer more particularly later on), which affect different parts of the country in different ways, and regulate the rainfall. The nature of the soil, too, has a great deal to do with determining the character of the climate; barren sandy districts being hotter and drier than those which are generally shaded and fertile; while low-lying, marshy jungle lands, are more steamy and malarious than such as are somewhat elevated and well-drained.

Premising that I shall only speak of two, the hot and the cold, seasons, I will now try and describe the climate of the year at the points of latitude before mentioned. I must first, however, explain the basis upon which I draw the line of demarcation between the hot and cold seasons. In London and the south of England, when the sun is in Cancer (on the 21st of June), we call it Midsummer. At this date, the point of vertical incidence of the sun's rays is about 28 degrees of latitude south of London. My conclusion, therefore, is that in any part of the world where for the time being the sun's vertical rays fall at a distance of no more than 28° of latitude, then in that part and at that time the warm season or summer has arrived. Thus, when the sun is on the equator, the whole

* Such as the territories bordering the southern side of the Himalayan range.

of the earth between 28° of north and 28° of south latitude will be enjoying its summer, the warmth of course increasing the nearer one gets to wherever the sun is vertical, as it always is at the equator on the 20th of March and on the 23rd of September.

DELHI. Situated in the heart of a continent and far from the sea, the North-west Provinces are intensely hot in the summer months, beginning on the 1st of April and lasting till the 15th of September; violent dust storms aggravating the misery of the hot land-winds which prevail during this trying time. On the other hand (taking Delhi as the central point upon which my remarks are based), a long cool season is enjoyed for the rest of the year, and, as above stated, even very cold weather during part of the time, ice being collected on the ground frequently in the early mornings.

CALCUTTA, being situated some seventy miles up the Hooghly, and consequently a good deal shut out from the sea-breezes of the bay of Bengal, and being moreover surrounded by a marshy district, possesses a painfully trying climate during the hot season, say from the 25th of February to the 15th of October. Towards the end of June it will be found even hotter than any part of the North-west Provinces, but being also far north. it possesses a long and refreshing period of comparatively cool weather during the rest of the year.

BOMBAY is the next step southwards The city itself being an island, possesses a proverbially moist climate. Its summer may be said to commence on the 15th February, and to last till the end of October. The months of December and January are delightful in Bombay, and, as nearly everywhere else in India, cool and bracing. The most trying months are May and October, the atmosphere being then hot and close, day and night. From June till the middle of August the climate is excessively damp, and some people find it enervating; but the heat is greatly alleviated by the rains and breezes of the south-west monsoon which prevail at this time.

The climate of Madras, though hotter, is generally considered preferable, owing to its drier and more bracing character.

MADRAS. I shall set down the summer season at Madras as beginning at the end of January, and lasting till the beginning of November; the climate being considerably modified after the beginning of October by the influence of the north-east monsoon. Madras has thus a very prolonged summer, of nearly ten months, owing to its southerly position; great heat, however, is ordinarily only experienced between the 1st of April and the end of September. The two months (or so) of cool season are thoroughly appreciated by Madrassees, as may be supposed, though this period is much milder and warmer than the same season in Calcutta, or even Bombay. The sun's rays fall vertically at Madras about the 10th of May and 1st of August.

COLOMBO. Being only seven degrees removed from the equator, and sixteen from the northern tropic, Colombo may fairly be said to have two hot seasons, and hardly any cool weather at all; though, of course, the months of December and January are, as elsewhere north of the equator, the coolest period of the year. The hottest seasons are from the 1st of March till the end of May, and from the 1st of July till the end of September. The first period is much the worst, owing to its being the dry season; while the latter is affected to a considerable extent by the rains and breezes of the south-west monsoon, between the 1st of June and the middle of August, and by those also which accompany the opening of the north-east monsoon, later on.

The climate of Ceylon is very humid, resembling in this respect that of the south-west of India, to which also it is similar as to vegetation, etc., and for the same reasons.

I must here devote some special notice to the monsoons,

or great periodic winds of the eastern seas, known respectively as the south-west and the north-east monsoon, of which I have already had occasion to make mention so frequently. Each monsoon is supposed to blow during half the year

That from the south-west commences about the middle of February, and lasts till the middle of August, but its effects are not very perceptible, nor does its strength apparently culminate in India, till about the first of June.

In the same manner the north-east monsoon, though actually prevailing from the 15th of August, is not greatly noticeable until the middle of October. In the case of each, some weeks before the great outburst takes place, there is in most years a premonitory manifestation of power in falls of rain and fitful gales of wind, which are known as the "little monsoons," but soon subside.

After this explanation it will have been rendered intelligible, that over the whole of Western India the heat must be considerably mitigated by the rains and breezes of the south-west monsoon (and especially after the 1st of June, when the latter has attained its full strength), coming, as those breezes do, from the colder regions of the south. Annually, with almost mathematical regularity about the last named date, does the wind begin to "blow great guns," the rain to fall, and the sea to rise, along the whole line of coast from Bombay to Cape Comorin, putting a stop to shipping operations at nearly every port south of Bombay * till its fury has subsided, and causing often great floods and inundations in different parts of Southern India.

The south-west monsoon would appear to act upon Western India, in precisely the same manner as the north-east trade winds on the south-east coast of Africa. Dr. Mann, of Natal, in a paper read before the Society of Arts, in 1867, states, that during the hot season, which extends in South

* Which has an excellent harbour, and is, therefore, comparatively independent.

Africa from October to March, the heat is much reduced, and there are almost daily falls of rain all along that coast, owing to the operation of this welcome trade-wind. In like manner, the south-west monsoon also arrives off the western coast of India in the beginning, and lasts through the remainder, of the hot season. In both cases the process is as follows:—Owing to the rising upward tendency of the atmosphere produced by the great heat of the land, a vacuum is created, into which the prevailing wind, provided in readiness by a beautiful arrangement, is steadily attracted. This wind coming directly from the sea, is of course laden with abundant moisture, part of which is poured down on the parched country; the larger portion, however being attracted and detained in either case by the range of mountains which, not many miles inland, runs parallel with the coast: for the remarkable resemblance is even thus far borne out, the Drakensberg Mountains of South Africa very accurately corresponding to the ghaut ranges of Western India.

While of the utmost value and importance to Western India, upon which it exercises a most beneficial effect in reducing the temperature and increasing the humidity, the south-west monsoon acts very differently on the country over which it passes after arriving a hundred miles or so inland. The wind is carried on; but passing over so large an extent of country, intensely heated at this season by the sun, is converted into a dry and scorching blast, and now begins to be known as the "land-wind." As a natural consequence, but making matters still worse, the moisture which at first accompanied it is evaporated, and passes away to cooler regions, where it can become recondensed into fertilizing rains.

It is a common belief, that the land-wind is the vehicle of noxious vapours, causing epidemic and other diseases in the districts over which it passes; and that such is the case seems more than probable, for during the months of May and

June, when the south-west land-winds prevail throughout Eastern India, fevers and cholera are always more prevalent than at other times. That exposure to the land-wind during sleep or at night is dangerous, I can myself testify; horses so exposed having been in the morning found paralyzed and useless, while men are sometimes stricken with violent neuralgia, rheumatism, or even waken to find the features of the face distorted by the same cause.

On the 15th of October, the north-east monsoon begins to be felt at Madras, and continues to expend itself for two months on the eastern side of the peninsula,* to which it brings a period of increased coolness in the beginning of the cool season, and usually a considerable rainfall, not unaccompanied with violent gales.

It was in October, 1864, that the Coromandel coast, at Masulipatam, was visited by the appalling storm-wave, which is estimated to have destroyed 37,000 lives; while in the same month of different years, the Bay of Bengal has been too often the scene of violent cyclones, many of which have caused terrible loss of life and shipping. The north-east monsoon produces an effect on the western half of the peninsula, corresponding to that produced by the south-west monsoon on the east; though with less scorching effect, the vertical incidence of the sun's rays having by this time passed to the south of the equator, and the country having become considerably cooled in consequence.

In years when the north-east monsoon is violent and prolonged, and accompanied with plenty of rain (which has not always been the case of late years), an enjoyable and healthful cool season may with confidence be reckoned on, all over Southern India at least.

* I must no longer defer explaining, that this term "peninsula" is constantly applied to Hindostan; and less often to describe that part of it lying south of an imaginary line drawn from about the mouth of the Kistna, on the east, to Goa on the west. In using the term in either sense, I conform to custom; though a glance at the map of India will at once show its inapplicability.

On the plains, the temperature within doors during the daytime would probably range in different parts of India from 70° to 80°, Fahr., *in the cool season;* that is, south of Calcutta, for of course farther north the thermometer would go lower. Under the same circumstances otherwise, but *in the hot season,* I should be inclined to give a range of from 80° to 105°, though a maximum of 110° is not unprecedented. At night there is a great variation, and the thermometer *all the year round* might range from 55° to 90°; the minimum in the cool, the maximum in the hot, season.

On the hills, the temperature ordinarily prevailing at any given elevation will be of course in some measure dependent upon the aspect of the locality, and its distance from the seacoast. Thus, we find on the hills of Ceylon a cooler climate than at the same elevation on the Indian continent, the sea being within a moderate distance on all sides in the former case.

The average temperature in fine, dry weather, indoors, at an Indian hill station situated from four to five thousand feet above the sea, may be set down as from 65° to 75°; that at from five to six thousand feet elevation, 60° to 70°; and five or ten degrees lower for every additional thousand feet. During the cool season,* at 3000 feet elevation, I have seen the thermometer at 47° at 5 a.m.; but this was unusually low: in the daytime, and in the hot weather, at the same elevation, it would perhaps rise above 80°, indoors of course.

Some more special description of the India hill sanitaria and their climate will be expected in this place; and this I will try and make as concise as is compatible with conveying to the reader a clear idea of the subject.

The sanitaria *par excellence* of Southern India (perhaps I should say of *India*) are Ootacamund and Coonoor on the Neilgherries, situated respectively at about seven and six thousand feet above the sea. The Madras presidency also

* At the end of December.

possesses Bangalore, a large military cantonment, with a delightful climate during part of the year, situated at something between two and three thousand feet elevation, on the Mysore plateau ; the Pulneys and the Shevaroy Hills have also agreeable stations, which, though comparatively young and unpretentious at present, are yearly growing into increased favour. Bengal possesses Darjeeling, within easy reach of Calcutta ; Kumaon has the charming hill-stations of Raniket, a military depot of Almora and of Naini Tal, whose numerous lakes—from which it derives its name—make its beauty unique among Indian sanitaria. Still higher north are the delightful stations of Mussoorie and Landour, whence the splendid landscape of the Dehra Dhoon valley, intersected by the Ganges, here a narrow stream meandering through its midst, presents a charming picture of tropical vegetation, intermixed with the foliage of a temperate climate, and yet more beautified by the grandeur of the not very distant view of the snow clad summits of the Himalayas. More northern yet, Simla with its wild and rugged scenery, with its pines and mountain-pictures, more magnificent by far than the grandest view in Switzerland, has long been the favourite resort of our Viceroys, and become the annual hot weather seat of the Indian Government. In the Punjaub, barracks for our European troops have been built at Murree, situated between the Jhelum and the Indus Rivers, and on the borders of Cashmere near Dhurmsala the sanitarium of Dalhousie, founded by the Governor-General of that name, is fully appreciated by the residents of Lahore. Again, the whole country of Cashmere is one delightful summer retreat, a panorama of beauteous spots, diversified here by charmingly peaceful valleys, there by wild and rugged mountain scenery, interspersed by picturesquely lying lakes and everywhere dotted with villages and towns, quaintly built, and inhabited by fine men with handsome features and women whose beauty is proverbial throughout the East, and is not surpassed by that of any other Asiatic race. Central India possesses Puchmurree and several stations situated on the ranges of the Vindhya and Mahadeo Mountains, while the breezy air of the heights enclosing the Nerbudda valley afford a welcome shelter from the heat of the plains below to the tired official of the Saugor and Jubbulpore districts. Then in a more westerly direction in the Rajpoot States is Mount Aboo, not only a delightful sanitarium for the European, but a famous place of pilgrimage for the Hindoo and the Jain. Its natural beauty is not the only attraction of this favourite retreat, for Mount Aboo is celebrated throughout Hindostan as possessing the most splendid Hindoo temple in existence, an edifice whose superb grandeur is scarcely equalled by any other of the many magnificent structures in India. Bombay is specially favoured in that it possesses, within easy reach of the presidency town, the hill stations of Mahableshwur, Poona, and Matheran, the last two being on the line of railway, and largely availed of for short holidays of a few days, and even for Saturday to Monday trips. The summit of Matheran Hill, elevated about three thousand five hundred feet, is attained by a pony ride up zigzag paths for six or seven miles, the prospect becoming wider and the air more invigorating at every turn. Several hotels, many private bungalows, a church, and a native bazaar form the settlement on the crown of the hill, all about which are formed roads and paths the most picturesque, wooded and shady, leading to various points whence the panorama in its varied features cannot but afford much delight to the visitor. Ceylon possesses Newera Ellia, some six or seven thousand feet above the sea, and situated forty miles from Kandy.

As soon as the much-dreaded hot season begins, the Anglo-Indian living on the plains, whom circumstances will permit, in whatever part of India, or who can make his business combinations so conform, bethinks him how much of this period he can spend, or send his family to spend, on the hills. It would be difficult to exaggerate the pleasure of inhaling the cool, bracing atmosphere of the hills after a long residence on the plains. It is like the inspiration of a new stock of life, and produces an immediate buoyancy of spirits, and increased activity of mind and body. Some persons are, in such circumstances, for the first few days, seized with an inordinate tendency to laugh, while others find it difficult to sleep at night.

Some of the hill sanitaria have not yet quite got over a reputation for feverishness at certain times of the year, owing in great measure to the luxuriant denseness of the vegetation, and also, probably, to the neglect of obvious sanitary precautions on the part of the inhabitants. But every year sees fresh land cleared, new houses built, new bazaars opened, and an increased population; all of which tend greatly to improve climates, which, but for the above drawback, would in some cases be unsurpassable.

The end of the dry and the commencement of the wet season, is the worst time of the year on the hills as regards salubrity; but this is not the time when dwellers on the plains are likely to turn their faces hill-ward, and this renders the fact of less consequence.

It is from most places now practicable to perform part of the journey to the hills by railway; and at the nearest station, country carts, with plenty of straw in them by way of cushions, coaches, or palkees are engaged beforehand to be in readiness to convey the travellers onwards. Some few of the sanitaria are not accessible to wheel traffic, and in this case, coolies, chair-bearers, or ponies will be in waiting at the foot of the ghaut (or ascent). For each person being *carried* up the ghaut, eight coolies or bearers will be required. Gentlemen frequently walk up, if fond of active exertion, and if the distance is not great; but as the ascents are usually very steep and long, a pony or horse should always be available in case of necessity.

Let us suppose ourselves arrived at the ghaut. Mile after mile we wind upwards along the zigzag road, ever and anon pausing under the shade of some overhanging foliage, to take breath, and to gaze in admiration over the far-reaching plain below. Away, for many miles, stretches the low country, partitioned into innumerable little patches of cultivation in every stage of progress. Some are dry and brown, others are lakes of glistening water, others are emerald green with growing rice. Here we see a stretch of barren forbidding country, not worthy of the ryot's efforts, and which produces nothing more valuable than a scrubby jungle. Here and there, there rises out of the level plain a miniature mountain, or chain of serrated hills, studded with sandstone crags and boulders, and bristling with scanty meagre vegetation ; while, in the far distance, some range of real mountains fades away into the very clouds, and shuts out the further view. Clumps of trees down in the valley among the ricefields, alone betray the existence of human abodes, few and small, which claim their shelter.

Still ascending, the air becomes lighter and cooler, and pleasant transient breezes give a foretaste of the bracing and rarefied atmosphere beyond. The road appears interminable, and still winds up and up above the very clouds, until we now find ourselves among the mountain tops, covered with dense forests ; fleecy masses of vapour passing silently through the foliage and onwards as if bent on some mysterious errand. Before us now appear new mountains, higher and higher still, at every turn ; the long ascent appearing to tantalize only to disappoint, and one height being surmounted only to disclose a further and greater task beyond.

However, everything must have an end, and at last having turned an angle of the road, there lies before us the long wished for station. The reader may give it any name he likes, most hill stations having a strong resemblance to each other. In front of the traveller is a shallow valley, or basin, not much more than a mile in length, surrounded by cloud capped hills. In its centre lies a little lake, the sloping sides of which are studded with numerous bungalows, with smoking chimneys and trellised porches. There, rises a pretty little church, while past it lies the road, coloured and buzzing with native life, and lined with bazaars on either side.

The bungalows are for the most part fairly comfortable, though not aspiring to the pretensions of houses in the plains. With their small windows, sloping roofs, and many chimneys, they put one in mind of English cottages. Families of two or more persons going to the hills, usually take up their abode in one of these; the rents ranging from fifty to a hundred rupees a month, furnished. The accommodation afforded is usually a couple of sitting-rooms, and the same number of bed and bath-rooms. These rooms are small, and the chimneys usually smoke persistently, but such drawbacks are overlooked in a climate which daily recruits one's health and strength, and which is consequently conducive to good appetite and spirits.

Bachelors and persons averse to the responsibilities of housekeeping, usually put up at the hotels, of which there are several in most stations.

The hill stations have luxuries of their own, in fine fresh English vegetables, milk, eggs, butter, and abundance of fruit. Indeed, at some of them, the first feature which strikes one, is the number and variety of fruit-bearing trees to be seen everywhere. On the roadsides, there are found orange, loquat, shaddock, lime, mulberry, or even cherry, apricot, apple, and pear trees, all of which produce abundant crops in their season. Strawberries, raspberries, gooseberries, and currants are successfully cultivated, while garden flowers, such as balsams, marigolds, ipomeas, roses, etc., find here their natural home, though probably introduced originally by English horticulturists. In gardens are produced roses, geraniums, stocks, asters, phloxes, salvias, dahlias, etc., etc., and no better soil or climate is required for more prosaic cabbages and potatoes.

Walking, which while on the plains is a weariness and a toil, is on the hills a treat thoroughly enjoyed; and within easy distance will be found different points commanding exquisite and extensive views of the country below. Such points are made the resort of frequent and hilarious picnic parties, which form one of the chief delights of hill-life. In addition to such enjoyments, dancing and croquet parties, concerts, flower-shows, and even sometimes "exhibitions," break the monotony. And by keeping always on the move in the cool and bracing air,—now gun on shoulder, on the look out for hares or partridges or larger game; or, again, to escort some of the gentler sex to admire a waterfall or some newly discovered prospect,—and by making the most of everything, the visitor may well contrive to enjoy himself thoroughly, and will eventually return to the plains strengthened and refreshed.

Though the dry seasons are sometimes prolonged for from four to five months, during which hardly a shower falls to refresh exhausted nature, and it may almost be said that the earth and sky have become iron and brass, the rainfall of India is very copious when it does come, and especially in certain districts. The rainy seasons exercise a most important influence on the climate, and the disastrous consequences which result from an unusually prolonged season of drought, or an inadequate wet season, may be imagined, from the fact that upwards of a million of people are supposed to have perished, from famine produced by this cause, in 1866, in Orissa and the Central Provinces alone.

To those who have never been in the tropics, it is difficult to convey an adequate idea of tropical rains. When we find such terms as "pouring rain" in ordinary use in England, with regard to every placid shower, they are liable to be misunderstood when used to describe a *really* heavy fall of water from the clouds.

In some parts of India, 150 inches of rain, as registered by the pluviometer, falls during a period of eight months—two thirds of this immense volume coming down within a third of that period.* During a fall of rain lately in Mādras, 3·01 inches fell in one day, and 3·35 inches in an hour and a half on the day following; or 6·36 inches in thirty hours! By comparing these figures with the actually registered rainfall in England, those of our readers who take an interest in the subject may come to a fair and correct conception of it.

The passenger landing from his steamer at either of the three presidencies, on a bright clear morning, will no doubt observe an awning secured over his seat in the landing-boat, a bark probably otherwise of very rude construction; and he should draw from the fact a lesson never to be overlooked as long as he remains in the country, namely, to *beware of the sun.*

I have little hesitation in asserting, that during the hot season it is unsafe for any European to walk out in the sun, *on the plains*, between eight o'clock in the morning, and four in the afternoon, and between ten o'clock and three, in the cool season, without at least the protection of an umbrella.

Strong and newly arrived Europeans, full of energy and spirits, often submit to even a trifling restraint of this kind with much impatience, if at all. They "do not *feel* the sun," they will tell you,—which may no doubt be true enough; but though they do not feel any inconvenience

* In Coorg, the average rainfall over a series of years has been 144 inches in the twelve months; of which only twelve inches fall from February to May; eighteen and a half inches from September to November; the remaining 114 inches coming down during the south-west monsoon, from June to August. There is no rain in Mercara (Coorg) registered in December and January, and only from half an inch to one and a half in November and February.

from it at the time, this does not prove anything. The sun of the tropics, if trifled with, *tells* on the system, whether felt at the time or not; and the European never becomes seasoned to its effects. In fact, the reverse is invariably found to be the case; *i.e.*, that the longer Europeans remain in the tropics, the *less able* they are to sustain the heat of the sun, and to resist other climatic influences, by which at the outset they would appear to be comparatively little affected.

This reminds us of the somewhat parallel and curious fact, that topers, when first they take to drinking, are able to imbibe larger quantities of alcohol without inebriation, than towards the end of their career; becoming *up to a certain point* apparently more and more seasoned, but ultimately being easily upset by a trifling dram. This would appear to show, that where there is at work an influence inimical to the constitution, the latter at first has a capability of resisting, which it cannot keep up when once its renovating power begins to be enfeebled.

Let none, therefore, flatter themselves, although they may appear to have escaped any immediate ill effects from undue exposure to the sun, that it necessarily follows they have "got off" scatheless. A person may escape a sunstroke or a fever, but who shall say when the seeds of disease may have been deposited in the liver, or how much more he may have increased his *predisposition* to suffer penalty on the next occasion? Prevention is better than cure; and surely every sensible person should avail himself of the former alternative, when only a trifling amount of care is required. What an amount of after-regret might have often been avoided, for some honourable and promising career cut short prematurely, had a little care and forethought been exercised in reference to this subject!

The numerous instances which from time to time come under one's notice in India, of illness being derived from wilful neglect of simple precautions in relation to exposure to the sun, almost suggest the expectation, that Government may some day take special cognizance of the subject in connection with their servants.

A young military officer or civilian, walks in the heat of the day to see a friend, or visit his club; shortly afterwards finds himself ill; and is finally, in numberless cases, ordered home by his medical adviser. The advice is endorsed by a medical board, and home he accordingly goes, for eighteen months or a couple of years, at the public expense. May not a question some day arise, whether Government should be made to pay for the result of what is, in such a case, disregard of the teachings of common experience on the part of their servant: always supposing, such wilful disregard could be clearly and formally proved?

There are few circumstances under which an umbrella cannot be carried, should walking in the sun become a matter of necessity; and to render this protection as efficient as possible, the umbrella should be covered with white calico; or better still, Chinese paper umbrellas, procurable in most bazaars, may be used in preference to cotton or silk ones. Should cricket, snipe shooting, or other sport be determined upon, incompatible with carrying an umbrella, the next best safeguard will be a good wide pith sun-hat, and a light quilting down the back.

The only system which entitles the European in India to expect to live as long and as hale as he would under ordinary circumstances at home, is one of careful adaptation, and any attempt to adhere in all respects to English habits will assuredly prove an utter failure The gardener is not surprised to find a vine, transplanted from Madeira to an exposed northerly English aspect, nipped by the frost, but rather concludes beforehand that it will be so. To prevent that result, he therefore takes the precaution of supplying the exotic with artificial warmth in a hothouse. No one, either, would be astonished at the failure of an attempt to acclimatize the horse-chestnut at Trichinopoly—or the Bombay mango in Greenwich Park, in place of its beeches. And yet one constantly sees Englishmen in India risking health and prospects by acts only suited to their native climate.

About the year 1862, while I was staying in Colombo, a melancholy proof was presented of the absolute necessity of care in regard to the sun. Capt. L——, staff officer of the fort, a peculiarly amiable and accomplished man and smart officer, had been engaged on duty one morning about the fort as usual, up till ten or eleven o'clock, without other head-covering than the ordinary foragecap. He came home to breakfast at the above hour, complaining of headache and other symptoms of indisposition; but his family thinking it nothing serious, no great notice was at first taken of the apparently trifling ailment. It soon, however, became apparent that these were symptoms of *coup de soleil*, and the gallant young officer actually died *the same afternoon*, leaving a disconsolate young wife and several children behind him; and to show how rapidly these events take place in the tropics, I may mention, that I followed his body to the grave at five o'clock *next morning*.

Hardly a hot season passes in India, without numerous deaths among Europeans, arising from the same cause; many of them probably brought about under circumstances similar to the foregoing, could one only sift the particulars in each case; while it is fair to infer, that very many cases of liver disease might be obviated were due and proper precautions taken.

Many persons suppose, that provided they keep the rays of the sun from the head, by wearing a pith hat, they are duly protected from all risk of sunstroke. But this is a fallacy, the poll and the spinal cord standing equally in need of protection. Perhaps the most frequent cause of sunstroke is the unprotected state in which the lower back part of the head is often left; this being, indeed, apparently regarded as a sort of neutral territory, of no particular importance, between the collar of the coat and the hat. The best protection is a flap or curtain, drooping from the hat down the back; and to protect the spinal cord itself, a tolerably thick coat should be worn. A medical friend of mine, holding a high professional position in the East, strongly impressed this point upon me, on one occasion, as of vital importance, recommending a light quilted pad under the coat down the centre of the back: a most valuable and practical suggestion, and one which should be universally followed by the young and active, who stand much in need of such precautions owing to their excessive liability to exposure.

The effects of the sun are much less felt on horseback than on foot; the explanation being, that in the former case one is further removed from the reflected glare and heat of the ground. The ground has a large share in intensifying the heat of the sun's rays, by reflection; and this fact should induce pedestrians, as far as possible, to choose the fields or grass for exercise, in preference to the roads.

It is admitted by many Indian medical men, that it is possible for sunstroke to be communicated to the brain through the eye, by the glare and heat reflected from a dusty road, even when the person is in all other respects fully protected. Of course, a case of this kind would be a curious one, but the possibility argues the advantage that may be derived from wearing green or blue spectacles.*

While, however, inculcating caution with regard to the sun at certain periods, and under certain circumstances, I would combat any notion that it ought to be avoided or dreaded as an enemy at all times, or when due precautions are taken.

* I have heard it remarked, that *blue* is the only suitable colour for glasses to protect the eyes from glare. The sunlight after penetrating the atmosphere, partaking of the colour of yellow, which, when blended with blue, becomes *green*—the most grateful colour to the eye.

When we remember the powerful vivifying influences exercised by the centre of the planetary system on all animal and vegetable life, it will be evident that anything approaching seclusion from its rays must be the reverse of salutary. The oldest of books tells us not only of "precious fruits brought forth by the sun," but also that "the light is sweet, and a pleasant thing it is for the eyes to behold the sun," while Job in his misery, says that he "went mourning without the sun." The plant grown in a cellar changes its natural greenness for a whitish yellow, and dies. Aged persons may often be observed basking outside their cottage-doors under the sun's genial rays, which they are evidently prompted to do by an instinct which tells them it will not merely warm, but also strengthen and refresh their frames. If I am not mistaken, I have somewhere seen, also, that of late years the medical faculty have found the direct rays of the sun, allowed to play on the naked body, a powerful agent in restoring energy to the nervous system, in cases of paralysis and nervous debility.

CHAPTER V.

INCOMES AND OUTLAY PROPORTIONED.—*Debt, necessity for avoiding. —Facilities for becoming involved.—To live on 300 rupees a month.—Houses and house-rent.—"Chummeries."—Furniture.—Conveyances. —Boarding-houses.—Hotels.*

HOWEVER proper and necessary it may be for officials of high standing, wealthy merchants, and others of large means, to live *en grand seigneur* in India, it is not possible (if it were desirable) for the Anglo-Indian beginning life on an income of from 250 to 400 rupees a month, to do so. In making any attempt to live expensively, he must inevitably run into debt; and, moreover, as every one in India seems to be acquainted with the affairs of every one else, the inadequacy of his income will be perfectly well known to all around him, and so far from bettering his position in society, he will be more likely to draw upon himself the unfavourable comments of his neighbours.

The prudent course for every one is, as soon as possible after arriving in the country, to decide upon the style in which his income will enable him to live, so that he may be able from the first (using a common expression) to "cut his coat according to his cloth," and so, above all things, to avoid getting into debt.

If once the Anglo-Indian gets into debt, he will have tied a millstone about his neck, chaining him to the country, and causing him ever again and again to postpone the long wished-for return home; he will have mixed for himself a bitter cup, the bottom of which will be always receding; for tastes freely indulged at the outset of a career, usually cling to a man through life; and even become more confirmed as he grows older; and extravagance, as a rule, grows at least in equal proportion with the income, and the necessary expenses which accompany it. It thus not seldom happens that the young civilian or mercantile employé, with his salary of £400 or £500 a year, and prudent habits, is really as well off as his superior with five times the income.

Few Englishmen begin life in India on much less than £300 or £400 a year, which, with care, even now is sufficient to procure all the necessaries of a bachelor *ménage;* and if it is not made so, there may be a fear that later on in life, when the bachelor has become the family man with large following and tenfold expenses, he will find as much difficulty as ever in making ends meet, however much his income may have increased.

Every facility is afforded the thoughtless and self-indulgent for getting into debt in India. Tradesmen often grant unlimited credit, and are only too well-pleased to allow young men, especially if members of the military or civil services, to "run up an account;" and no habit is more apt to grow, than one of gratifying every wish as it occurs, when this can be done without even the trifling hindrance of having to produce the equivalent in ready cash: an immediate self-denial being ever more grievous than a prospective difficulty.

Perhaps the cumbrous silver currency may have tended to bring about the existing inordinate growth of the petty credit system in India. However, be that as it may, as a matter of fact, when an Anglo-Indian buys anything, he invariably has it "put down to his account;" and this being the case, no doubt often buys a great many things he could have done very well without, and indeed would never have thought of buying, had it been necessary to pay for them on the spot.

Even in church, many people at the offertory bestow little "chits" or pro notes, to be presented for payment during the week, in lieu of cash. This gives the church authorities unnecessary trouble; but it may be questioned whether the collections do not gain on the whole: it being possible, that a donor may sometimes put down his *name* for a larger sum than he might feel disposed to give in cash, *incognito*.

Indebtedness among Anglo-Indian officials, has of late years attracted the attention of Government, which, in consequence, has made it the subject of one or two public orders—no doubt with the feeling that such a condition must interfere with the *morale* and spirit of untrammelled independence which ought to characterize its servants; and this must be my apology for dwelling so largely on the subject.

There are certain well recognised though unwritten laws with respect to domestic outlay in India, to break which is regarded, in some measure, as an offence against society. For instance, no one drawing an income much under "a thousand a month" (£1200 a year) is supposed to have a right to indulge himself or his wife with a carriage and pair; and any one ignoring this law is calmly set down by society at large as on the high-road to ruin. A similar rule applies to champagne dinners, and numerous other little insignia of wealth; and these rules are not, perhaps, without a certain wholesome effect, in discountenancing needless extravagance among the young and inexperienced.

It is not so much the mere expense of regaling one's friends once in a way with a few bottles of champagne, or of keeping a carriage and a pair of horses, which renders these luxuries unsuitable for persons of small means, as the concomitant expenses which they involve. Thus, a gentleman who lives some distance from his place of business, must necessarily keep a close carriage to convey him there; while if he is married (and an open carriage would not otherwise be thought of), the occasional use of a similar conveyance will be required by his wife when indulging in the luxury of a morning's shopping, or when paying calls during the heat of the day The carriage and pair would thus necessarily be an extra, and not the only equipage; a large stable establishment being thus at once necessitated. The latter, again, will be found quite incompatible with a moderately rented house, a small staff of servants, or even with a plain quiet table: for extravagance, once allowed to gain access to the stables, will inevitably before long extend its influence to the rest of the establishment.

I shall not suppose any of my readers capable of the folly of aiming at an outward show of luxury at the expense of real home comfort.

No bachelor or person of small income is expected to reciprocate the hospitalities of the rich; while, at the same time, there may always be a place at the quietest table, and homely entertainment for a friend, or even for two or three, upon occasion.

Under these circumstances few men need be in debt, or live with discomfort within their means, the regular expenses having been once strictly proportioned to the monthly salary. Supposing the latter to be 350 rupees, the following is something like the calculation I would lay down for a single man (or even for a married couple) *in Madras*:—

Rent of a small bungalow	Rs. 60
Horsekeep, including wages of horsekeeper and grasscutter	30
House servants and gardener	50
Bazaar account	100
Liquors, etc., ice and oilman's-stores	40
Sundries	10
Dhobie	6
	Rs. 296

This for those who wish to live in a house by themselves; and the calculation would suit equally well for either Bombay or Calcutta, were it not (as will be seen later on) that no houses suitable for Europeans are obtainable in the latter cities at so low a monthly rental as 60 rupees. In Madras, however, a habitable bungalow for persons of moderate pretensions can be got for even less; while at up-country stations, small houses are often available for from 15 rupees and upwards; 50 or 60 rupees a month, in these cases, being only asked for comfortable and capacious ones.

In England, a comfortable suburban, or country-town house, sufficient to accommodate a quiet, moderately-sized family, may be rented at between £40 and £60 a year. In Madras, a residence affording the same accommodation would probably be £160 or £180. In Bombay, the rent of a house equally good would be double the last-named amount, and in Calcutta nearly so; but in the large cities of the north-western provinces rents are somewhat less, while in most of the smaller towns and in all the outstations they are very considerably so.

House-rent seldom exceeds 350 rupees per month (or £420 a year) in Madras; while very large and comfortable abodes can be secured for 250 rupees (£300 a year), unfurnished of course, but surrounded with a considerable area of ground in the way of park or "compound."

In Calcutta and the Western Presidency, rents being so high, it is next to impossible for a person of moderate income to rent a whole house; and the result is, that "chummeries," of three or four bachelors living together and sharing expenses, are the most common expedient. A house of two stories, containing, on the ground floor, drawing and dining room; on each side a bedroom, dressing-room, and bathroom, with verandahs; and about half as much accommodation upstairs in addition (which in Madras would be rented at 150 to 200 rupees per month), would in Calcutta probably be occupied by two families, dividing the rent, which would not be far short of 400 rupees, unfurnished While no house fit to live in at all can be had in the European quarter of the latter city under 200 rupees a month.

During the speculations of 1864–5 in Bombay, house-rent reached an incredibly high point, and numbers of respectable persons had no resource but to camp out in tents, or to live at the hotels; and though some decline has since taken place, they may still be called exorbitant; more especially, seeing that the Bombay houses are inferior in every way to those of Madras and Calcutta. For the most part they are merely bungalows of one storey, hardly a bedroom possessing a punkah, and such a luxury being hardly, as a general rule, even found in the dining-rooms; although all such accessories are universal in Madras and Calcutta houses.

All the houses occupied by Europeans in Madras are situated in the environs, the Luz, Adyar, Nungumbaukum, etc., all of which are from three to five miles distant from "Black town," in which all business is transacted; and a close carriage for conveyance to and from business is, therefore, indispensable to every one.

Nearly the whole European population of Calcutta reside in the quarter called "Chowringhee." In consequence of the steaminess of the Calcutta climate, it is commonly considered unsafe for Europeans to sleep in rooms on the ground floor; and all the houses have, therefore, upper stories. In addition to rent, residents in Calcutta have to pay a water rate, lighting tax, and police rate; while in all the principal towns, taxes are imposed by the municipalities, in addition to those levied by the State.

By two or more bachelors clubbing resources and living together, several items of the expenditure, which would otherwise fall on each, become divided among all: *i.e.*, house-rent, the wages of gardeners, cook, butler, waterman, mussalchee or tannycatch, sweeper, etc.; while the bazaar bill is probably not increased more than half as much for each additional individual, as it would amount to for one person only. Each person living in the house would have to keep his own dressing boy or bearer; and an additional matey (kitmutgar or hamal) might perhaps be required in a house occupied by more than two persons.

Chummeries, of course, are only lasting arrangements where the associated parties happen to be of congenial tastes and habits. When a spirit of conformity, and of mutual tolerance and forbearance is wanting, they soon break up.

The following calculation of the monthly house expenses of a couple of persons living together in a house by themselves, is applicable to either Calcutta, Bombay, or Madras. It is supposed in this case that means are not particularly straitened, and that comfort and moderation are equally kept in view.

House-rent	Rs. 225
Town rates, etc.	25
Bazaar account	165
Keep of two horses, including horsekeepers, grass-cutters, etc.	75
House servants	150
Ice, liquors, oilman's-stores, etc.	110
	Rs. 750 = £75.

This total in Calcutta, or perhaps 800 rupees in Bombay, is intended to include the cost of every comfort, and is, therefore, not extravagant.

With strict economy and a little self-denial, probably 180 to 200 rupees might be clipped off, if desired, in the presidencies last named; while for Madras only, a still more moderate estimate would suffice; say as follows:—

House-rent	Rs. 125 to 150
Bazaar account	100
Keep of two horses	65
House servants and gardeners	90
Liquors, oilman's-stores, etc.	80
Sundries and contingencies	25
	Rs. 485 = £48 10s.

485 rupees in this case, or not much over 500 rupees at any rate, probably providing nearly as much comfort

and accommodation for two persons as would be procurable in Bombay or Calcutta for 600 or 700 rupees.

It would in all cases be desirable, in the first instance, to furnish the house, and to buy such means of conveyance as may be decided on, leaving only the current expenses to be provided for; for although both furniture and conveyance can always be hired, such a method of obtaining their use entails a heavy drain on the income without any ultimate advantage.

For 1200 or 1500 rupees, ample furniture can be procured for a small bungalow, such as is rented in Madras for about 60 rupees a month. Of course, one would not go off straight to the best European cabinetmaker's, and order the articles required, out of hand, at shop prices. Here, as throughout, a little management and prudence must be exercised. In every large town auctions are constantly taking place, at which secondhand furniture can be picked up, and by visiting a house where such a sale is about to take place while the furniture is on view, marking down in the catalogue the articles required, and buying them if obtainable at moderate prices, much money may be saved. Bedroom furniture can generally be obtained through the native brokers, for about half the price the European shopkeepers would demand,—quite good enough for all practical purposes in the meantime.

With regard to horse and conveyance, about 700 or 800 rupees will probably procure both—the latter secondhand, of course. Horsekeep being 30 rupees per month, including coachman, an outlay of about 1000 rupees (or £100) is involved during the first year; whereas by hiring, merely, the same conveyance for the same time, at 60 rupees a month, £72 is run away with, and at the end of the year one is no richer than at the beginning. In Bombay and Calcutta the arguments in favour of buying one's own conveyance (if one is required) are far more forcible, the rates of hire being much higher than the above.

But there are other domestic arrangements which the newcomer may enter into, should they appear preferable to those previously suggested.

For instance, respectable families are sometimes found willing to take in a private boarder; or he may reside permanently at a club, hotel, or boarding-house. Hotel living, however, possesses few recommendations in India. The hotels often belong to natives, who do not understand the comfort of us Englishmen; than whom perhaps no people are more fastidious and hard to please, especially abroad. These native hotel-keepers, moreover, are ever anxious to seize upon an immediate profit, not being sufficiently far-sighted to perceive that the most profitable course in the end, would be to yield the maximum of comfort and good entertainment consistent with a moderate profit. They are, further, too lethargic to attend actively and closely to details, which are consequently left to a number of often inferior servants, selected for their willingness to accept low wages; and, as a general result, such hotels are found lacking in order, quiet, cleanliness, and comfort—drawbacks which, though of comparatively slight moment to the passing traveller, are sufficiently serious to the permanent resident.

The charges, however, are moderate enough: about 6 rupees per diem for rooms and board, exclusive of liquors, for a single person; and probably during the hot season, when the presidency towns are more or less neglected in favour of the hills, board and lodging might be obtained in a hotel, by arrangement, for from 90 to 120 rupees per month, without liquors.

In the Madras hotels there was until recently no *table d'hôte*, though this has long been the system in nearly all other parts of India. Each guest was confined to his own rooms, in a solitude depressing to a stranger in a strange place. The "solitary system," as this might be called, had the further disadvantage of necessitating poorer fare for a number of distinct tables, than would, with no additional expense, have been admissible upon a *table d'hôte*. The latter has, however, now been introduced at all the principal hotels.

No married couple in Bombay or Calcutta, with an income of less than 500 to 600 rupees a month, should think of occupying a whole house; they should rather try and arrange to join resources with another couple in their own position and take a house with separate sets of rooms; failing this, they might enter a boarding-house, or take private apartments in a hotel. A man and wife with very small means, might probably obtain one room in a boarding-house (in this case the only private room they would have), the use of a public sitting-room common to all the inmates, and meals at the *table d'hôte*, for from 150 to 200 rupees a month, without liquors. Income tax, servants, ice, and one or two little extras, would run away with at least 50 rupees more; liquors, say wine, beer, and soda-water, 50 rupees; while at least the same further sum would be required for "gharry-hire," medicines, and small articles of clothing, such as gloves, boots, etc. A total of 300 or 350 rupees a month is thus made up. Of course this arrangement would not be very comfortable in some respects, but still it might be submitted to for a beginning.

In some cases the attendance of a medical man is retained by an annual fee, averaging, for a young married couple in the presidency towns, about 300 rupees.

Conveyances in Calcutta can be hired at 12 annas (1*s.* 6*d.*) the first hour, and 6 annas (9*d.*) for every hour or part of an hour succeeding. This is a sensible plan, and a moderate charge compared with that made in Madras, which is only by the day or month, the charge being there 3 rupees per day (or any part of a day), or 75 rupees per month; though native livery-stable keepers are often contented with 2 rupees 8 annas, and 60 rupees respectively.

Gharries can also be engaged by the month in Calcutta, if desired, for about 90 rupees; and in Bombay at

130 to 150 rupees; or, in the latter city, at 6 rupees a day.

Horsekeep, including horsekeeper and grasscutter's wages, costs in Calcutta and Madras about 30 rupees per month; while in Bombay, where all things are comparatively dear, the cost must be set down at 50 rupees, or two-thirds as much again.

CHAPTER VI.

HOUSEKEEPING.—*Housekeeper necessary.—Currency, weights, measures.—Market purchases.—"Commission."—Bazaar accounts.—Stores and storerooms.—Liquor book.—Butcher's meat.—Poultry, fish, game.—English provisions.—Liquors.—Ice.—Fruit and vegetables.*

THE first thing to which I will refer in connection with the subject of housekeeping, is the mistake fallen into by most men, and by too many ladies, on first entering upon an Indian life, of waiving all personal interference in the details of their households, in favour of the head servant.

This sometimes arises from indolence; sometimes, perhaps, from an idea of the impossibility of ever being able to master the intricacies of a subject, the terms, quantities, and materials of which are foreign and strange; and probably, sometimes, there is also a false notion of the increased dignity supposed to arise from an assumed superiority to domestic details, and from a pretended indifference to economy.

With regard to gentlemen who decline superintending their own domestic affairs, there are extenuating circumstances: probably they never kept house for themselves at home, and are unprepared to do so abroad; preferring to put up with the consequences They should, however, remember, that among those consequences, must surely be reckoned a largely increased expenditure; though, should this be a consideration of no importance, they will, with a good butler, probably be able to live comfortably enough.

But with ladies, the question ought not to be so easily disposed of; household management being obviously a part of their sphere, to neglect which must necessarily, in the end, bring its own retribution. Some ladies, while willing to admit, that when in England they daily superintended the more delicate operations of the kitchen, ordered the dinner, or even upon occasion made the pudding,—as soon as they come to India, think it necessary to be completely ignorant as to the meal about to appear on the table, leaving such details entirely to the butler; while they consider it an ample concession to duty, to honour the butler's bazaar book with a superficial inspection, once a week, or once a month.

Now, surely this is a wrong state of things altogether

There are very few ladies in England, in the enjoyment of health, and those few certainly not worthy of imitation in this particular, who consider it *infra dig.* to order the family meal, or to superintend the household, and there can be no reason why the case should be otherwise in India. On the contrary, if economy and a close attention to matters domestic are called for at home, they are much more so in India, where work and anxiety are doubly arduous; where money is more dearly earned, and more quickly spent; a rupee in India, in point of fact, going very little further than a shilling in England.

The *laissez faire* system, however, on which some households are managed in the East, might lead one to suppose the reverse of all this to be the case.

Looking at the number of Anglo-Indian households, in which the butler reigns supreme, as manager and virtual master (doubtless extracting from the office a yearly profit in many cases ten times his nominal wages) one wonders that this class of servant should ever be induced to take service in a house where the mistress discharges the duties of a mistress, and keeps a strict check upon consumption and outlay, and where the pickings and perquisites must necessarily be reduced to a minimum.

The following hints are intended for the guidance and instruction of those who have made up their minds, on arriving in India, to take the arrangement of their household affairs into their own hands.

It will, in the first place, be necessary for the housekeeper to become familiar with the relative value of rupees, annas, and pies. The pie is equivalent to half a farthing English, the anna to three-halfpence, and the rupee to two shillings—exchange at par. Consequently, the table stands thus:—

12 pies=1 anna.
16 annas=1 rupee=2 shillings.

The next lesson, should be the table of weights and measures current in the locality to be resided in. This information I cannot undertake to give here, owing to the fact that a different table prevails in almost every district in India. The weights and measures used in Bengal differ entirely from those of Bombay and Madras. Thus, the "maund" in Calcutta is 82⅛ lbs.; in Bombay, 28 lbs.; in Madras, 25 lbs.; in other parts, 32 lbs.; and so on.

An immense amount of confusion and inconvenience will be obviated, when some satisfactory scale of weights and measures, to be common to the whole of India, is introduced and officially recognised. The matter has occupied the attention of Government, off and on, and has been carefully studied, for many years past, but nothing seems to have been yet decided on. And yet there can be no great reason why a uniform table of weights and measures should be more difficult to introduce than a uniform coinage, which has nevertheless existed for generations.

A "seer," current measure in all three presidencies, equals about 2 lbs.; a "viss" about 3 lbs.

The housekeeper should next learn the normal market prices of all common articles of consumption, and this may be best done by consultation with those already possessed of experience in such matters; or by study of the bazaar lists which are regularly published in the presidency towns.

A great difficulty stands in the way of every housekeeper, in the fact that all purchases have to be made through either the cook or the butler, on whose honesty it is therefore necessary (often in spite of one's judgment) in some measure to rely. Even though one may have a very good general idea of the market prices, these are constantly varying, according to supply and demand; and there are, besides, always two or three prices for the same article according to its nominal quality. If cheapness is insisted on by the housekeeper, it will be the aim of a dishonest butler to make his profit by buying inferior articles, and charging for them as for those of the best quality. Meat, fowls, butter, etc., are commonly classified as "first," "second," and "third sort"; there being a considerable margin between the price of the one or the other. It is, therefore, as may be supposed, difficult to convict a servant of overcharging in a particular instance.

The leg of mutton may be as hard and tough as leather, but such a butler will declare that it is of the "first sort"; and though you may feel tolerably sure in your own mind that it is part of an old goat, and, acting on that conviction, deduct a few annas from the charge made, you cannot *know* whether positive justice has been done; or whether your servant may not himself have been cheated in his purchase. Should such be the case, as is at least possible occasionally, why then you are in the unpleasant position of appearing to wish to cheat him, which is certain (however innocent your real intention) to induce reprisals on his part; as he will not fail to "make it up" with interest on the first opportunity.

This element of doubt and uncertainty, however careful, conscientious, and painstaking the housekeeper may be, will always be found tending to create suspicion and dissatisfaction. Of course, it arises mainly from the character of the native servants, who in this one particular matter of housekeeping, it must be admitted, are systematically dishonest; for the plain reason, that they cannot, apparently, be induced to consider an overcharge on a purchase made for their employers (which does not go beyond a certain per-centage) as a dishonest act, or as other than a perquisite to which they are rightfully entitled.

An English lady in India writes on this subject: "One of the most disagreeable feelings in India is that of constant suspicion induced by the native character; the mistress of a house is compelled to look after the most trifling details, or peculation will surely creep in; an extra quantity of oil, or eggs, or wood, will be demanded on the most trivial pretexts; one feels ground down by these petty cares, and life becomes a wearisome struggle against small encroachments.

"Of course, there is a bright side; the unwearying patience and gentleness of all domestics with children, the kindness of horsekeepers to their horses; the way in which cooks accommodate themselves to having meals ready at all kinds of irregular hours, and the manner in which all servants submit to the querulousness produced by the climate in Europeans,—these, and many other points, are greatly to be praised; but one returns, sooner or later, to the old grievance."

It is a great mistake, however, to take the matter to heart to this extent, the best plan being from the commencement to determine to accept all such trivial annoyances—which are, to a certain extent, inseparable from an Indian life—with the utmost stoicism and equanimity. It is among the natural effects of the climate to make one magnify small evils and anxieties, as well as to cause querulousness; and both of these effects should be sedulously guarded against by the Anglo-Indian who would live in health and happiness.

In order to evade this kind of worry, I at one time made a contract with my butler, to supply the table at a regular fixed sum monthly, allowing a fixed extra charge for every guest entertained at breakfast, lunch, or dinner, and leaving him to make a profit—provided the fare supplied was satisfactory. This plan did not answer, however, for the simple reason that I found the butler (though, to do him justice, he supplied the table very fairly) to be making a considerable profit, which I was shrewd enough to bethink me was just so much money thrown away. I came to the conclusion therefore, that I might as well make the profit for myself, by taking the management of affairs into my own hands; and this is what every one should do if possible.

If the cook is an intelligent and punctual man, of average honesty, all matters connected with the kitchen will be better arranged directly with himself, and not through the butler; and to render this practicable, it will be advisable to employ one who has some knowledge of English. By dealing with the cook direct, instead of through the butler (the latter being the most common course), one per-centage on the cost of every article bought in the market will perhaps be saved; for, be it remembered, nearly every Indian servant considers a per-centage of one anna or so in every rupee he spends for his master a perfectly legitimate commission; though, as he is well aware his master takes a different view of the subject, he does not openly profess to charge it.

A missionary of South India remarks upon this peculiar system, as follows:—"You are charged more than the proper price of articles, the difference being pocketed. If a man bring straw for sale, your servant may bargain with him to ask so much, provided he allows *him* a certain proportion. The proportion taken varies from 3 to 24 per cent.; except in the case of *spendthrifts*, where it is much greater. Servants generally attempt to justify it under the name of *commission*. It is almost impossible to check it entirely, for a shopkeeper prefers making an allowance to a servant, to ensure the continuance of your custom."

This system enters into all one's small money transactions with the natives; and, although obviously based on dishonesty, is almost impossible of suppression; seeing that even should you go shopping yourself in person, in five cases out of ten the shopkeeper (native of course) will add so much to the price of what you get, with a view to returning the overcharge to your servant on a future occasion, with the object of obtaining the permanent custom of the house; or he will even return it to yourself if this is insisted on, with the same motive.

A horsekeeper receives from the farrier from two to four annas every time the horse is shod; the butler exacts his commission privately for every rupee's worth bought from a hawker at the door; and so on throughout. Nor can it be supposed, that the farrier or the hawker pay the commissions without having previously included it in the original charge, so that it does not come out of *their* pockets, but out of the purchaser's.

Such being the case, if the bazaar account go through the hands of the cook into those of the butler, and thence into those of the housekeeper, the latter is sure to be doubly mulcted, each servant considering himself entitled to a per-centage *sub rosâ;* and an imposition, on the usual scale, of at least two annas per rupee will thus be involved. Even however, if the accounts are taken directly from the cook, there is always still a chance of his charging the butler's commission, or "dustoorie," as well as his own, with a view to a subsequent private settlement, particularly if these worthies happen to be on friendly and confidential terms with each other.

Instead of the common plan of glancing over the servants' account, it will be found a much better one to take down the bazaar list yourself in writing every day, requiring the servant to dictate every separate item; and this *vivâ voce* system will afford an excellent opportunity and means of checking overcharges, all of which, when palpable, should be strictly suppressed. A suitable occasion will also be thus afforded the housekeeper, of noticing anything that may have been amiss in the cooking, of ordering the supplies and meals for the following day, etc.

A system of this kind, if carried out in a deliberate and business-like manner, will also be found to have the effect of bringing about great care and nicety on the part of the cook in the discharge of his important functions; for the efficiency of the cooking arrangements does form an important feature in the comfort of every household.

On the other hand, when the cook is treated merely as a machine, never coming into contact with his master or mistress, he naturally ceases to consider himself a responsible agent at all, and will take little or no pride or interest in his work. How can any other result be looked for should he, as is often the case, receive all his instructions through his fellow-servant, the only bond between himself and his master being manifested in the occasional transmission of an angry message from the table, or the infliction of a fine; either of which tokens of relationship will be seldom required, if the course above recommended be adopted.

Every housekeeper should have a convenient lock-up storeroom (or, as it is called in India, a "godown"), in which to keep all household stores which need not necessarily (owing to their perishable nature) be bought in small quantities daily. There will not, as a rule, be much difficulty in obtaining this desideratum, plenty of outbuildings and godowns being usually attached to every Indian house. The storeroom, however, should be inside the house if possible, it being neither pleasant nor comfortable for a lady to have to cross the yard in hot or wet weather.

A stock of the following articles, and probably of some others, may be laid in monthly; the daily allowance of each or any being properly measured and weighed as given out to the cook, butler, or housekeeper, every morning:— oil for the lamps, curry stuffs, rice, potatoes, sugar, tea and coffee, cocoanuts, salt, spices, onions, currants and raisins, and oilman stores ; also grain for the horses

These articles should be purchased in the bazaar, at the printed tariff rates for "first sort," and carefully weighed and measured when taken into store. All this appearance of careful, painstaking accuracy, goes a great way in making the servants also economical and exact ; and the more particular they see you in such matters, the cheaper will they buy the stores, and the less "commission" will they themselves charge.

The quantity of every separate article necessary to be got in for the month, and given out daily, can be easily ascertained by inquiry among thrifty friends, and by comparing the experience and advice of several housekeepers together. Those who have a reputation for economy, and are at the same time known to keep a good table, are the best qualified for consultation in such a matter.

By adopting the above course, the number of articles to be brought *daily* from market will be much diminished; the cook's or butler's temptation to peculate being thereby reduced, and the bazaar account being much simplified. In fact, the only things which need then be got daily will be meat, poultry, eggs, vegetables, charcoal, firewood, etc.

Oil has great attractions for the natives, and I doubt whether the most honest and respectable servant could resist the temptation to help himself to a little cocoanut oil, should any come in his way. They use this, gingelly, and castor oil indiscriminately, for rubbing over their bodies, for dispensing for the same purpose to their families, and for burning at night in their houses and godowns. A sharp look-out should therefore be kept; and the less cocoanut, gingelly, and castor oils brought into the house the better. Paraffin or kerosine oil is now much used in India, and has great advantages. It is useless to the natives for lubrication, and cannot be burned without a special kind of lamp, such as they never possess; as it is also very cheap, and gives an excellent light, it is very economical in every way. Specially constructed shades must be used, however, with kerosine lamps, which are otherwise quickly blown out by punkahs, drafts from open doors, etc.

Cocoanut oil also gives a very nice, clear, smokeless light; and is therefore much used for burning. Gingelly gives a smoky and inferior light, but does not congeal, which cocoanut oil does with extraordinary readiness, rendering it useless in cold weather for lamps. Castor oil is cheap and inferior, but burns very slowly, and hence is mostly used for servants' lights, in the pantry, cookhouse, and stables.

For kitchen and out-of-door use, common lard may be used. It is to be obtained in the bazaars under the name of "pig's fat," and when melted down at home and skimmed, becomes clear, and burns without any disagreeable smell; being generally only about two annas a bottle, it is much cheaper than oil. When oil is thick or muddy, it can be clarified with salt. Hog's lard would at least have the recommendation of being no temptation to servants, more especially Mussulman ones, should they be employed.

With regard to bread, butter, and milk, which are supplied daily by the baker and cowman, and paid for monthly, the best plan is always to get precisely the same quantity every day, so that there can be no room for fraud or exaggeration in the monthly bill. Thus, three loaves every day gives just that number multiplied by the days of the month; so with bottles of milk, "cups" of butter, etc. If a larger supply than usual is required on any particular day, the extra quantity should be paid for in cash at once, so that the monthly bill may never vary.

Grain should be kept in boxes lined with tin or zinc, to keep out the rats and mice; and due precautions should be taken with regard to every article to exclude the ants, which are very troublesome and extraordinarily numerous.

People living in up-country stations, where there is no market, usually arrange with a shopkeeper in the nearest town to supply them with everything they require, to be paid for monthly. In this case, a bazaar book is kept, in which every article required is entered by the housekeeper; the purveyor, when supplying it, setting down the price opposite, and the amount being totalled up at the end of the month.

Tea, sugar, and coffee in daily use, should be kept in a locked case, duly divided into compartments, in the dining-room; larger supplies, together with wines, beer, and spirits, should be kept in the storeroom; such wine, etc., however, as is open and actually in use, should also be kept in a cellaret or in the side-board; so that it may not be necessary to open the storeroom oftener than about once a day; and the key of the side-board will of course remain with the housekeeper.

If the storeroom is not provided with bottle shelves, the liquors may be kept in a separate godown; and as it will be necessary sometimes to send the butler to this receptacle without the housekeeper's presence, the best plan, if he is a respectable man, is at once to entrust the key to himself, a wine or liquor book being kept in duplicate, one copy by the butler, and the other by the housekeeper. All liquors received into the cellar should be entered on one side, and all issued for consumption on the other; separate columns on each page being ruled for beer, porter, sherry, port, champagne, brandy, soda water, etc. The entries should be made *every time* any liquor is taken out, by the butler, and taken down by the housekeeper once a day; and "stock" of the actual quantity of each kind of liquor remaining in store should be taken at least once a month, care being taken that this agrees with the figures in the book.

Servants frequently take advantage of a tiffin, or dinner party, when a good deal of beer and wine has been used, to exaggerate the quantity; the apparent consumption in these cases, to judge by the butler's account, being sometimes fabulous. This should therefore be guarded against; and on a clear case of the sort being proved, the cost of the liquor evidently abstracted deducted from the butler's pay, in spite of all protestations.

Beer in bottles should never be put on a stone or plastered floor, or it will turn flat and ultimately sour. The best plan is to lay the bottles down on their sides, two or three deep if necessary, on wooden shelves. If the beer is newly bottled, it will ripen more satisfactorily in this position than in any other. Before being used, a few bottles should be taken and placed upright on a wooden board or bench, and allowed to stand for a week to settle; care being taken that it is not shaken or laid down again, when being iced, or under any circumstances. Beer or porter once iced, unless drunk at the time, should be kept for a week or two before being used, as otherwise it will be found to have turned flat.

In large towns there will be no difficulty found in obtaining such supplies as are required of the common necessaries of life; but in up-country stations, or in the jungle, this is often by no means the case, and "the food question" then becomes one of much anxiety.

There are for the most part properly conducted markets in all considerable towns, and bazaars at least in smaller ones, where mutton, fowls, butter, vegetables, game, fruit, and grains are exposed for sale.

BUTCHER'S MEAT.—Beef is not at all times procurable, but is generally sold about once a week in every station where there is a sufficient number of Europeans to render the slaughter of an animal worth the butcher's while. Very little beef is used among the natives, and under the circumstances it is not often to be got of really good quality; what is sold in the markets being, as a general rule, the remains of some old bullock worn out under the yoke, or of some dilapidated cow. Occasionally the slaughter of "a fine English stall-fed cow" is advertised;

those who wish for joints or pieces putting down their names beforehand for the quantity required, the price usually being from 4 to o annas (*6d.* to *9d.*) per lb. Of course tolerable beef can always be got in the presidency towns.*

Mutton seldom fails; but as goat's flesh is cheaper and much used by the natives, the difficulty, as a general rule, is to get the former tender and good. There is no difficulty in distinguishing goat from sheep mutton in a cooked state, as the former is then found to be remarkably tough and high flavoured, though there is little difference in the appearance of the meat when raw. Indian sheep are usually small and lean, yielding joints of only about half the size of those obtained in England; nevertheless, if well-fed, the mutton is sweet and well-flavoured, especially in the hill districts, where pasture is rich and abundant, but seldom equal in the general estimation of Anglo-Indians to genuine Southdown. The "Patna mutton" obtained in Calcutta is noted for its excellence.

In India, mutton is hardly ever sold by the pound, but nearly always by the joint, the price being regulated by its apparent size and quality, at the discretion of the butcher. In Madras, a good leg of mutton costs about 1 or 1½ rupees (2*s.* to 3*s.*), while inferior ones may be bought as low as 12 annas (1*s.* 6*d.*).

In Calcutta, the price of the same joint ianges between 2½ and 6 rupees (5*s.* to 12*s.*), but it will here be found much larger. The price of the saddle in Calcutta ranges between 6 and 15 rupees (12*s.* to 30*s.*), while in Madras it would be got for 2½ rupees (5*s.*), and is seldom dearer than 5 rupees (10*s.*), according to size and quality. The price, however, is in most cases quite arbitrary and uncertain, being just as much as competition and demand will admit of the butcher's asking. In Bombay, the saddle

* In some districts, the sale of beef is prohibited by law, out of respect for caste prejudices. This is the case in Coorg, for example.

(as well as other joints) can be had weighed, at 6 annas (*9d.*) per lb., the leg, loin, and shoulder at 5 annas (*7½d.*), and the breast, neck, and head at 4 annas (*6d.*), all "first sort."

In Ceylon, mutton may be considered scarce, no sheep being reared in the island. As much as 30*s.* is sometimes paid for the hind-quarter, which at another time might be obtainable at from 12*s.* to 15*s.* Beef, however, is there procurable in any quantity, though generally speaking of very inferior quality, at from 4*d.* to 6*d.* per lb.

BUTTER is an article difficult to procure of good quality, except on the hills, where it is sold by European settlers, who make dairy-keeping contribute to their support. The native tendency is to palm off buffalo butter (of which the "ghee," which enters so largely into their diet, is made) for that made from cow's milk. In the adulteration of milk and butter, the native of India almost equals the proverbial proficiency of the London dairyman, though not quite, fortunately for Anglo-Indian ladies and their children. Native-sold milk is largely watered, and subsequently thickened with crushed plantains, rice-flour, etc., the same ingredients being generally mixed with the butter, which is besides coloured with turmeric.

To guard against these practices, an effort is generally made to induce the dairyman to bring the cow and milk it at the door, in presence of the servants; but even then, the milkman, who invariably insists on using his own can, often puts water into it before entering the compound. Watered milk can be detected with the lactometer, a neat little instrument sold in all the shops; while the presence of rolong, rice-flour, and so on, in the butter, is to be discovered by the rough, granulated appearance which they give it.

POULTRY.—Fowls, ducks, geese, turkeys, and pigeons, are generally procurable in every properly conducted market; fowls in every roadside bazaar. Large fowls, for boiling or roasting, are generally priced from 8 annas to a rupee each, according to size and condition. Geese are from 3 to 4 rupees (6*s.* to 8*s.*) each, in Calcutta and Madras, and about 5 rupees (10*s.*) in Bombay.

Madras is noted for its capons, which are both cheap and excellent, being priced from 1 rupee to 1 rupee 12 annas (2*s.* to 3*s.* 6*d.*) each. Small chickens, suitable for curries, can be got for from 3 to 5 annas (4½*d.* to 7½*d.*) apiece. Turkeys fattened and ready for the table usually cost from 7 to 10 rupees (14*s.* to £1) each, the latter price ruling mostly about Christmas, when this bird is of course in great demand. Ducks vary in price, from 1¼ to 2 rupees per pair.

In the mofussil or elsewhere, where peafowl are procurable, those who may have the opportunity should try a roasted peacock occasionally, as a substitute for the turkey, having it first well hung for forty-eight hours or more, according to the heat of the climate. The peacock is a magnificent table bird, possessing a flavour something between that of the pheasant and the turkey, and having a depth of breast exceeding that of the finest "gobbler" ever dressed. The peahen is smaller and inferior to the cock, but still capable of affording an excellent dinner to a considerable party.

EGGS are plentiful enough all over India, but very small, and most people also consider them flavourless as compared with English ones. In making puddings, cakes, etc., allowance must be made for these defects, putting in two for every one mentioned in an English recipe or cookery book. Many people keep English fowls, by this means securing fine fresh eggs for the breakfast-table, and a pleasant morning recreation for themselves in superintending the arrangements of the poultry-yard. Rearing fowls is well worth while for another reason, *i.e.*, that well fed and cared-for fowls are much better eating than those ordinarily procurable in the bazaars.

FISH.—I must not omit to make some mention of the variety of excellent fish with which the shores of India are plentifully provided; and which, when dried and salted, form the staple animal food of the bulk of the native population. The most important variety is the rohoo, otherwise called the mahseer or Indian salmon, very similar to Scotch salmon in taste, but not in the colour of its flesh, which is white. The hilsa, or Indian pike, found in the mouths of the Ganges, is also esteemed a great delicacy; and no breakfast-table at Bombay or Calcutta, when the mango-fruit ripens, is complete without the delicately flavoured mango fish, a kind of sardine.

Another important variety is the seer-fish, which is not unlike the cod in flavour and consistency; and is usually boiled and served up at dinner in the same way as that fish at home.

The next in order of popularity is probably the pomphlett, a very delicate and sweet-flavoured fish, in shape like the turbot, but seldom exceeding two or three pounds in weight. This is generally served up as above, or "soused" with vinegar, green chillies, ginger, and onions. Next come soles, which are the same as those we get at home, and make a nice breakfast dish. In addition to these, there are mullet, whiting, and other descriptions, which need no particular remark.

Prawns, shrimps, and crayfish are plentiful on some parts of the coast; and are made by the native cooks into capital curries. In Bombay and Calcutta, where prawns are of a very large size, they often appear on the table in the form of cutlets, prepared in an excellent manner and tasting deliciously.

Oysters are also procurable, but are by no means of superior quality, being exceedingly small, beardy, and protected by great uncouth shells, so that in an uncooked state they are hardly worth attention.* Being, however,

* An exception must be made in favour of those taken at Mahim, near Bombay, which have a very delicate flavour and are habitually eaten from the shell.

generally very cheap, when once a quantity have been shelled in the kitchen and scolloped, or made into patties, they are not so much to be despised. In Calcutta one occasionally meets with oysters brought from the Burmese coast, which are of an enormous size, but they are repulsive in appearance, and either rough flavoured or insipid.

Crabs are plentiful, and differ in no way from those procurable at home.

GAME.—In many parts of India, game is marvellously cheap and abundant. Early in the season, snipe are no more than six annas (9*d.*) per couple, while later on any number can be bought at half that price. Teal range from three to six annas each (4½*d.* to 9*d.*), while wild ducks can be bought for about eight annas (a shilling) apiece. I have bought partridges, on the hills, from native sportsmen, at four annas (6*d.*) per brace, and hares at eight annas each. Besides these, spurfowl, junglefowl, peafowl, florican, and other excellent game birds are frequently snared and shot by the natives, and hawked about among the bungalows at hill and up-country stations. The numerous jungles all over India afford excellent fields for the sportsman; they abound in large game, such as the roe, the antelope, the neilghae (lit. blue cow, half deer half cow) and other deer. In the central and north-western provinces especially, they are very plentiful, and wild cattle, the descendants of once domesticated animals are also frequently to be found. The wild boar also is constantly to be met with, and in Bengal pig-sticking—a sort of steeple-chase after wild pigs, each rider being armed with a long spear—is one of the most exhilarating and exciting of sports, not unmixed with a spice of danger to give it zest.

BREAD.—In towns it is always easy enough to get very fair bread, though Indian bread generally is somewhat spongy, and lacking in solidity and flavour, as compared with what one gets at home. It is also occasionally complained of as being gritty, owing probably to the native stone mills in which the flour is ground. The spongy lightness of Indian bread must no doubt arise from the rolong which is mixed with the flour of which it is made, and from the toddy which is used for raising it, instead of yeast. This toddy is a sappy exudation of the palm-tree, which, when taken fresh from a cut in the tree, is a delightful and wholesome drink; as it gets stale it takes a smoky flavour, and when fermented it becomes an intoxicating spirit.

English Provisions, or, as the natives call them, "Europe provisions," are of course dear as compared with home prices. But the rates charged by many storekeepers in India are so unnecessarily high as to render it advisable to have regular supplies sent from England; and the best way is to have assorted shipments despatched at stated times, modifying the quantities and varying the selection from time to time, as experience and taste may suggest.

In the shops, English hams, bacon, and cheese are sold at from 1 to 1½ rupee per lb. all round, and when one remembers that excellent cheese and bacon can be got at the English dealer's for from 10*d.* to 1*s.* per lb., it must be concluded that the Indian purveyors make a handsome profit at the former prices, even allowing for the fact, that a proportion of such articles sent out from England no doubt arrive in the country in a damaged state.

"Country"* ham and bacon may be priced low enough as far as I know; but I would here warn the Anglo-Indian housekeeper, that it is as a rule unfit for food, unless reared and cured by European settlers on the hills. Pigs kept by natives are the foulest of feeders, and being quite unrestrained, and hardly ever fed except with offal and refuse, devour all the garbage and filth in the neighbour-

* Everything produced in India on the spot is known as "country" produce. People born there are said to be "country" born, and so on, as distinguished from all that traces its origin to Europe.

hood where they are kept. Their flesh, under such circumstances, cannot but be highly poisonous. Who shall say how much the cholera, and other epidemics which devastate the country year after year, may not owe their origin to the consumption, by low-caste native communities, of swine and other equally foul-feeding animals and poultry (for unless supplied with proper pasturage, *and salt*, these are as bad as the swine), which one sees wandering at large among the native towns and villages.

From what I have myself seen of the tastes of Indian cattle and poultry, to say nothing of the pigs, I have sometimes been inclined to vow never again to eat animal food in the tropics.

People just arrived from England are sometimes surprised to find apple, damson, greengage, and gooseberry tarts set down on the dinner table quite as a matter of course; every kind of home fruit being obtainable in a preserved state at all the shops, at from twelve to fourteen annas (1*s.* 6*d.* to 1*s.* 9*d.*) per bottle. These fruits keep their flavour well; and always recall agreeable home associations. Indeed, the Englishman abroad owes a debt of gratitude to the enterprise of such firms as Crosse & Blackwell, and Hogarth, whose pickles, preserved fruits, meats, soups, tin hams, tongues, bacon, and indeed every kind of oilman's stores, are probably unsurpassed, and for soundness generally to be depended on. This is more than can be said of *all* the preserved provisions that occasionally find their way out, and those who seek to obtain excellent quality combined with extraordinary lowness of price, will probably be disappointed. Agents entrusted with the shipment of stores will usually, for their own sakes, select such as are pretty sure to turn out well. Of jams, Moir's were the best I remember coming across in India. These were generally in small one and two pound *tins*, and retained the original flavour of the fruit in a very marked degree. In marmalade, Keiller takes the lead.

Beer, Wines, and Spirits.—Bottled pale ale is deservedly popular among Anglo-Indians; the price, at either of the three presidencies, ranging from five to six rupees (10*s.* to 12*s.*) per dozen. Allsopp's and Bass's "East India Pale Ales" are among the oldest established, and probably the most largely patronized brands; but Furze, Flower, Aitken, Tennent, and Ind & Coope, have each their partisans among beer connoisseurs. A very capital brand has lately made its appearance, called Anglo-Bavarian East India Pale Ale, and is well suited for Indian consumption on account of its fine tonic properties. It has also the advantage of being a trifle lower priced than Bass. Of porters, Guinness's stout probably takes the lead, and is usually recommended for invalids. Next come Blood, Wolfe & Co's, Reid & Co's, etc. Porter differs but little from ale as to price.

Many persons prefer "country" bottled to English bottled ale; and if the beer can be got sound in the wood, direct from trustworthy importers, and is well bottled by experienced hands, and above all kept to ripen afterwards, for from four to six months, it is pleasanter to the palate, and probably more wholesome also, than what comes out from England in bottle. The latter is apt to become very gaseous and somewhat sharp and tart, especially when too long in bottle.

The cost of Allsopp's and Bass's ale in wood at the presidencies is about 80 rupees (£8) per hogshead, each hogshead producing about twenty-four dozens and a half, when bottled. The cost of empty bottles is from 8 to 12 annas per dozen; the charge for washing them 5 rupees (10*s.*); corks cost 5 rupees more, and bottling 5 rupees; bringing up the entire cost of the hogshead in bottle to 112 rupees 6 annas (£11 4*s.* 9*d.*), or say, 4 rupees 10 annas (9*s.* 3*d.*) per dozen. Some saving in cost may therefore be effected by buying in wood; but the largeness of the quantity which must be taken at one time, and the length of time the beer has to be kept before it is ready for use, are drawbacks to laying in a stock in this way to all except the heads of households in which a considerable quantity is drunk.

Of wines, perhaps the principal one drunk is sherry. Fair dinner sherry may be had at from 16 to 18 rupees per dozen, and better classes for after-dinner drinking at from 20 to 28 rupees. Port is very little used among Europeans, and is too rich and heavy to be a favourite in a hot climate. Well-to-do people usually give their friends champagne on the occasion of dinner parties. The price of this kind of wine varies a great deal, but I should say fair champagne ought to be procurable for about 34 to 40 rupees per doz. (68*s*. to 80*s*.)

Brandy is a useful thing to have in the house, not merely with a view to "brandy and soda," but in case of sudden illness; and as it may at any time be required medicinally, I should advise the housekeeper never to buy any but what is known to be of really good quality. Exshaw's No. 1 quality has been generally conceded the first rank among brandies in India; its cost, however, is high—38 rupees (76*s*.) per doz. Courvoisier's is rapidly making its way into favour, being very pure, and moderate in price. Hennessy's, Martell's, and various other brands can be got, of sufficiently good quality for all practical purposes, at a reasonable price.

Claret has of late years been coming more and more into favour among Anglo-Indians, more particularly the light breakfast clarets, which are cooling and grateful to the palate in hot weather. Large quantities are imported direct from France to the seaport towns, but the duty on importation is at present exorbitantly heavy, being two rupees per dozen bottles, or one rupee per gallon, thus adding largely to the cost of what ought to be a cheap, as it certainly is a palatable and wholesome drink. As but a comparatively small revenue can be collected from this item of the customs, it is hoped that the Indian Government will eventually see the wisdom and advantage of doing away with the impost, or at least of reducing it to the level of that charged upon beer. Fair *vin ordinaire*, or breakfast claret, ought to be obtainable at from 8 to 10 rupees (16*s.* to 20*s.*) per doz.

I would take this opportunity of suggesting to all Anglo-Indians who drink labelled, English-bottled beer, wines, or spirits, the propriety of their defacing systematically the label of every bottle opened, with the view of discouraging the present nefarious and fraudulent trade carried on by some of the native shopkeepers to a very serious extent. These poisoners, for so they deserve to be called, buy up from the servants of Europeans, or in the bazaars, all the empty bottles with good labels on them they can find, and refill them with the most villainous concoctions, which they then pass off as the original contents. Persons who suspect anything of the kind can generally tell whether the fraud has been perpetrated by examining the cork, which, of course, if the original one, will be stamped with the same name as that on the label. But the plan above recommended, if pretty generally adopted, would render the trick complained of impossible.

ICE.—I must go no further without mentioning this article,—the Anglo-Indian's greatest luxury. A constant supply is kept up at the three presidencies by vessels from the United States. Sometimes a single vessel lands no less than 1400 tons of Wenham ice. The loss during passage and landing cannot, I should imagine, be much under 30 per cent.; and yet, in spite of this item in the cost, and freight and charges, the company who have the monopoly of the supply, and are lessees of all the Government ice-houses, are said to make a fair profit, selling it as they do in retail at, in Madras, 1¼ anna (1⅞*d.*), and in Calcutta and Bombay at one anna (1½*d.*) per pound.

How the Anglo-Indians in former times managed to get on without ice, and how those who live on the plains of the mofussil still do so, is a puzzle to those within easy reach of the icehouses to-day, who have come to regard it as a positive necessary of life, and who bewail the hardship should the supply now and then fall short for a few weeks. Every household in the towns where it is kept (except perhaps some of them for a month or two during the cool season) consumes several pounds of ice daily, a glass of water being seldom taken without a lump having been put in to cool it; while wine and beer are kept in the icebox for the same purpose. Europeans also, who live in the mofussil, but within access of the presidency towns by rail, commonly receive regular supplies direct from the icehouses.

In localities where ice is to be had, every dining-room should have an icebox lined with zinc, with a hole at the bottom to allow the water to drain off.

Many lives must from time to time have been saved in India by ice, seeing that the prevailing climatic disorders of Europeans, such as apoplexy, fever, etc., are those in the treatment of which this article seems to be instinctively called for as the natural remedy. We cannot therefore be too thankful that we live in a time so energetic and enterprising, in which distance and locality are no longer elements of difficulty in the accomplishment of anything; for surely it is interesting and remarkable to find the very emblem and peculiar property of the frigid zone an article of common daily consumption in the tropics.

FRUITS AND VEGETABLES.—Of Indian fruits and vegetables there is a great variety, and all should be used and enjoyed in their season.

The finest fruits are the mango, the pineapple, and the melon; but the custard apple, the soursop, the pomegranate, the rambutam, the loquat, and the guava, as well as grapes, are also good in their respective turns.

The plantain is universally eaten, and is wholesome, nutritious, satisfying, and cheap. Europeans sometimes eat them mashed up with milk and sugar, when they are an excellent substitute for strawberries and cream.

The American ice ships usually bring a large supply of apples, but these last only for a short time; though they are very good when first taken out of the ice. Good apples, as well as strawberries, and several other English fruits, are grown on the hills. The orange, the lemon, the shaddock, and the citron, also flourish on the hills in abundance.

Of vegetables, the most useful to Europeans is the potato, which is grown in great perfection on the hills, though no great elevation above the sea-level is absolutely required. On the Neilgherries, I have known potatoes, as fine as any that could be grown in England, sold freely at a shilling per maund of 32 lbs. The usual price in Madras is about an anna (1½*d.*) per lb., and in Bombay from half to one anna per seer. Cucumbers, pumpkins, and vegetable marrows are also plentiful; while supplies of fine cabbage, peas, cauliflower, beetroot, celery, etc., are obtainable from the hills. Almost anywhere on the plains, however, French-beans, lettuces, radishes, tomatoes, parsley, mint, etc., can be grown in one's own garden, all the year round; as well as peas, carrots, cabbages, etc., in the cool season. The great desideratum in an Indian vegetable garden is plenty of good water.

The principal Indian vegetables are the onion, the brinjall, the bondekoi, the moorenghey, and several species of the gourd tribe unknown in England, all of which are very excellent if well cooked.

In Ceylon, the art of making vegetable curries is thoroughly understood—indeed, far better than on the continent of India.

To the above list of Indian vegetables I must add the excellent farinaceous yam and the sweet-potato, also the curious knol-kohl, which seems half turnip, half cabbage.

CHAPTER VII.

SERVANTS.—*Respectful subserviency, patience, neatness, "manner."—Masters and servants.—Fertility of resource.—Native Christians.—Anxiety of servants to please.—Trustworthiness as carriers.—Apparent contradictions.—Swift messengers.—Emulation.—Avoidance of showing suspicion.—Responsibility for safe custody of property.—Board and lodging.*

ONE of the first matters to engage the attention of the new-arrival in India, will be the selection of servants. But before proceeding to give advice on this subject, I wish to offer a few general remarks connected with it.

It is a great mistake to imagine, that the native servant, any more than his fellow-countryman of higher degree, is devoid of ordinary feelings or sympathies. True, he is not strictly honest or truth-loving; but are the uneducated people of the lower orders of any country (England for example) greatly noted for these characteristics? What is the origin of that sarcastic reference to "the cat," occasionally heard in "home" domestic circles? Who purloins the half-burnt candles; finishes up the cold joint; sometimes waters the brandy, or keeps a surreptitious key for the beer-tap; or, even worse, entertains forbidden policemen and stalwart "cousins" in the culinary regions?

"The cat" then is hardly more troublesome in India than at home. No one pretends to argue, that the average man or woman servant in Europe is free from faults; and why should we expect to find perfection in Govindoo, Ramasamy, Diego, or Hyder Khan?* No; Thomas and Betsy have their faults, which is about as much as can be said against their fellow-servants of dark complexion.

* These names are intended to represent respectively servants of Calcutta, Madras, and Bombay. Hyder Khan is a Mohammedan cognomen.

But both have their virtues too, which we must be at least equally careful to remember. Whether the English or Indian servant has the larger proportion of faults, is a question I am not prepared to decide, the faults of each being of different character.

Thomas constantly disgusts one with his affectation and self-conceit; the housemaid not only worries her mistress with her carelessness and constant breakages, but when reproved for these faults, frequently responds with impertinence, or "gives warning." In towns especially, female servants have it all their own way, and keep their employers in salutary subjection by their airs and exactions. A London nurse lately, within my knowledge, "gave warning," because she was required to be home by eleven o'clock, when supposed to be attending church on Sunday evening. Such strictness was intolerable

Now, such a spirit as is thus often shown in England is rare among Indian servants. The latter are indeed at times stupid, lazy, and careless, much given to small peculations, and by no means regardful of the truth; but they also possess characteristics, which in servants "cover a multitude of sins," being as a general rule willing, respectful, good tempered, and anxious to please their employers.

It is important to remember, that good masters make good servants, and that bad masters and bad servants as a rule go together. In saying "masters," we of course include also mistresses; nor do I mean by "good masters" specially indulgent ones, but such as are systematically judicious as well as kind.

Too much indulgence is as bad for the *morale* of a servant as too much harshness and severity; and this rule probably applies to servants of all countries.

Some people fancy that "natives" are only to be kept in order by harshness, such as they would never think of using towards domestics in England; but to act on such a principle must inevitably breed dislike, and though it may be submitted to for a time will only be so for reasons not to the master's advantage. Good native servants are always possessed of self-respect, and therefore will not brook systematic ill-usage for a longer time than is absolutely necessary; though, if on the whole treated with consideration, they will show no resentment at occasional ebullitions, which would without fail pique an English servant into throwing up his place.

The placid, yet not withal pert or disrespectful indifference, with which the irritability (which is a common effect of the climate on Anglo-Indians) of a master is borne, is often quite a study. Seldom will a native servant "answer back" in the way an English one would, especially if he thought himself in the right when scolded; nor will the former ever resent a scolding in the roundest terms, if he be a decent, respectable man, and sees that it has been justly incurred. On the other hand, in extreme cases, where an injustice has (whether unconsciously or otherwise) been committed, and where his sensibilities have been more than ordinarily wounded, he will probably remain silent while the storm lasts, but return an hour or two afterwards, and quietly request his discharge.

Native servants are commonly neat and methodical, especially if they find great importance attached to these qualities; and also, it may be added, scrupulously honest with regard to all that is placed specially under their care. They are sometimes marvellously quick in construing—nay almost in anticipating—the wishes of their employers, and extremely ready in carrying them out under circumstances of difficulty.

To these good traits the Indian servant adds, that he is naturally possessed of tact, discreetness, and what is known as "manner," in, I think I may say without fear of contradiction, a far higher degree than Europeans generally of the same rank in life.

No Belgravian footman will show a visitor into the

drawing-room, or open the door of a carriage, with more dignified politeness, than the head servant in a well-conducted Indian household. No English valet will with more quiet promptness bathe your feet, or lay out your evening dress, and retire as soon as he sees his presence is no longer desired, than your "boy," or "bearer."

But in India, as elsewhere, before one can expect to be comfortably situated with regard to servants, it is first of all necessary to take pains to get good ones, and next, to instruct and initiate them at the outset in all the various duties they are expected to perform.

Young men coming straight from the English home-life, and thrown on their own resources for the first time, can hardly be expected to be particularly *au fait* in the treatment of servants, and Indian servants. Then, to make matters worse, they frequently begin by getting disreputable attendants—the floating scum perhaps of the English-speaking native population, whose drunkenness, trickeries, and general misconduct tend to disgust their masters with the whole class.

It is thus that bad servants make bad masters; for a man whose whole experience of servants is derived from those who have proved themselves idle, dirty, dishonest, and intemperate, is naturally inclined to regard all servants as "tarred with the same brush," and to entertain for all, in consequence, feelings of mingled contempt and dislike. Such feelings lead to a corresponding treatment; and this is probably one reason for our finding so many young Europeans, not long in the country, in the habit of addressing their domestics in terms of severity, when they would be better served, and altogether more comfortable, were a different course followed.

The tone of some of the "sketches" of Anglo-Indian life, which appear in print from time to time, incidentally shows that the treatment servants experience in India is by no means invariably kind or judicious.

An instance of this is presented in a work called "Gup," which it will be remembered was brought out some years back. The authoress had long been resident in India, and was familiar with the life and localities treated of. Well, she does not appear to have been at all shocked or surprised by the conduct of a gentleman whom she describes as kicking the native butler down stairs for some trifling fault, the said butler being in the act of carrying a tray with dishes, etc., and of course falling headlong amid a crash of broken crockery. One might have expected, that such a circumstance would hardly be referred to otherwise than in terms of reprobation; but that the writer should expect her very lenient view of the matter to be taken by the average English reader appears to argue her belief in a wrong state of feeling on the subject, as being entertained by the majority of English people.

Only the other day I happened to take up an article, entitled "Reminiscences of India" by an old officer, the prevailing tone of which implied the utmost contempt for all natives, or, as he calls them, "black men." Speaking of some medicine which the doctor of his regiment was anxious to prescribe for him, the author says: "He knew it was no use to send me medicine, which I should only have hidden under my pillow, or *thrown at the black servant's head*," etc. Elsewhere he relates: "As I was not likely to see a European for many weeks, I asked our doctor what I was to do with my *black men* (the italics are mine) if they were seized with the disorder (cholera). He gravely told me, that I had better always begin by giving the patient a table-spoonful of laudanum, with a tea-spoonful of calomel to follow. All I shall say is, I did my best for the poor fellows, and not always without success, but *it was fortunate there were no coroners' inquests in that country to pry into the results*."* (My italics again.)

* The reader should be made aware, that these quantities are about five to ten times the ordinary doses given to adults.

The evil lies in the fact, that such references are supposed to be highly humorous; but persons who consider their servants entitled to no better usage than is naturally implied in such anecdotes will never keep respectable people about them, or be at all well served.

On this subject, an experienced observer writes: "I am often told that it is a proof of weakness to show consideration for servants—that the better a native is treated the more ungrateful he is; but I cannot divest myself of the idea, that he is, if a very bad specimen of 'a man and a brother,' at all events a fellow-creature, and I really cannot persuade myself or others that it does well to treat him like a brute, to deny him every opportunity of relaxation, or to prevent his having his meals or sleep in peace." A very proper view of the subject.

The quickness and fertility of resource of the native servant, under difficult circumstances, is a point specially deserving of mention. On a journey, they are hardly ever at a loss, and will contrive to provide a satisfactory meal on the shortest notice, with the most slender materials and appliances. Three stones from the road-side, arranged by the cook under a tree, will form a fireplace; a few sticks, a fire; and an earthen chatty, purchased for something over a penny, at the nearest bazaar, will be made to do duty for saucepan, kettle, or fryingpan, as may be required. With such appliances, or little more, a good dish of curry and rice, a stew, or cutlets, will be prepared at the first halt, the necessary materials for the dish being everywhere procurable.

It is not at all an uncommon circumstance, on the unexpected arrival of hungry visitors in the jungle, fatigued perhaps by a long ride, for a hearty cooked meal to be set before them within the space of half an hour. This is accomplished somewhat as follows; perhaps the last supplies of mutton, or beef, got from the nearest market town, are exhausted, likewise the bread, butter, etc. But no matter.

The cook instantly seizes a couple of fowls, calmly strutting before the cook-house door. These are killed, plunged into a bucket of hot water (in aid of plucking), opened out, and grilled; and hence is produced a dish (sometimes called "spatch-cock," but more commonly by the appropriate title of "sudden death"), by no means unpalatable to the hungry stomach, when flanked by a smoking dish of sliced potatoes, some rice flour "chupatties,"* and washed down with a bottle of pale ale. All this is done in the time an English domestic would require to grumble over the dilemma of the establishment; and in situations where, be it remembered, fresh provisions cannot be bought, and consequently where, to the uninitiated, nothing short of a miracle would appear likely to produce a meal.

Many native servants are also excellent nurses during sickness, and will watch night and day by the bedside of a master, whose habitual treatment of them has entitled him to such a solicitude, and this they will do in a noiseless unobtrusive way, admirably suited to the sick-room.

It is a common thing to warn new arrivals against taking as servants natives who profess Christianity; but nothing that has come under my notice, during my long experience, warrants me in endorsing the caution. There can obviously be no reason why native Christians should, as a rule, make worse servants than heathens, while there are powerful ones why they *ought* to be better. It is probable, however, that the strong prejudice so commonly entertained against native Christians of the lower orders, has not originated without at least some foundation; and this I take to be somewhat as follows. Many of the so-called native Christians are either born of nominally Christian parents, or have become so themselves for some material advantage, their knowledge of the principles of Christianity being, however, almost nil.

* Cakes.

Stories are told of the Portuguese and Dutch, in former times, taking out boat-loads of natives some little distance from the shore, in order that wholesale baptism might be facilitated to the utmost, no previous instruction or probation being required. Once baptized, however, the proselytes were of course called "Christians," and their descendants also. Although missionaries are often, nay generally, now-a-days, sufficiently strict in their examination of candidates for baptism, still it may happen that natives, principally from the lowest ranks of life, from time to time profess themselves converts from interested motives; and such of course cannot be otherwise than inconsistent, and even morally inferior, to the honest among the heathen around. Having once declared themselves "Christians," they are abandoned by their relatives, and are moreover emancipated from the restraints of caste and social ties; and being uninfluenced by the new obligations they pretend to have taken upon themselves, such converts are naturally disreputable and intemperate.

But surely *all* native converts are not to be placed in this category. There are exceptions to every rule, black sheep in every fold; and it is hardly fair to condemn an entire class, because a proportion of its members deserve opprobrium. Instead of adopting so narrow-minded a course, I shall recommend the reader rather to act upon the following valuable opinion of an excellent Indian missionary, who says: "When *truly converted* native Christians *can* be procured, they are by all means to be preferred. The best native Christians, as a rule, however, are not accustomed to domestic service. *Nominal* Christians are not more honest than heathens, and sometimes drink, which the latter as a rule do not. Heathen servants are to be preferred to bad Christians."

When in India, I should never have thought of inquiring, before engaging a servant, what religion he professed. It seems to me, that it would be equally absurd either to refuse to employ, or to engage, a man *because* he professed one religion or another—say Christianity. In the one case you dishonour Christianity, in the other you encourage hypocrisy, and offer inducement to designing unprincipled persons to bring Christianity into disrepute.

The honesty or otherwise of native servants is a puzzling question, owing to the many contradictions an analysis of it brings into view.

A man who would at one time appear incorruptibly honest, you will perhaps find, at another, guilty of the pettiest deceits, or even thefts.

When a new servant is taken into the house, everything should be given over into his charge; he should be made to take a list, and this should be checked at intervals; and he should understand, distinctly, that he is held responsible for anything that may be lost. You may then make your mind easy, even though the man be not particularly honest in other respects.

Many persons even make over their money into the servant's charge, taking from him what they require from day to day; but this is perhaps carrying the principle unnecessarily far.

A man who appears to be thoroughly trustworthy in great matters is often quite the reverse in small ones, and will not hesitate to cheat you in the bazaar account, or to help himself to your stores. Common coolies in the planting districts are often unhesitatingly commissioned to carry bags of money, as much sometimes as 1000 rupees, alone and unguarded two or more days' journey through the jungle. When in charge of coffee estates at one period, if in want of money to pay the work people, I would sometimes call a coolie out of the field; and handing him a cheque for £50 or more, request him to run into the town, a distance perhaps of twenty miles, and bring out the cash from the bank. Next day, this man (whose wages were only *7d.* or *8d.* per diem) would return with the money tied up in his handkerchief, perfectly correct, being well satisfied with the customary present of a shilling for the responsibility incurred. Large sums too are continually brought up the ghauts, from the Malabar coast to the South India coffee districts, in the same way.

These money carriers are sometimes knocked down and robbed, when passing through the villages, but seldom if ever abscond; although of course such sums would enrich any of them for life. And yet, anomalous as it may seem, the same man who would discharge such a responsibility with perfect accuracy would probably not hesitate to steal a few measures of rice, or a pound of coffee or salt, should an opportunity of doing so occur, without much seeming risk of detection.

Natives of the coolie class,—about whom a word more,—are often splendid runners, and will often carry a letter or a parcel as far and as fast as an average European on horseback. Did space permit, I could relate many feats illustrating this assertion, but one will suffice.

When engaged in superintending some fieldwork one day, I found myself short of tobacco; and being then an inveterate smoker, at once beckoned to a Tamil coolie, working close at hand, and giving him a written slip, and explaining how things stood, told him to run into Kandy (Ceylon), 14 miles distant, deliver the note, and bring out the required article. It was now near noon, and a present was promised if he was back by seven in the evening. Before the time named, my messenger was back, his face glowing with evident satisfaction at having accomplished the feat.

I always found it a good plan, when requiring any unusually severe task from native servants of any class, not only to promise a reward if it were satisfactorily performed, but to take them into confidence, by explaining the circumstances creating the urgency. A sort of friendly sympathy for the occasion was thus established, producing more intelligent and willing service than would be the case were they treated merely as machines.

Thus, when living out in a jungle, I would sometimes have occasion to say to a messenger, required to bring out provisions an ordinary two days' journey in half the time, "Several gentlemen are coming to dinner to-night, and there is nothing in the house to eat; run with this order to ——, and bring out the things to-night, and I will give you a present." When the intended messenger gave a ready response, and promised to return within the time named, he almost invariably did so, unless delayed. But if he appeared to demur to the task as too arduous, I would dismiss him as "a lazy fellow," and select another messenger. By these means a spirit of emulation was created. Of course, it should be made a rule never to impose a heavier task in this way than experience has shown to be practicable.

Horsekeepers have commonly a character for intemperance and excessive trickiness, but they are not *always* deserving of it, especially if well looked after. They have, generally speaking, a hard life of it,—the custom being for them to run a great deal after their master's carriage or riding horse, and perhaps this in some measure accounts for their tendency to drinking. In up-country stations it is not an uncommon thing for one of these men to bring your steed saddled to the door, take your carpet-bag on his head, and run at the rate of six miles an hour for fifteen or twenty miles. He will then take the animal, rub down and feed it, and make the return journey on the following day.

Indian servants generally are, as a rule, anxious to please; and if they find they can succeed in doing this, they readily identify themselves with the family in which they are employed, taking a real interest in its welfare and credit. This is shown by the common adoption among them of the plural pronoun, in speaking of their master's property or belongings.

Thus they would say, "our horses," "our garden," and even "our children," when speaking of those of the establishment.

It is, however, desirable to be cautious in showing approbation of their conduct. In a general way I should be inclined to say that they cannot stand much praise. It takes them completely off their legs, and tends to make them conceited and troublesome. The true principle seems to be to keep before them that they are but unprofitable; while, at the same time, care is taken to show approval of good conduct and faithful service, by a general off-hand friendliness of manner, and *practically* as well by little occasional presents, etc.

In dealing with servants, or indeed with natives of any class, it is very injudicious to show suspicion of their honesty, unless, owing to previous undeniable convictions, it is impossible to keep up even an appearance of confidence; but in this case a servant ought by no means to be retained. Be as watchful and cautious as you like,—the more so the better,—but do not let this be apparent. A man is ten times more likely to act uprightly if he believes himself to be trusted, than if he perceives he is already looked upon as a thief *in posse:* some men indeed, in the latter case, will be piqued into a course of systematic plundering and deceit, which can neither be detected nor guarded against.

It is also to be remembered that in Indian houses, owing to the large number of servants, there are great difficulties in the detection and conviction of thefts, and suspicion may often fall on the wrong person. It should therefore be made a rule never to accuse, without proof positive, a servant of having *stolen* anything that may be missing.

It is better to call the head servant, and tell him such and such an article has been *lost,* and that you insist on its being found; gently reminding him that he is responsible for its safety. In most cases, especially if it be seen that the loss is looked upon as important, this will lead to restoration.

The effect of making a native responsible for one's property is remarkable, and may often be turned to account under trying circumstances. On one occasion, when travelling hillwards, and having arrived at the foot of the ghauts, where the cart-road ended, and where coolies had been engaged to be in readiness to convey my baggage to the station, I was taken aback by the said coolies flatly refusing to take up the boxes, etc., on the plea of their being too heavy. There was no possibility of getting a fresh set of men; and every argument to overcome their obstinacy proving in vain, I turned to the duffadar (or head man of the gang) and said: "Now these coolies have been engaged to carry my luggage to ——, which, as they nevertheless refuse to do, I shall hold you responsible, and will trouble myself no further, leaving you and the coolies to do as you like." So saying, I forthwith started up the ghaut by myself, leaving duffadar, coolies, and baggage in the middle of the road. Of course I knew nothing about the duffadar; and had he and his gang then and there set to work, taken possession of my effects, and carried them off to their villages, I might never have heard of any of them again. But I knew my friend would be little likely to take this view of the matter, and relied on the effect I had often previously found produced by a similar course to that which I had now taken. Had I remained on the spot, I might have argued till doomsday without producing any effect, and the coolies would have gone off and left me to shift as best I might. But, once I departed, the onus of looking after the baggage devolved entirely upon *them*, and I knew they would not leave it, at the risk of being afterwards held answerable for casualties.

Nor was I wrong in this calculation. Calmly proceeding on my way, I reached —— early in the afternoon; and towards dusk, one box after another made its appearance, until all had been duly laid down before me in the bungalow verandah; the maistry himself bringing up the rear, and making his salaam in token of having discharged the obligation laid upon him.

One great convenience in relation to Indian servants, as compared with English ones, is, that no provision has to be made with regard to their board or lodging. In the large towns, nearly all the higher servants have houses of their own, to which they retire after the duties of the day. Indeed, although there are in most parts of India ample outbuildings on their master's premises, they prefer this arrangement. It is only necessary to have one or two servants to sleep *in the house* at night, and one or other usually takes it in turn to do so, spreading his mat on the floor of the entrance hall or in the verandah, which is all the accommodation required. The cook sometimes makes himself comfortable on a shelf in the kitchen; otherwise, he leaves a deputy in charge of the pots and pans. The horse-keepers should *always* sleep in the stables, and one or two spare horse-stalls will suffice for them.

But, though it is thus necessary for some few of the servants to live within the compound,* the licence ought *never* to be extended to their families, seeing that an average Indian establishment contains from fifteen to twenty servants. Taking the lower number, suppose each of these to be married (and every native of sixteen and upwards *is* married), and we have fifteen wives; half of them probably will have from two to three children a-piece, say eighteen children—making in all forty-eight souls; to say nothing of inevitable relatives and hangers-on, adding probably ten to the number. It must evidently be undesirable, if only from a sanitary point of view, to permit such

* "Compound" is a term applied to all the ground attached to and surrounding an Indian dwelling-house. The word is said to be a corruption of the Portuguese "campania."

a colony to live within fifty yards of one's house: but there are other objections, such as constant squabbling and fighting, children crying, tomtom (and wife) beating, and so on, all destructive of the order and harmony of a well-regulated household.

CHAPTER VIII.

SERVANTS.—" *Characters."—Bad memories.—Servants in Madras—In Calcutta—In Bombay.—Tables of wages.—Butler.—Khansamah.—Matey.—Kitmutgar.—Dressing boy.—Bearers.—Ayahs.—Durzee.—Durwan.—Chokkra.—Tannycatch.—Multiplicity of servants.—Causes.—" Custom " and caste.*

THE question now presents itself:—How are good servants to be got?

In England and elsewhere, the common method is to be guided by the written "characters" in possession of the applicant for employment; but in India these are not at all to be relied on, unless they happen to be in some known handwriting, or to have been given by persons accessible to direct inquiry; and such is not very often the case.

By a curious coincidence, it generally happens that the characters presented for review are all of a date antecedent to one's arrival in the country; and such, it may be taken for granted, are either borrowed for the occasion from *bonâ fide* recipients, or purchased in the bazaar. The forgery of false characters is quite a recognised calling in all the large Indian towns, and I have been told that one for any position, or a "begging letter" to suit any circumstances (however harrowing), can be bought for from four annas to a rupee. Some of the ingenious rogues who concoct them occasionally do a little business in the way of composing petitions on their own account; and I remember an instance, in which "a blind widow lady in reduced circumstances" whose petition used to come round periodically, turned out to be a retired native butler.

It does not always follow that a palpably transferred or fictitious character bespeaks a bad servant; nor that a man who possesses genuine though only modified testimony as to his antecedents, may not sometimes turn out to be a very fair servant after all. As a rule, all servants looking for situations will produce good characters; and, therefore, any who present such as convey only "faint praise," argue themselves unusually ingenuous.

The great majority of candidates for places, are also, strange to say, quite unable to remember any of their immediate antecedents. Up to the dates of their characters, say four, five, or eight years back, memory seems to have stood them in good stead, but the interval is a blank in their history—judging from the difficulty usually found in extracting any tangible information on the subject. The only replies to be got in these cases, are that they have been "in their country," a very common expression; but where their country is, and what they have been doing there, are unfathomable mysteries.

The explanation no doubt commonly is, that these place-seekers have left their last berth on not over good terms with "master" or "missus."

Where it is not practicable to refer to the *bonâ fide* giver of a character, most men, if recommended by some other decent servant, will be worthy at least of a trial; and where a man has an open, intelligent countenance, not a particularly "down-look," and is generally neat and respectable in his appearance, he will probably be found equal to the average in other respects—while trial will best prove whether he is competent for his duties. Good servants are generally able to introduce others; and, while writing, I have in my mind's eye, an excellent Indian butler, who was always somehow or other able upon the shortest notice to produce a respectable and trustworthy servant for any vacancy. Any friend, therefore, who already has a good butler, will be able in due time to put the new arrival in the way of getting such servants as he may require.

The three great capitals of India are Calcutta, Bombay, and Madras; and the social customs prevailing in each, extend in great measure over what are commonly known as the Bengal, Bombay, and Madras Presidencies; though the Bengal Presidency proper, or province of Bengal, forms only a small part of the territory over which Calcutta, to all intents and purposes, exercises the influences of a capital. This practically, though hardly nominally, includes the Punjaub and North-west Provinces; though each of the latter provinces possesses an important local capital of its own, as Lahore, Allahabad, Delhi, etc.

In the same way, Madras extends an influence to Cape Comorin on the south, to the Central Provinces on the north, and to British Burmah on the east.

The social influence of Bombay, may be said to begin on the western coast at Sedashegur (Carwar), and extends northwards as far as Beloochistan; being bounded on the east by Scindia and the Deccan, and on the north by the Punjaub and Delhi.

This at least appears to me about the most convenient division, for the objects aimed at in the present work; and having made this preliminary explanation, I now purpose giving some account of the servants required in each of the three presidency towns, taking it for granted this information will be found more or less applicable over the respective territories with which those towns are connected.

To begin with Madras: the following is intended to be a list of servants required in the house of a married couple, without children, in comfortable pecuniary circumstances:—

1, Butler; 2, matey; 3, boy, or dressing-boy; 4, ayah; 5, cook; 6, cook's matey, or market-boy; 7, tannycatch; 8, waterman; 9, totee, or sweeper; 10, and 11, two gardeners; 12, a bearer (two are sometimes employed); 13, punkahman, for day work; 14 and 15, two punkahmen, for night work (for each bedroom); and supposing the stable establishment to consist of a one-horse office carriage, and an open carriage and pair for evening drives, the following additional servants—16, coachman (perhaps two); 17, 18, and 19, three horsekeepers; 20, 21, and 22, three grass-cutters (women).

If no open carriage and pair be kept, but only a single-horse close carriage, then two horsekeepers, and two grass-cutters can be dispensed with; but every horse kept necessitates keeping also a horsekeeper and a grasscutter to attend to it.

Washing is done out, for which a dhobie is paid so much monthly.

The above list gives a complement of 18 men and 5 women servants; costing from 135 to 150 rupees a month; (as per list of wages which is given later on).

In small or bachelor establishments, or where economy is aimed at, the following servants will be dispensed with:— 1, matey; 2, one gardener (or perhaps this servant may by arrangement be made chargeable to the landlord); 3, bearer; 4, the day punkahman; and if only one close office carriage is kept, perhaps 5, 6, and 7, three horse-keepers; and 8, 9, two grasscutters, leaving the coachman to take care of the horse as well as the carriage, in which case he will require one or two rupees a month extra pay. In houses where there is no lady, of course no ayah (10) will be required. Under these circumstances too, the servants will be content with smaller wages than would be looked for in the larger establishment.

It will thus be seen, that in a small and thriftily managed household, the number and cost of servants may be much reduced, and that a quiet and unostentatious bachelor, in Madras, may manage to get his curry and rice cooked, his bed made, and his shirts washed, by no more than 10 or 11 men, and at a cost not exceeding 60 or 80 rupees a month.

In Madras, nearly all the upper servants speak English more or less perfectly; it being considered indispensable that the butler, the matey, and the ayah should do so.

The number of servants employed in Calcutta, is even

greater than in Madras, as the following list of those ordinarily required in a comfortable household, where there is a married couple, will show.

1, Khansamah; 2, kitmutgar; 3, cook; 4, mussalchee; 5, bazaar coolie; 6 and 7, two bearers; 8 and 9, two (sometimes four) punkahwallahs; 10 and 11, two mallees (or gardeners); 12, bheestie (or water-carrier); 13, durwan (or gatekeeper); 14, mehter (or sweeper); 15, ayah; 16, mehteranee ayah; 17, dhobie; 18, durzee (or tailor); and for the same stable establishment as set down for a similar Madras household, providing for two carriages and three horses, 19—25, a coachman, three syces (or horsekeepers), and three grasscutters.

This gives a complement of 20 to 22 men, and 5 women servants, costing from 175 to 200 rupees per month.

A bachelor of quiet habits, might reduce the number and cost, by dispensing with 1, kitmutgar (or rather by inducing the khansamah to combine kitmutgar's duties with his own); 2, one bearer; 3, one mallee; 4, the ayah; 5, mehteranee ayah; and 6, durzee; and in the cold weather, with 7 and 8, all the punkahwallahs; and finally, 9, with the durwan, whose duties could be taken by the mallee; bringing down the total cost to 80 rupees a month, or perhaps, with careful management, to less.

A moderately sized household in Bombay, similar to those of Madras and Calcutta above described, would comprise the following servants:—

1, Butler; 2, dressing-boy; 3, hamal; 4, mussalchee; 5, cook; 6, bheestie; 7, mallee; 8, sweeper; 9, ayah; 10, coachman; 11 to 13, three horsekeepers; 14 to 16, three grasscutters, giving a total of 12 men and 4 women, at a cost of from 175 to 200 rupees a month, without including dhobie (probably 15 rupees more); and also without punkahwallahs or bearers should such be employed, which indeed is rarely the case, but which are included in the Calcutta and Madras lists.

A few Madrassees are also employed in Bombay, being preferred to those born on the spot. Indeed, it is no exaggeration to say, that the Madras servants, like the Madras houses, are, taken altogether, the best in India.

The following table shows the servants employed in each of the three presidencies, and their wages. The class of house containing such an establishment, in each case, is intended to be one where the status of comfort and position aimed at is that of tolerably well-to-do people in society.

Madras.	*Calcutta.*	*Bombay.*
1. Butler, at 10 to 15 rs.	Khansamah, at 1c to 15 rs.	Butler, at 17 to 20 rs.
2. Matey, at 6 to 8 rs.	Kitmutgar, at 8 rs.	Hamal, at 10 rs.
3. Dressing-boy, at 6 to 8 rs.	Sirdar-bearer, at 8 rs.	Dressing-boy, at 12 to 15 rs.
4. Cook, at 10 to 15 rs.	Cook, at 10 rs.	Cook, at 20 rs.
5. Market-boy, at 5 rs.	Bazaar coolie, at 6 rs.	Market-coolie, at 8 to 10 rs.
6. Waterman, at 5 to 6 rs.	Bheestie, at 5 rs.	Bheestie, at 16 to 20 rs.
7. Tannycatch, at 4 rs.	Mussalchee, at 5 rs.	Mussalchee, at 5 rs.
8. Sweeper, at 5 rs.	Mehter, at 6 to 8 rs.	Sweeper, at 6 rs.
9, 10. Two Gardeners, at 5 and 6 rs.	Mehteranee ayah, at 6 rs.	
	2 Mallees, at 6 and 9 rs.	2 Mallees, at 10 rs. each.
11. Ayah, at 10 to 12 rs.	Ayah, at 10 to 12 rs.	Ayah, at 18 rs.
12. Dhobie, at 9 rs.	Dhobie, at 10 to 12 rs.	Dhobie, at 15 rs.
13. Coachman, at 7 rs.	Coachman, at 10 to 14 rs	Coachman, at 12 to 15 rs.
14–16. 3 Horsekeepers, at 6 rs.	3 Syces, at 6 rs. each.	3 Syces, at 8 to 10 rs. each.
17–19. 3 Grasscutters, at 4 rs.	3 Grasscutters, at 4 rs.	3 Grasscutters, at 6 rs. each.
20. Bearer, at 7 rs.	Bearer, at 6 rs.	
21–23. Punkahmen; one at 5 rs., 2 at 3½ rs. 24.	4 Punkahwallahs, at 5 rs.	
25.	Durzee, at 12 rs.	
26.		
27.	Durwan, at 7 rs.	

The following list is intended to represent the establishment of a young bachelor, desirous of living with quietness and economy.

Madras.	*Calcutta.*	*Bombay.*
1. Butler, at 10 rs.	Khansamah, at 10 rs.	Butler, at 15 rs.
2. Dressing-boy, at 6 rs.	Sirdar-bearer, at 8 rs.	Dressing-boy, at 12 rs.
3. Cook, at 8 rs.	Cook, at 8 rs.	Cook, at 15 rs.
4. Market-boy, at 5 rs.	Bazaar coolie, at 6 rs.	Market coolie, at 8 rs.
5. Waterman, at 5 rs.	Bheestie, at 5 rs.	Bheestie, at 15 rs.
6. Tannycatch, at 4 rs.	Mussalchee, at 5 rs.	Mussalchee, at 5 rs.
7. Sweeper, at 4 rs.	Mehter, at 6 rs.	Sweeper, at 6 rs.
8. Gardener, at 6 rs.	Mallee, at 7 rs.	Mallee, at 10 rs.
9. Coachman, at 7 rs.	Coachman, at 10 rs.	Coachman, at 12 rs.
10. Grasscutter, at 4 rs.	Grasscutter, at 4 rs.	Grasscutter, at 6 rs.
11. Horsekeeper, at 6 rs.	Syce, at 6 rs.	Syce, at 8 rs.
12, 13. Punkahmen for night work, at 3 rs. 12 an.	Punkahwallahs, at 5 rs.	
14. Dhobie, at 5 rs.	Dhobie, at 5 rs.	Dhobie, at 7 rs.

Some explanation must now be given of the respective duties of these different attendants.

The butler superintends all matters connected with the table, receives visitors, looks after the horsekeepers and other inferior servants, and sees to the carrying out of orders generally throughout the house.

Looking after the horsekeepers is by no means the least arduous or important of his duties, as these domestics will too frequently steal the horses' food unless well looked after; and shirk cleaning, watering, and walking them out. Nothing is more provoking to the owner of a valuable and faithful horse, than such delinquencies on the part of those specially employed to care for it. The best guarantee that your horses are properly treated, is to have them fed in front of the house, making it a part of the butler's duty to be present while the grain is being measured out and given to each.

He will also have to see that the punkahmen are duly in attendance; and, if in the hot season, that the "tatties" are properly watered.

The khansamah's duties answer almost exactly to those of the butler. Among them, are attending market every morning to purchase provisions for the day's consumption; these purchases being made in accordance with the instructions of the master or mistress of the house. He, as well as the butler, occasionally makes the pastry and confections; and both are always responsible for all plate, glass, crockery, kitchen utensils, etc., belonging to the establishment.

On the matey devolve the duties of dusting and cleaning the furniture, plate, knives and forks, and washing up the plates and dishes. In small houses, one man is sometimes got to act both as butler and matey, and is then called the "head-boy"; but servants willing to combine both offices are generally of rather an inferior stamp. A thoroughly respectable butler will seldom undertake to do so.

Sometimes a boy is kept to supply the place of a regular matey; but the few rupees saved by this arrangement are more than compensated for by constant breakages of china, glass, etc., which follow; to say nothing of petty thefts of oil, sugar, and other articles which come within reach of the make-believe matey. These matey-boys are, besides, invariably dirty and unpresentable; and, therefore, unfit to wait at table, which a respectable matey should always be prepared to do when required.

The kitmutgar answers in many respects to the Madras matey; waits at table, and generally assists the khansamah.

There is usually a kitmutgar attached to each person living in a house where there are two or more bachelors. In some small Calcutta houses, a Mohammedan servant is employed, who takes upon himself the combined offices of kitmutgar and head bearer.

The mussalchee's and hamal's duties are principally washing up the dishes after meals, cleaning knives, and doing pantry work generally.

The dressing-boy, as will be inferred from his title, occupies a similar position in the Indian household, to that of the valet in Europe, only that he is, perhaps, a more useful attendant than the latter, not being so apt to take airs, or to assume the fine gentleman. He has charge of his master's room, wardrobe, etc., and is responsible for its contents. Such being the case, he is necessarily present when the sweeper or any other servant may have work to do in these rooms; has to see that they *are* regularly swept, the bath filled, etc. He calls his master in the morning, assists him to dress, and sees that the horse has been got ready for the morning ride, if such be the recreation contemplated. He then makes the bed and puts the room in order; lays out his master's dress for the day; sees that the clean shirt is in a fair state of preservation, and that no buttons are missing.

When "master" returns from his morning walk or ride, all is thus in readiness for the toilet; and on his leaving after breakfast for the office, the morning paper is duly put into the carriage—it being always one of the chief responsibilities of a good "boy" to see that "master" never forgets anything. In the event of any oversight or omission, the average master will turn to his satellite with —"Boy, why didn't you put my tonic in the carriage this morning?" "Why did you let me forget about leaving those boots at the shoemaker's?" "Why didn't you tell me the cigars were finished?" and so on; "boy" usually becoming more and more mindful as time wears on, until his master feels very much dependent on his humble services.

Once master has been got safely off to his office, the boy is released from personal attendance till evening; but it must not be supposed that his duties for the day are yet ended. Probably, after first taking his own breakfast, a good dressing-boy will now proceed to overhaul his master's wardrobe; some garments require to be put out in the sun, as a preventive measure against mould or moth-holes; some require brushing, others have stains to be sponged off; buttons must be put on; while under-linen is found to have been frayed by the merciless energy of the dhobie, and must be put into the hands of the tailor. If there is to be a dinner party in the evening, the inevitable black suit and accompaniments will be laid out, etc., etc. In fact, the "dressing-boy" is a most useful and invaluable servant, if willing and well-trained in his duties. What the ayah is to her mistress, that is the "boy" to his master,—a constant satellite and bodyguard, within doors; and in a very short time he adapts himself to all his employer's whims and idiosyncracies.

If a youngster, his ambition often is to become a butler; and with this view he keeps his eyes and ears open, gradually becoming versed in the intricacies of the more dignified office. This remark, however, refers solely to Madras and to Christian servants in Bombay. In Bengal the offices of khansamah and sirdar bearer are incompatible, the former being invariably a Mohammedan and the latter a Hindoo, to whom performance of the duties connected with his master's table would be an utter abomination, and entail certain loss of caste.

The dressing-boy generally begins life at the age of twelve or fourteen, and will continue at his post till he is eighteen; when, if he has the above ambition, he will probably get a matey's berth for a year or two by way of preparation. Sometimes, however, he has no such prospective views, and is content to continue a "boy" long after the period of boyhood is past. With a kind and judicious master, and if naturally of a good disposition, he will frequently become much attached to his master's family, and not uncommonly, the dressing-boy of twenty years back, has become the "bearer" or faithful companion, guardian, and playmate, of his employer's children.

Bearers.—The principal of these in Calcutta is known as the sirdar-bearer, he being the personal attendant on the master of the house, in this respect answering to the Madras dressing-boy. The subordinate, or matey-bearers, are engaged in the morning in dusting the furniture and cleaning the lamps: duties which in Madras devolve on the matey, or in Bombay on the hamal or mussalchee.

From ten o'clock, one bearer takes up his position at the front door to wait for visitors. In large households, another is usually in attendance about the house, ready to carry a note or message, or for any other little task for which an extra attendant could by any possibility be required; but the number of bearers generally depends on the number of people living in the house.

They are, as a general rule, a very trustworthy set of men; prompt and reliable messengers, and excellent custodians of a vacated house or office, or indeed of any kind of property. They are usually natives of Cuttack, Behar, or Orissa, or of the Coromandel coast from Masulipatam northwards.

As their name indicates, their original caste or calling is that of *bearing* or carrying palanquins, in doing which they excel, as to endurance and precision of swing; particulars in which the ordinary coolie can never compete with them.

Four men of the bearer caste are usually employed in Calcutta, during the hot weather, as punkahwallahs; and one is always on duty, day and night, ready to pull in whatever room a punkah may be required.

We next come to the ayah, who occupies no unimportant sphere in a household where there are ladies or children.

When well treated on the one hand, and not spoiled on the other, by a capricious or over-indulgent mistress, the ayah is usually a very faithful and affectionate attendant—not only willing to wait upon her special charge, but also to perform many little offices about the house when required. For instance, she will often make the "early tea," and, what is more, make it better than a man-servant would do; a woman in these cases paying an attention to boiling the water, and such essential minutiæ, which could hardly be looked for in the stronger sex. She generally quite identifies herself with her mistress's interests, looks after her property with a jealous anxiety, and is always ready to report any improper proceedings which may be going on among the other servants—against whom, if necessary, she will unhesitatingly range herself on her mistress's side; unless, indeed, she happen to be the butler's or cook's wife, which is, all things considered, not an arrangement greatly to be desired.

Under such circumstances, the ayah is not generally a favourite among the other servants, though they will keep on good terms with her, owing to her supposed influence at head-quarters.

The duties of an ayah are to superintend the cleaning of her mistress's rooms, assist her in dressing, take charge of her wardrobe, etc., and be her nurse in sickness. Ayahs, of course, have their faults as well as other servants, among which are a general tendency to get out of the way, run off to their godown, or slip away to have a gossip in the bazaar. They are, however, take them all in all, good and useful creatures.

The mehteranee ayah is in most cases the mehter's wife, or a woman of the same caste. She is only employed in Calcutta, as a rule, where the lady's ayah is a Mohammedan, and consequently declines more in the way of work than to "do" her mistress's hair, and assist her to dress. Mohammedan ayahs being thus fastidious are better avoided, Hindoo women being much more useful and obliging.

The principal duty of the mehter or sweeper is to attend to the bathrooms, and to keep clean all the drains, etc., about the house.

The durzee is the household tailor, who mends the linen, and makes the dresses of the ladies and children. He comes to work about ten a.m., and leaves again about six p.m. This functionary requires looking after, as he is much given to bringing in other work with him, for doing which of course he intends to get paid outside. Another common trick of his, is to draw his pay by the month, and then absent himself every now and then on plea of sickness, all the while working for higher wages for some other family. The only guarantee against this, is to stop his pay for every day he is absent from work.

Whether the durzee is a necessary appendage of the Anglo-Indian household, readers must decide for themselves when they arrive in India. Few ladies in England employ a sempstress to work permanently in the house, but then of course a European sempstress would cost more than the durzee; and again, ladies can hardly perhaps be expected to be such industrious needlewomen in India as at home.

The durwan is a Calcutta institution. He is generally an up-country Hindoo of the kshetriya or warrior caste,* though some people, especially those who employ Ooriah bearers, employ an Ooriah durwan, still a kshetriya by caste. The durwan is generally provided with a lodge or gate-house for his abode, and here he is supposed to remain constantly on guard, seeing that no unauthorised persons enter the "compound," and that nothing is made off with by any of the servants. He has also to be on the look out for visitors, admitting them, and giving notice at the house of their arrival.†

* The kshetriya caste is the second of the four great caste divisions of the Hindus. Having emerged from the *arms* of Brahma, the kshetriyas are the warriors or military class, and rank next to the brahmins.

† If the lady of the house does not intend to receive visitors, the durwan closes one half of the gate, taking his seat outside. Should visitors drive up, they are thus stopped, and informed that his mistress does not receive. The visitor then leaves his card and passes on. If the durwan has not had such orders, the gate is opened at about eleven o'clock, and he seats himself inside at the door of his lodge, with a gong. On the appearance of a carriage containing visitors, he

Besides his pay, the durwan usually makes a snug income by exacting a per-centage from all hawkers, etc., who make sales within his domain, whether to the master or the servants. This allowance or commission is called "dustoorie," and is generally at the rate of about one pice (or a farthing and a half) in the rupee. This corresponds with the system referred to elsewhere, as prevailing with regard to butlers, etc., and is not to be evaded. It enters into every transaction, and is so universally recognised, that dealers even allow "dustoorie" to the purchaser who buys beyond the premises, after his bargain has been made.

The durwan is generally a great usurer, and the banker of the other servants; not in the sense of taking care of their money for them, but of lending them money, at the moderate charge of one anna in the rupee per month, or say only seventy-five per cent. per annum! Objectionable as these practices are, it will nevertheless be better for the master of the house not to interfere. He cannot possibly put a stop to them, and the wisest plan, therefore, is to feign ignorance, since to appear to know of and not try and prevent abuses, may be understood as equivalent to countenancing them.

I must not close this chapter without referring to another domestic to be met with, on one pretext or other, in most Anglo-Indian houses, but not included in the foregoing lists. This is the "chokkra," or small boy, a creature both useful and troublesome to a degree. His occupations

looks in, and if he finds a gentleman only, gives his gong one stroke; if there be a lady and gentleman, or a lady only, two strokes; and three strokes for the doctor's carriage.

When the carriage draws up at the door, the bearer receives the card, and shows the visitor into the drawing-room. In some houses, however, where there is no durwan kept, the bearer takes in the card first, while the visitor remains in the carriage, and should the bearer, on his return, deliver "salaams," this is to be understood as an invitation to "walk in."

are indiscriminate, such as helping about the house, "bringing fire" for master's cheroot, pulling off the latter's boots, breaking an occasional lamp or plate, or helping himself to the jam, sugar, or anything tempting left in his way; in fact, he makes himself as generally useful as his naturally mischievous propensities will allow. In a house where dogs are kept, this youngster will be their special nurse and attendant—and indeed where such pets are kept, a boy to wash, feed, and exercise them is absolutely necessary.

The number of servants maintained in even the most moderately conducted Anglo-Indian establishments has always been a cause of surprise to people living at home—many of whom are accustomed to be attended upon by only a couple of maids, willingly dividing between them all the work of the house—and often no doubt leads to a suspicion of extravagance in their friends abroad, which does not really exist; or which, if it does, is perfectly unavoidable.

Could the cook or butler, who makes the daily purchases at the market, be induced to carry home the basket containing the provisions purchased, a "market-coolie" could of course be dispensed with; but no power on earth would prevail on either of the former to demean himself by carrying anything more burdensome than a red pocket-handkerchief over his shoulder, or a cotton umbrella in his hand. To carry a basket would be a fatal indignity, and for ever lower him in the eyes of the other servants, as well as in his own. "That coolie business, ma'am," the cook would deprecatingly reply, if asked to do so. A "market-coolie" must, therefore, be kept; and in addition to taking him to market, the cook at once imposes on him all sorts of odd jobs about the cookroom, and he thus becomes a sort of cook's assistant.

This being so, one would have supposed that no more hands would be required in the kitchen; but a third domestic, called in Bengal the mussalchee, and in Madras the "tannycatch," is also, it soon appears, indispensable; in Madras the former is generally a female, but in Calcutta and Bombay always a man; in all the three presidencies the office answers in some respects to that of the scullery-maid, and his or her business is to pound the rice for the table—and probably, if the truth were known, for most of the other servants as well—clean the pots, keep hot water always ready, etc. One may hold out for a time against this superfluity, but submission is sure to follow in the end. The kettle, otherwise, will never be boiling in time for "early tea;" the rice will be gritty; the dinner invariably late, etc.; all being represented as infallible proofs of the indispensability of a tannycatch. Few decent cooks, indeed, will accept service without such assistance being allowed.

The multiplicity of Indian servants, arises from causes which it is at present difficult to overcome. Caste has, no doubt, a good deal to do with it, and as the prejudices which it authorizes in this case are on the side of an excessive subdivision of labour, without any simultaneous reduction of emolument, they are of course all the more tenaciously held to.

It might have been supposed, that when once a caste native was permitted to undertake domestic service under Europeans, it would matter little whether he dusted the table, or swept the floor; put the family dinner on the table, or lit the evening lamp; handed round a full dish, or washed an empty plate. But, in point of fact, there is considered to be the greatest difference between any one of these offices and any other; for while a servant will look upon the one as his proper duty, he will consider himself dishonoured in performing the other.

The next greatest tyranny to caste is "custom," for which every native of India is a determined stickler. Ask your butler to wash a plate or dust the table, and in nine cases out of ten, he will politely but firmly reply, "That not my custom." Nor must we fly into a rage, and dismiss him on the spot, as will often be the first impulse in such a case, for his successor will act in precisely the same way.

It is possible, that much of the precedent which has created the "custom" in such trivialities, may have arisen from want of system or extravagance, and that the absurdity of the result is patent to all; but it matters not. In former times, when every Anglo-Indian was a *rara avis* in the land; the man of power and dispenser of patronage; when living was cheap, and servants were contented with the smallest of wages, in consideration of the various *sub rosa* advantages to be derived from connection with the great sahib,—the latter was probably willing enough to add to his dignity by keeping round him a large body of retainers; and perhaps partly in this way, a great number of distinct domestic appointments came to be created.

Now-a-days, however, a great deal of this is changed, and the average Anglo-Indian would gladly sweep away all superfluous household parasites. But this it is not so easy to do. That some reform may be ultimately accomplished in this direction, when popular prejudices have been in a greater degree borne down by civilization, and the growth of practical "common sense" ideas, is more than probable. Something towards bringing about this result may be done by every one who will bring his attention judiciously and quietly, but persistently, to bear on the subject.

A Calcutta resident wrote to me lately as follows:—

"The number of our servants is simply ridiculous, and the work each has to do hardly appreciable. It would be a great blessing if the number of idle hangers-on in every house, could be diminished." An opinion in which, I imagine, all will coincide.

CHAPTER IX.

CHILDREN.—*Absence of Nurseries.—Consequences.—Send them home.—Why.—Education.—Native associates.—Native conversation.—"Chee-chee."—Hygiene.*

THE want of proper nursery accommodation is a very great defect in many Indian houses. Seldom is there any play-room apart from the ordinary sitting-rooms where the children can exercise their lungs and limbs without disturbing the rest of the family; and this is the more serious a drawback, that, as a rule, the rooms all open one into another, and are only separated by light screens which close hardly more than half the doorway, so that no retreat is quiet or secure.

Add to this want, the invariable over-indulgence by servants, and frequent want of judgment shown by the parents, and Anglo-Indian children will be understood to be often a positive annoyance, instead of (as they should be, if judiciously brought up) a source of constant pleasure and amusement.

Some parents seem quite indifferent to noise and riot, however unrestrained, in their own children; and perhaps, therefore, can hardly be expected to appreciate the annoyance which may thereby be inflicted on their friends. I have known some, who made it a rule *never* to check any amount of romping, shouting, or screaming, on the part of their children, under the impression that nature required these demonstrations for the due development of health and strength. The result, of course, is to render their house a perfect Babel. Hither and thither, through drawing-room, dining-room, and bedrooms, rush the obstreperous little creatures, tumbling over couches, upsetting the table ornaments, and scattering toys in every direction.

If a caller appear, he is immediately made the common prey; remarks are passed on his personal appearance, and peculiarities, if he has any. Or, if the visitor be a lady, her fan or cardcase is immediately seized upon, and inspected not too gently; and the whole visit is disturbed by a succession of juvenile demonstrations of one kind or another, varied with a running fire of mild and unavailing remonstrances from "Mamma;" all this, as may be supposed, not being highly favourable to conversation.

That some proper and distinct arrangements are not made for the comfort and amusement of the children, as is the case in England, arises partly from carelessness, and partly from a fallacious idea on the part of the parents, that having so much to try them, in the heat of the climate, etc., children require every possible indulgence to compensate. The fact is, however, that children are very indifferent to the heat, or, at least feel it much less than adults; nor are they either better or happier for total freedom from restraint, which on the contrary only ends in making them selfish, irritable, and obstinate.

By being constantly present, too, during the conversation of their elders, children are apt to become precociously sharp and old-fashioned, losing the sweet shyness and simplicity which become their age; and it is doubtful whether those allowed to grow up under such circumstances to the age of five or six years, ever entirely get over the bad effects of their early Indian life.

On the other hand, quite as much harm may be done by parents, who, while anxious to guard against the misrule adverted to, are, however, unwilling to take the trouble of devoting that *continuous* attention which is necessary to the proper training of their children; and who fall into the mistake of continually snubbing and punishing them for great or trifling faults alike. Though such treatment may perhaps prevent the little ones from becoming a nuisance to society, for the time being, it effectually hinders the due unfolding of their minds and hearts. Failing to find sympathy in their parents, they are naturally thrown back upon the ayah and other native servants; so that I have actually seen Anglo-Indian children, who, on being sent to England for education at the age of seven or eight, had as little idea of good manners as if they had been brought up in the backwoods; and who were unable to speak a single unbroken sentence in their mother tongue.

Anglo-Indian fathers lead too busy a life, in a trying climate, to have much time or inclination for special attention to the development of their children's minds, so that the whole onus and obligation fall on the mothers; many of whom, however, after a time begin to find themselves incapable of extending their supervision beyond the physical culture of the young people, whose higher qualifications, one way or other, are thus hardly done justice to. Education in its larger sense comes to be postponed, the parents comforting themselves with the reflection, that by-and-by the children will be "sent home" to school, and that the arduous task will thus devolve upon others—paid for undertaking it.

This necessity is a serious consideration for married Anglo-Indians; for it seems to be universally admitted, that every child must be sent home, before much more than half-a-dozen years have flown over its head, if it is to be brought up as a useful and intelligent lady or gentleman. It is a necessity arising from physical as well as mental causes; the climate of the tropics being apparently quite antagonistic to the development of an undeteriorated and robust European constitution, even could the best intellectual culture be obtained.

Nor, setting physical considerations aside altogether, does it appear that the best instruction in India will compensate children for the want of an English bringing-up. They may be sent to the best schools (and there are many excellent institutions of the kind in India, where a thorough *book education* would be conveyed), or the best private instructors may be employed for their benefit; but however well their heads may be stored with classics and mathematics, there will always be a "certain something" wanting, which is to be found in the regular English schoolboy or girl A boy will grow up timid, unstable, and helpless, and in some cases even unaccountably deceitful and meanspirited, where one would wish to see a ready, frank boldness of manner; while a girl will be reserved and *gauche,* either driven into a confused giggle, or an attempt to withdraw, on every occasion of being spoken to; and neither the boy nor the girl, in nine cases out of ten, will grow up into a respected man or woman.

This may appear strange and difficult to account for, but what we must chiefly look to are facts taught by actual experience; and, while writing, I call to mind instances in support of my conclusions.

Education does not consist merely of a certain course of book or class instruction; it is what is picked up by the mind and heart on all sides, and from every associate, principally during the earlier years of life. When one finds a child, in a Christian home, surrounded by embodiments of purity, affection, and the best growths of religion; and he is thence sent to a school in which the insensible effects of such influences are confirmed and acted upon by judicious and accomplished teachers (the child being meanwhile surrounded only by playmates similarly circumstanced, while all are completely secluded, for the present, from contact with aught that belongs to a less pure and refined atmosphere)—in such case, *education,* in the full sense of the word, is presented under the most favourable conditions, and there must be something radically defective in a character and disposition which do not ultimately do a certain amount of justice to it.

In India, a conjunction of all these conditions is impossible. The virtuous happy home, and the school unexceptionable as to teaching, may no doubt be there, but there are still the inevitably bad associates out of school hours. For the staid and comparatively cultured nurses and other attendants of the English home, are substituted the horse-keepers, the matey boys, or even the ayahs, from association with whom the child cannot be kept, and whose influence on his *morale* must be more or less injurious.

Indian servants are naturally very subservient to their employer's children; and yielding to every whim, however unreasonable, in a short time turn the youngster into a self-indulgent and capricious tyrant on a small scale. Nothing can be worse for children than this premature experience of mastery. Made to be ruled and led, in India they find themselves the directors of their appointed care-takers, and the result is easily imagined. Then, the pliant obliging nature of these servants naturally attaches the children to them, and it is not unheard of to find the latter preferring the society of their native attendants to that of their own parents; and as the private morals and conversation of the domestics are seldom of the purest, the minds of the children cannot fail to be in some degree contaminated. I may in this place state—what I think I have not mentioned elsewhere—that the language of the vulgar in India is corrupt, and interspersed with obscenity to an extent almost incredible. Where the lower orders in other countries vent their vocal immorality in profane and blasphemous expressions, those of India use language of ribaldry, the possibility of one's children hearing which is an idea horrible to contemplate.

But there is another danger: by being constantly with native servants, children pick up the "ways" of those who often belong to all but the lowest class of natives. Human nature is highly imitative; child nature especially so; the tendency being always greater to copy what is bad than what is good. Among these "ways" will be found a disregard for candour, and a quickness at framing falsehoods which cannot perhaps afterwards be eradicated.

However careful, trustworthy, and affectionate the ayah or other nursery attendants may be, all Anglo-Indian parents, giving their deliberate and serious attention to the subject, will no doubt agree with me, that the less their children are left to the exclusive care and companionship of native servants, the better. Left too much among the latter, an English child will only too soon learn the native language, and, as a necessary consequence, lose much of the innocence of childhood.

The acquaintance of English children with the vernacular tongues, cannot, in my opinion, be too strongly deprecated; nor will the reader be surprised after what has been stated above. But even were there no other objection, such acquaintance will interfere with their proper cultivation of, and purity of accent in, their mother tongue; give a disagreeable, whining intonation, and a nasal enunciation. Some parents, unmindful of the many drawbacks which must, up to a certain age, accompany such proficiency, occasionally point with pride to Johnny's or Charley's progress in Tamil or Hindustani; but there is in truth no real cause for congratulation. Far better to keep them totally ignorant at their age of so muddy a stream, which, if required, can be much more correctly and intelligently learned in after-life, on their return to India after an English education. The nasal twang and shrill unmusical tone of voice so generally found in native women of the lower orders, give a most unpleasing peculiarity of tone and pronunciation, often noticed in Anglo-Indian children, and one which may, if care is not taken, cling to them through life.

The general ill effects of an Indian bringing-up on children of pure English blood, are very forcibly implied in the term "chee-chee," which is commonly applied to them in Bengal. Without lending any approval to its use, I may explain that "chee-chee" is an ejaculation of disgust, used by the natives of India upon all occasions; and the origin of the application of the term to Europeans born and brought up in India, is probably their constant habit of using it themselves in the same manner.

With regard to the hygienic management of Anglo-Indian children, I need say little here, the subject being referred to elsewhere by a professional pen; but I may recommend, that they should always be allowed to enjoy as much out-of-door exercise, freedom, and fresh air, as are compatible with guarding against undue exposure. Let them not be kept too much out of the sun-light, but allow them to run about the garden within the hours permitted to adults, always taking the precaution to give them light broad-brimmed hats, of pith, or some other suitable material. A mistake is sometimes made, of almost totally secluding children in India from the light of day. Some parents seem to argue that if much exposure to the sun is injurious, even a little can hardly be beneficial. And what is the course they adopt in consequence of so illogical a conclusion?

Aware that their children should at least have open air and exercise, they insist on the little unfortunates being taken out of their beds at dawn, and hurried out of doors, often into a foggy atmosphere, loaded with unhealthy gases, which the sun has not yet risen to dissipate. Colds, fevers, and dysenteric affections are the not uncommon result, while the general appearance of such children is wan, sickly, and spiritless. Only half awake, they are walked up and down for an hour or so, and then taken indoors, to be confined in carefully-shaded rooms and verandahs till sunset, when again they are taken forth, for the slight remnant of daylight out of doors.

This is very injudicious management. No child should be taken out of doors *till after sunrise*; and then not till after receiving some nourishment, such as a bowl of bread and milk, some weak tea and "appas," or something equally light and strengthening.

To avoid chills, let them be clothed in loose light flannels, or drill suits with flannel underneath. Linen clothing next the body should be religiously avoided. At night some loose garment should be worn, as they are apt to throw off the bed clothes during sleep, and are then liable to cold when the morning breezes begin to pour in. Children are apt to suffer very severely from musquito bites, against which every care should be used to protect them.

It has often struck me, that Anglo-Indian children are ordinarily indulged with far too stimulating a diet. The youngest are given broths, etc., almost before they are weaned; and those slightly older are constantly fed on meat, etc., where in Europe farinaceous food only would be considered suitable. Wine and beer too are not uncommonly given. Altogether, this would seem to be a very unnatural state of things; but, of course, a medical man alone is competent to express a decided opinion regarding it.

CHAPTER X.

TRAVELLING.—*Long distances.—Railways.—First and second class travelling.—Refreshment arrangements.—Bullock coaches.—Country carts.—Dàk gharries.—Palkees.—Wild animals.—Horseback.—Travellers' bungalows.—Pepper-pot.—Travelling supplies.—Marching.*

THOUGH travelling in India is daily becoming more simple and less fatiguing, owing to the extension of the railway system, and to the daily increasing improvements in roads, bridges, and conveyances all over the country; still it differs in many respects sufficiently from travelling in Europe, to render it a subject on which a few hints may be found useful.

During the hot season, journeys on the plains are to be avoided if possible; or at least not undertaken in the expectation of their proving a source of enjoyment. People in India, however, seldom travel merely for the sake of enjoyment, the cause generally being, in the case of officials, a change of station at the call of authority; in the case of the general public, a change of climate in pursuit of health.

By whatever means the journey is accomplished, fatigue and expense, even now, are never-failing attendants,—as might be expected, having regard to the heat of the climate, and the long distances which generally speaking have to be traversed. From Bombay to Calcutta, 1470 miles; from Calcutta to Peshawur, over 1400; to Lahore, 1200; to Simla, 1100; from Bombay to Madras, 700; Madras to Secundrabad, 450; the Neilgherries, 370; to Beypore, 400: such are some of the "flittings" which the Anglo-Indian has commonly to undertake.

In early times, horse, elephant, and perhaps camel-back, and palankeens, were the usual modes of conveyance. Now, the railroads constitute the principal highways, and have superseded most of the old trunk roads; elsewhere, journeys are performed in horse or bullock conveyances, though occasionally on horseback; while palkees are still in general use in some parts of the country.

First, I will say a few words on railways in India, the subject being one of the first importance as affecting the well-being of the country.

At the end of 1869, there were 5000 miles of open railways in India, constructed at an expenditure of (principally English) capital amounting to £85,000,000 sterling, or at the rate of £17,000 per mile. The actual net profit on the whole mileage averaged 3⅛ per cent. per annum, while most of the companies being guaranteed a dividend of 5 per cent., the remaining 1⅞ per cent. is in such cases made good to the shareholders, by Government. The objects kept in view by the Government in lending this guarantee, are:—(1) The facilities afforded by the railways to military movements; whereby a material saving is effected, not only in the cost of moving the existing forces from one station to another, but also in the reduction of the strength of the standing army which is thus rendered practicable; the troops being concentrated in a few large stations, while the smaller ones within easy reach by rail are abandoned.* (2) The increase of commerce and industry, and consequently the additional material wealth, prosperity, and increased tax-paying capacity of the people, which the railways tend so largely to promote.

The number of passengers in 1869, was about 16,000,000, forming a comparatively small proportion out of a population of 150,000,000. But the natives are every year becoming more awake to the advantages of railway travelling, so that as more of the minor branch lines (many of which are now in course of construction through the popu-

* Another consideration, is the reduced wear and tear in moving about troops by rail, as compared with the old wearisome marches, during which so many men were always sacrificed to sunstroke, fatigue, etc., each soldier (humanity apart) costing the State £100.

lous parts of the country) are completed, the number of passengers may be expected to swell rapidly and largely. The proportion of European to native passengers is of course exceedingly small, the total receipts from the fares of the former in 1869 being less than £90,000.

The great majority of native passengers travel third-class, most of the remainder second-class, while only a few, principally persons of wealth and distinction, travel first-class. All Europeans, excepting soldiers, artisans, etc., are expected to travel first-class. The fares charged on the different lines average somewhat as follows:—first-class 2¼*d.*, second-class about three-farthings, third-class about three-eighths of a penny, per mile; from which it will be seen, the difference between the first and the other class fares is very heavy, the intention being apparently to force Europeans of the better class, who wish to avoid contact with natives of the lower orders, but who otherwise might be tempted by the lowness of the fare to go second-class, to travel first-class; and also to deter natives and poor Europeans from doing so.

This intention, however, is not always fulfilled, many respectable Europeans, especially those who have families to move about, being unable to afford the higher fares, for long distances; while a few, considering the difference between the two class fares disproportionate, travel second-class "on principle."

I have myself tried both first and second-class travelling on the Indian lines, and the following are the conclusions arrived at in consequence. (1) A gentleman travelling alone or with other gentlemen, by day, and in the cool weather, to whom the saving to be effected is an object, may very well travel second-class, provided there is not likely to be an unusual crowd of natives travelling about. (2) Ladies and gentlemen forming a party sufficiently large to occupy the whole or the greater part of a compartment, also by day, may also go second-class without much discomfort. (3) But, as a general rule, ladies in India ought always to travel first-class; also gentlemen by night; and (4) all Europeans, at all times when they can afford to do so.

I remember on one occasion making a night journey of some 200 miles in a second-class compartment, and the impression left by my sufferings will not be easily effaced. Large numbers of the natives were at the time moving about in all that part of the country, in consequence of some religious festival. The railway company too, ran no third-class carriages at night, so that all were obliged to avail themselves of the accommodation which, in a moment of rash economy, I had chosen.

The second-class carriage in which I travelled was a large van to hold fifty passengers, divided in the middle of every second bench by a wooden bar for the back. Not foreseeing a crowd, I had installed myself on the bench farthest from the engine, laying down rug and cushions, and fondly looking forward to a comfortable as well as inexpensive journey; but at every succeeding station fresh native passengers dropped in, with bundles, baskets, boxes, bunches of plantains, etc., and the carriage gradually filled; first one bench and then another, had its full complement of occupants, until at last my domain began to be encroached upon. First one sleek Hindu, then another, then a couple more, closed in upon me, till cushions, rugs, etc., had to be bundled up, and I was finally reduced to being one of a row.

I am imbued with no instinctive repugnance to Hindus or Asiatics in general, nor do I belong to that class of Englishmen, which, according to Baboo Keshub Chunder Sen, "regards the natives as one of the vilest nations on earth," and who not only "hate the natives with their whole heart, but take a pleasure in doing so." At the same time, I must admit, that my cosmopolitan leanings were put to a severe trial upon this occasion.

Many of the natives are addicted to practices which make them anything but agreeable *compagnons de voyage* in close quarters. In the first place, they lubricate the body with oil, sometimes cocoanut, but often castor or margosa oil; the two latter kinds having a most fœtid and, to a European, a most disgusting and nauseating smell. Secondly, being often fat, the natives perspire very freely, which they can hardly be blamed for, but which intensifies the effect of the anointment.

Another of their habits, to which the European never becomes fully reconciled, is that of chewing a mixture of betel-leaf, tobacco, areka-nut, and chunam (lime), which causes a copious red expectoration, which is freely distributed on all sides, and dyes their teeth of every shade from crimson to jet black. This gives the mouth an appearance, from a European point of view, hideous and revolting, but which among themselves is considered positively beautifying.

But worst of all, is their habit of eructating on all occasions, without the least attempt at restraint. Nothing is more surprising to an Englishman, accustomed to look on such an act as a gross breach of good manners; but the natives argue, that after a substantial meal, this is an appropriate method of venting their satisfaction—as it were by way of grace. Of course, natives who have mixed much among Europeans, would not offend in this way before them, but any of even the most refined would freely do so among his fellow-countrymen or in his own family.

If, therefore, the reader will please to imagine himself in a railway carriage—the thermometer meanwhile at 80°—containing some forty or fifty fellow-beings, all more or less characterized by the above peculiarities, he will probably resolve never to travel in such company in India. But the years which have passed since the trying journey above alluded to, have brought great improvements with them, and I believe that second-class railway travelling in India is now fairly comfortable and tolerably free from objectionable companionship.

The first-class carriages usually are comfortable, and on the whole quite equal, if not superior, to the generality of those in England. The windows are supplied with silk curtains, venetians, gauze blinds, and glass, to be used at pleasure, with the view of excluding the dust, glare, and heat ; this, however, is an impossibility, as the air must be admitted, and the small particles enter with it, penetrating into every pore, and causing great discomfort in every way. First-class travellers by night are provided with sleeping carriages, four persons, each supplied with a berth, being allotted to each compartment. In the morning, the upper berths, which are shelf-like, and connected with the sides of the carriage by hinges, and raised and fastened by bolts when required, are let down, and form the back cushions for the lower seats.

With every appliance, however, travellers still cry out in such a climate for further improvements, and there is now a talk of supplying first-class carriages in the hot season with tatties, or window-screens made of the sweet smelling Kus-Kus grass, which, if kept wetted by a mechanical contrivance, will add greatly to their coolness and comfort. Anything which will answer this purpose is much needed, numbers of Europeans dying annually on railway journeys from the heat and its effects.

The most objectionable feature in connection with the Indian railways, until recently, was the extreme defectiveness of the refreshment arrangements. These were for the most part decidedly bad,—in the face, as must, however, be acknowledged, of great difficulties. But now, there are reasonably good refreshment rooms at all the chief stopping stations, and in particular, on the main lines between the great Presidency towns, abundant accommodation is provided, and abundant time allowed at suitable hours for breakfast, tiffin, and dinner, with lavatories and all other needful arrangements for comfort. A couple of hours before arriving at a station for dinner, it is customary for a guard to go to each first and second-class carriage to learn how many Europeans purpose taking dinner, and the number is then telegraphed on, so that on arrival the *table d'hote* is ready and waiting, with enough entertainment for all. For a short journey, it is always easy to carry a few sandwiches and a little sherry and water in the carriage, as at home. For long marches, in parts of the country which can boast of fair cart-roads but no railways, the pleasantest way of travelling is by "bullock coach." Anglo-Indians living in the mofussil often keep their own coach and bullocks, especially those whose duties involve much moving about within their districts; but these conveyances are to be had for hire in most mofussil towns. They are square two-wheeled vehicles, set on springs, with roofs extending somewhat on all sides over the actual top, as a shade from the sun in day travelling, or protection from the rain. The seats are placed at each end, the hinder one, which lies across the door, being movable, to admit of exit and ingress. When the conveyance is to be used at night, the space between the seats is boarded over, making a false floor extend over the whole of the interior of the vehicle, and upon this the bedding is laid down for the night's repose. The bullocks are yoked to a pole, the driver sitting in front under an awning.

After a short apprenticeship to this kind of travelling, one can sleep calmly through any night journey, notwithstanding unlimited jolting, most irregular paces, and the sustained volley of inexplicable sounds addressed by the driver to his team,—by dint of which, and sundry tail twistings, thumps, prods, and occasional digs with the great-toe nail, he prevents their falling asleep.

Indian bullocks have two important merits—they are very surefooted and possess great powers of endurance. A pair of them will go on steadily, at the rate of three miles an hour, from eight o'clock at night till six o'clock in the morning. Occasionally, in an unusually dark part of the road, they will take themselves and their charge over the bank into a paddy-field or into a ditch, or now and again they will quietly lie down in the middle of the road, when they think they ought not to be asked to proceed farther; but they never stumble, thus possessing one advantage over most of the horses available for this kind of work.

I can remember, on one or two occasions, when travelling at night by bullock cart, waking up to find myself landed upside down in a ditch; but as the speed is not great, there is generally speaking not much danger. These upsets, however, are far from pleasant, especially as (having usually divested one's self of boots before lying down to sleep) one may chance to leap barefooted on a heap of stones, or into a mudhole or bramble-thicket.

When travelling long distances in this manner, and *time* being an object, it is usual to have relays of bullocks posted at every stage, some seven, eight, or nine miles apart; and by this means, the journey can be accomplished with considerable rapidity, as having only a short distance to go, the cattle will trot the greater part of the stage—and, although heavy clumsy-looking animals, with long dewlaps and large humps, ordinary bullocks trot remarkably well. There is a smart style of bullock with which the natives are fond of driving about, which will trot some ten miles within the hour with a light gig.

In most districts, it is the duty of the village authorities to see to the supply of bullocks and coolies to European travellers; but though they will generally do so on a civil application being made, it is, as a rule, better to be provided with a formal authorization from the nearest European revenue officer, or magistrate, before setting out.

Where a bullock coach is not procurable, or indeed at any time for those who are not fastidious as to mere appearances, the common cart of the country will serve as a conveyance equally well. This is a long cart without springs, on two wheels, covered over the top and at the sides with an awning of plaited cocoanut leaves, but open at the ends. By first putting under the mattress a layer of straw about a foot deep, a comfortable and easy bed may be formed for the night, or a couch for the day. It is usual to lie with one's head to the bullocks, and a portmanteau or carpet-bag will make a capital pillow.

Should several persons be travelling together, one of these carts, owing to their narrowness, will be necessary for each. I would also remark, that those who take it into their heads to walk occasionally, when on the march, by way of change, will do well to keep behind and not in front of their cart—especially at night, if going through a village, or travelling along a road much frequented. I give this caution, having once had a pair of blankets and other articles laid down for my night's bed, whipped out of the cart by some expert unknown, while innocently strolling on in advance of my conveyance.

"Dàk gharries," as stage travelling conveyances are styled in Northern India, are often drawn by horses, but the latter are usually very wretched animals; in my opinion bullocks are to be preferred, owing to their surer footedness, sleeker sides, and altogether less ill-used appearance, though they perhaps take longer on the road. The lower-class natives do not, as a rule, know how to appreciate horses, and are apt to take advantage of their comparative willingness to overdrive them cruelly. For bullocks, however, they seem to have some sort of regard, and moreover find it useless to try and urge them beyond a certain pace.

Of all modes of conveyance, perhaps palkee travelling is the easiest. Beyond a slight regular swaying, there is no motion, with a well-trained set of bearers. The palankeen itself I need not describe, as by picture or description it must be familiar to every one. The best class of bearers are the Teloogoos and Ooriahs of Eastern India. Palankeen bearing is their caste employment, and they therefore take to it naturally. With an ordinary set of them, five or six miles an hour may be got over on level ground; fresh relays being usually provided in readiness at the different stages, in the same way as with bullocks for coaches.

While running along, the bearers keep up a monotonous chant, which enables them to keep time and step, and thus facilitates their progress. One man, the leader, generally improvises the song, the rest taking up the refrain or chorus. There are several stories as to the tenour and character of these ditties, which tend to show that the improvisatore does not always refer to the slumbering and unconscious passenger in the most complimentary terms. One of these is so rich (though, I may add at the same time, so apparently improbable) that it is worth repeating. Once upon a time, a civilian who had been some years in the country without having picked up much knowledge of the language, was much non-plussed by a new Government order which came out, rendering it compulsory for him and others in his position to pass a certain examination at Madras within a given period. The time elapsed, but he was still as ignorant as ever. However, trusting to the chapter of accidents, he set off for the dreaded ordeal.

On the way down, thinking over the probabilities of being "plucked," and of consequent hindrance in his profession, his ear was insensibly attracted by the song of the bearers, repeated mile after mile, and which unconsciously became indelibly stamped on his memory. Arrived at Madras, Mr. —— presented himself at the boardroom, where he found the examiners (little wiser in the language than himself) arrayed in state. Being now told that he was to be examined by a native moonshee, he repaired to a private room with this individual, thoughts of possible bribery and corruption dimly flitting through his mind as his only chance of safety.

The moonshee's first request was, that "the gentleman" would give a *viva voce* specimen of his linguistic powers. A bright thought here occurred to our friend, and he forthwith began vociferously to pour forth the song of the bearers of the previous day The stratagem was entirely successful, for it turned out to be no other than a string of vituperation so gross, that the moonshee, fancying it to be directed at himself, at once stopped Mr. ——, and endeavoured to appease his apparent wrath, by assuring him of his perfect confidence as to that gentleman's attainments.

Palkee travelling is by far the best means of locomotion for invalids unequal to jolting or exertion, and indeed one may often pass more restless and disturbed nights in bed in India, than when gliding smoothly along the moonlit roads, or forest paths, lulled into unconsciousness by the monotonous chant of the human team. When the nights are dark and wet, one or two bearers usually precede the palankeen with torches.

A great many wonderful stories are told, of night travellers by palkee through the Indian jungles being attacked by tigers, wild elephants, etc.; but the majority of these may be set down as romance. In many parts of India a tiger is never heard of, nor an elephant either; and though I have travelled at night in neighbourhoods where there were both, I unfortunately never encountered any adventures of the kind wherewith to embellish the present pages.

The most alarming sounds at night, are generally the dismal howl and insane exultation of troops of jackals, the wild yell and discordant cachinnation of the hyena, or the screech of the night-owl, none of which are certainly very inspiriting, and perhaps have given rise to some of the fancied narrow escapes of travellers from more formidable enemies.

A "rogue elephant"* is the most formidable customer one can encounter unprepared, as he is almost sure to assume the offensive. But when elephants are met in herds, as they sometimes are,—only in Ceylon, however, or in the Terai, on the borders of Nepal,—they are seldom dangerous, and will disperse quickly at the approach of even a single man. A friend of mine, who lived in Ceylon, had once an awkward adventure with some of these animals, tending to show, however, how harmless and peaceable they are when not molested.

My friend was a coffee planter, and resided in the Medamahanewera district. One Sunday morning, on his way to visit a neighbour residing some five or six miles off, he was cantering pleasantly along through the forest, when at a sharp turn he found himself immediately confronted by a herd of five or six elephants standing right across the road. The horse he was riding, if not the most frightened, was at least the most prompt and decided of the party; stopping short, he sent his rider flying over his head up to the very feet of the herd, turned round and galloped homewards. Mr. N—— was not much hurt by the fall, but feeling himself perhaps in an embarrassing position, and thinking it judicious to leave the next move to the party in the majority, he lay quite still. The elephants were evidently as much taken aback as himself; but after a momentary hesitation, the leader of the herd stepped forward and deliberately applied the end of his trunk to the prostrate coffee planter, apparently for the purpose of closer examination; and the result being evidently most unsatisfactory, drew back, raised his proboscis on high, and uttering a shrill trumpet-blast, led the way into the jungle, the whole herd following as fast as they could stampede. The inci-

* A "rogue" is an elephant turned out of his herd for misconduct, and hence doomed to a solitary life. They are always very savage.

dent, though it takes longer to describe, probably occupied only a few seconds.

The Anglo-Indian in robust health, and when not pressed for time, would probably most enjoy travelling on horseback, especially with a pleasant companion or two. For my part, I know of no greater pleasure than an Indian journey, at the rate of fifteen or twenty miles a day, on a good, strong, willing, and surefooted horse, accompanied by a friend similarly mounted. Starting at morn, or in the afternoon, when the sun's rays are becoming oblique, the ride may be accomplished without fatigue and with much real enjoyment. Six or seven miles an hour is quite fast enough for man or horse, and is a pace admitting of ample opportunity for cracking jokes or spinning yarns, or in the case of those who are so addicted, for smoking pipes.*

When making a journey in this way, it is necessary always to look closely after your steed's welfare. The horsekeeper, grasscutter (the latter when travelling should always be a man, not a woman), together with the coolies carrying the *impedimenta*, should start several hours in advance, according to the length of the march, in order that they may be on the spot when the halting stage is reached. Thus the animal can be at once rubbed down, get his feet washed, and receive a good feed as soon as he arrives. With this view, it is always well to walk one's horse the last mile or two, so as to bring him in cool.

Nothing is so injurious to a horse as to stand in his sweat after a journey, and this is always unavoidable should the horsekeepers not have come up; and nothing is more

* Lord Mayo, the late lamented Viceroy of India, appeared by all accounts to have been an excellent horseman, sometimes, by his forced *marches à cheval* of from sixty to eighty miles a day, completely knocking up all his staff.

There is little doubt that a man who can ride eighty miles a day in India—and Lord Mayo had done this—can get through a good deal of other kinds of work as well, if occasion requires, unless he be a mere Sir Harry Towers, which the late Governor-General certainly was not.

annoying than to feel that the animal which has brought you along so cheerfully, is being neglected, while your own comfort has been provided for. If the journey ends at a friend's bungalow, and one's own horsekeeper has not turned up, another may sometimes be got to attend to the animal; but not under other circumstances.

It is one of the great differences between English and Indian travelling, that in the former case the horse's feed and attendance are found in readiness at every halting place, while in India they have to accompany the animal from day to day.

The halting-places in India deserve some special mention. I refer to the dàk, or travellers' bungalows, provided by a considerate Government for the use of travellers, in a country which is unable to boast of inns or hostelries, except at a few of the chief cities frequented by Europeans.

These institutions are an invaluable boon, and even where, as is sometimes the case, not kept up in very good style, or affording luxurious accommodation, are not only invaluable, but perfectly indispensable. In Europe, the traveller on the highways finds an inn every four, five, or six miles, can choose his own stages, and stop at any distance on his journey as may be most convenient. But this is not the case in India: there are no roadside inns, except in one or two isolated cases on a very small scale; and one might travel from one large town to another and never find a possible halting-place, or obtain a comfortable meal, were it not for the traveller's bungalow. Even many considerable towns possess no hotel maintained by private enterprise.

The travellers' or dàk bungalow is usually a one-storied house, surrounded by a deep verandah; it is often divided into two sets of rooms, each consisting of a sitting-room, a couple of bedrooms, and the same number of bathrooms. There are also plenty of outhouses, providing accommodation for servants, cooking, and animals. As before remarked, this establishment is erected by Government for the special use and advantage of European and Eurasian travellers.

The furniture of the travellers' bungalow is not—as might be supposed, seeing the building is open to the public at large—of the most luxurious or costly description; but the sitting-rooms are provided with plain table and chairs, and the bedrooms with cot, bedding, and toilet apparatus, which is all that could reasonably be expected.

The bungalow is usually situated some little distance off the high-road, in the centre of the village from which it takes its name, and being often the only house having at all the look of having been built for the use of Europeans, is at once recognizable. One of them will be found at every tenth or fifteenth mile along all the main roads of India. Each is put in charge of one or more servants, paid by the collector, or chief revenue officer of the district; and a book is kept in which visitors can record their approbation, or the reverse, with regard to the accommodation provided for them and the attention and civility, or otherwise, they meet with while there.

In some districts (as in the Deccan and Mysore) the accommodation and attendance are provided gratis, it being, however, expected that a gratuity will be presented to the servants, who, in consequence, receive very low wages. Elsewhere, a fee of eight annas or a rupee (one or two shillings) per diem is exacted from each visitor, the amount thus realised going toward the expense of maintenance. The servant in charge is called "peon," "mussalchee," "sepoy," or "butler," according to the *locale;* and if he be a pushing, enterprising person, he usually keeps on hand a stock of beer, brandy, tea, sugar, tin meats, etc., for the use of travellers, making a considerable profit by their sale. As unfortunately, however, such is not always the case, and as it does not do to be entirely dependent for one's dinner, at the end of a long journey, on uncertainties, prudent people usually carry a supply of such provisions with them. This is the more easy if the journey is being performed by wheel conveyance, as there will generally be room enough for the provender basket; but if one is travelling by palkee or on horseback, the stores will have to be brought on by coolie.

As in England, at every village inn the traveller may safely reckon on being able to obtain a meal of bacon and eggs, so in most Indian villages where there is a bungalow, it is possible to buy a few fowls, some eggs, rice, salt, and curry materials. It is hardly safe to count on being able to get much besides; but with a few accessories, such as a tongue, a pig's cheek, a tin of English bacon, or a good plum pudding, which may be brought from home or indeed anything good that will keep, and a bottle of wine or beer in addition, carried with one, a tolerable dinner may be eked out with such materials as the above.

Some travellers, not fond of "roughing it," carry their whole complement of kitchen servants with them on the march; but this is a troublesome plan, and more pleasure may often be got by a little rough-and-ready living for a short time, especially with a travelling appetite.

A famous expedient by which old hands at Indian travelling provide themselves with an unfailing and substantial dinner always at hand, is the *pot au feu*, or "pepper-pot." This is so excellent and ingenious a contrivance as to be entitled to some description.

The "pepper-pot" is thus contrived:—First get a medium sized iron pot, lined with enamel. It ought to have a lid fastened by a hinge, and fitting tightly when closed. To prevent a tendency to burst when the pot is at the boil, there should be a little valve on the top of the lid, free to rise to the pressure of steam from below. So much for the pot; next for its contents. The evening before starting on a journey, put in a fowl, one or two pounds of mutton chops, some potatoes and onions—in fact any meat and any vegetables; add a due proportion of water, salt, pepper, and spices, and then allow all to boil slowly, or stew, for as long as is necessary. Now add a little Worcestershire or Harvey sauce, for piquancy, and the whole is ready. Take the pot with you, and on arriving at the halting station, heat it up again, and *set it on the table.* After dinner, let your servant kill and dress another fowl, add it, or some chops, steaks, a hare, jungle fowl, or anything else of the same kind that may be obtainable, a few hard-boiled eggs, vegetables, salt and pepper, and boil again; next day repeat the process *da capo,* and your pepper-pot will last the whole journey, giving a savoury meal whenever required.

Some travellers look upon the pepper-pot as sacred, and never allow their servants even to look into it, the lid being kept padlocked. This is not a bad plan if your servants are low fellows, and not to be trusted, otherwise it is demoralising, and hurts their feelings, without affording any adequate compensation. In Bengal, however, where caste exercises so great an influence, there is no fear that any servants but native Christians and men of the sweeper caste will ever purloin edibles cooked for the European. All but Mohammedans will even refuse to touch not only meat, but plates and cooking utensils which have been used for food.

Bread, tea, coffee, sugar, mustard, and pepper, are articles never procurable at roadside bazaars, and seldom at bungalows, and should therefore be carried. For those who cannot take tea or coffee without milk, this may be kept in the form known as "Swiss or desiccated milk," which is to be had in the towns, and is really an admirable substitute for the fresh article.

When marching with a regiment, or in the district on revenue duty, it being necessary to camp at night, tents will be required—a large double-poled one for a family, a small one for a bachelor and a small one in addition for servants. It is a good plan to have an additional tent to send on in advance, but this can be dispensed with if necessary.

"The bandies and small tent should be sent on the previous afternoon, leaving out only the actual necessaries which can be packed in a couple of cowrie boxes, and carried by a coolie, and the bedding, chairs, and table, which will be only one cartload. Before going to bed, everything should be put into the cowrie boxes, except the teapot, kettle, and cups, which can be packed up in a moment; the tentpegs are loosened at the first bugle, so that the tent may be struck before the second sounds."

All servants taken on a journey, should have their comforts and wants attended to, otherwise they will be knocked up and fall sick; and as long as the march continues, they are each entitled to a daily allowance in cash, in addition to their regular pay, wherewith to provide themselves with good food on the road. After any unusually long or weary march, or in wet weather, it is a good thing to give them each a bowl of hot coffee, or a little spirits and water. All native servants, moreover, when taken to the hills, should be provided with warm clothing, otherwise, from motives of economy, they will only take with them their usual cotton garments, and certainly fall sick.

As an obvious precaution against fever or sunstroke when travelling, a general rule should be made, to travel only in the morning or evening, and never during the heat of the day; otherwise both men and animals will certainly be knocked up. The morning is the best time for riding, and the day's march of 20 miles can easily be done between half-past five and nine o'clock. For bullock-cart journeys, the night is the best time, and can for the most part be passed in sleep.

In hot weather, the day may be passed under the shade of large trees in the bungalow compound, or within doors, as may be most pleasant and convenient; and in case it should be overlooked, I may remind the traveller that he had better carry some interesting book with him, to while away the hours, as books are seldom to be found at dàk bungalows. Another thing the Anglo-Indian cannot go wrong in carrying with him on the road, is a small supply of simple medicines, such as quinine (made up into three or five grain powders), chlorodyne, spirits of camphor, liquor ammoniæ, and ipecacuanha powder. Even should he not require them himself, his followers may; or he may possibly fall in with others in need of medical relief, and life may perhaps be saved by his being thus provided.

Elsewhere in the present work, full and explicit instructions are given by my friend Dr. Mair, as to the immediate treatment of the more common and climatic affections, in cases where professional advice is not accessible; and of this proportion of medical science every Anglo-Indian will do well to make himself master.

CHAPTER XI.

HORSES AND DOGS.—*Value of horses in India compared with that at home.—Arabs.—Capes.—Australians.—Persians.—Pegues.—Respective values.—Horse's food.—Kooltie.—Bengal gram.—Paddy.—Grass.—Hay.—Stables.—Shoeing.—Dogs.*

ALTHOUGH it seems to be a common idea that horses are cheaper in India than at home, I cannot help thinking that the reverse is the case. But the fact is, it is always difficult to get a really good horse cheap anywhere; while on the other hand, it sometimes turns out that a long price has been paid for a bad one.

Whether at home or abroad, a considerable amount of care must be taken if it is intended to avoid the latter contingency. And first of all, let it be remembered, with regard to riding-horses, that an animal free from tricks, with a good mouth and temper, and at the same time cheerful, active, and well up to his master's weight, is a treasure indeed. In fact, few horses combine all these virtues, and one which does is a paragon, and worth a large price in any market. All dealers know this very well, and such an animal, therefore, is little likely to be sold, as the saying is, "for a song."

There is a great choice of breeds in India, large numbers of horses being annually imported, not only from Affghanistan, Cabool, and Persia, but also from Arabia, South Africa, and Australia.

Of all breeds, that which makes the best riding-horse for the tropics is undoubtedly the Arab. For docility, high spirit, and excellence of pace, he is unmatched; and in addition, he possesses powers of endurance adapted to the climate of India, which could hardly be expected in animals bred far from the tropics. At the same time the drawback is, that the Arab is a very expensive animal: from £80 to £120 being often paid for good blood, and higher figures for weight carriers. But, once bought, the Arab is hardier, more lasting, and altogether more satisfactory, for those who can afford the price, than any other horse; and will often be in good condition and spirits, and fit for gentle work, after he is twenty-five years old!

The Cape horse is possessed of much endurance and docility of temper, but, as far as I had opportunities of judging, is somewhat deficient in fire and spirit, and liable, like the Australian, to knock up when much exposed to the sun.

The Australian horses are powerful animals generally, and when well descended possess many of the excellent qualities of their English ancestors. They have, however, two serious defects: namely, unsuitability to a hot climate, and a propensity to which many of them are addicted for "buck-jumping." This most dangerous trick, or "vice," is one which may exhibit itself at any moment unexpectedly; perhaps not for the first time until the animal has been ridden, without manifesting any such tendency, for a twelvemonth. The "buck-jump" consists of a sudden curvature of the back, and a simultaneous spring with all four feet off the ground, and will often unseat the most practised rider; indeed many Australians, though quiet in other respects, and in harness, cannot be ridden at all owing to this propensity, of which it is quite impossible to break them when once they have discovered it. A gentleman who passed several years in the Australian bush, informed me, that it is not an uncommon thing for a stockman out in quest of sheep or cattle, to find his horse, after having gone steadily and cheerfully enough for eight or ten miles, suddenly commence a deliberate series of springs with the obvious intention of throwing his rider. Owing to this circumstance, Australians generally are in somewhat bad odour as riding-horses, and are more commonly used in harness, for which they are admirably adapted; it being, however, always to be remembered that in India, like ourselves, they are exotics, and should not be exposed to the sun more than can be avoided, especially in hot weather.

The Persian horse is ordinarily a gentle and tractable animal, though occasionally, if badly used, becoming very vicious. They are noted rather for powers of plodding endurance than for spirit, ardour, or speed. The native dealers seem for the most part never to think of breaking in their horses with a view to creating a good "action"—even if they are not ignorant how to do so; and the consequence is, that both Arabs and Persian horses, but especially the latter, are sometimes given to tripping, which renders them, in the absence of any largely compensating virtues, suspiciously regarded for the saddle.

A very good class of animal is produced in the countries north-west of Bombay, and along the shores of the Persian Gulf, by crossing the Arab with the horse of the country. These horses are called "Persian Arabs," or "Gulf-Arabs," and their value is regulated by the degree of Arab blood their appearance and powers would argue them to possess.

For those who are unambitious enough to be content with a pony, the Pegu is really a first-class animal, probably unsurpassed by any other breed of ponies in the world. These animals, which usually range in size from 12½ to 13½ hands, are brought over, as their name indicates, from Burmah, to the eastern coast of India, and owing to their well-known excellent qualities always find ready buyers, at prices varying from 200 to 350 rupees each; their willing ardour, splendid action, strength, and powers of endurance rendering them worth prices which might otherwise seem high for animals of such small calibre. For hill-work and bad roads, the Pegu pony is unequalled, while he is also a good weight-carrier, being frequently equal to thirteen or fourteen stone, and at the same time a match for anything of his size in speed. A good strong Pegu pony will carry a man weighing twelve or thirteen stone, thirty miles a day, without showing any disposition to knock up, if well fed and cared for.

A friend of mine, in the Southern Indian hills, has one of these indomitable little creatures which he himself has ridden for the last fifteen years, and which must now be at least thirty years old; and yet, only two years ago it acquitted itself with credit in a scurry race.

In price, Australian horses of good breeding range from £40 to £80; Cape horses from £40 to £60; Persians from £30 to £40; Arabs from £50 to £130; country-bred horses from £20 to £30; and Pegu ponies from £20 to £50.

Horses in India are usually fed on a grain called "kooltie" (Hindustani), or "kōlloo" (Tamil); or on "Bengal gram." In Ceylon, the feed is more commonly "paddy" (rice in the husk), or "paddy" *and* "Bengal gram" together.

"Kooltie" is a kind of small, flat, brown pea, similar to that yielded by vetch in Europe, and requires to be boiled for several hours until it has become quite soft and pulpy, and swollen two and a half times its original bulk, before it is given to the horse. The usual allowance is four measures (each weighing 2 lbs.), or altogether about the seventh part of a bushel, of the raw grain, per diem; this, when boiled, produces exactly ten measures, or say, roughly, one peck and a half English; which should be given in two portions at least, half in the morning and half in the evening; or else, which is perhaps better, four measures (boiled) morning and evening, and two in the middle of the day for "tiffin." As kooltie takes so long to prepare, the feeds for the following day ought, when on a journey, to be boiled at the halt of the night before.

Bengal gram is an excellent nutritious grain, in taste and consistency not unlike the common small beans upon which horses are fed in England, but in appearance resembling the grains of Indian corn or maize. It ought to be ground, or soaked for an hour or two, before being given to the horse; or it may be subjected to *both* processes, to render it more easy of digestion. The allowance of gram is usually from three to four measures; but less of it is required than of kooltie, which should be remembered. It is rather a heating food to be given alone, and is better combined with paddy: say two measures of gram to four of paddy.

Paddy alone is not bad feeding for young horses that can masticate and digest a sufficient quantity of it to keep them in health. To assist the latter process, it is necessary to have it thoroughly well pounded, or ground, after having been sifted to free it from stones and dust; and lastly, it should be moistened with water.

Of course the reader, in feeding his horse, will in great measure be influenced by local custom; and give whatever food may be ordinarily in use in the part of the country in which he resides. It may not, however, be out of place to give here the following results of my personal observation, as to the comparative merits of gram, kooltie, and paddy, as food for horses.

Bengal gram is *strong* food, and will enable a horse to go through a great deal of work, but (as in the case of beer with ourselves) under other circumstances is too heating to be given alone, for a permanency. Kooltie, I should be inclined to think more suitable as food for cows than for horses, its tendency seeming to be to soften and to produce fat and flesh, rather than sinew and muscle; it must, however, be stated, that over a great part of India the horses get little else. Paddy is nourishing and wholesome food for horses with good digestion; it is not, however, sufficiently nutritious for those that have to go through much hard work. Of all foods, however, the mixture of paddy and gram is no doubt the most wholesome and strengthening on the whole. Some horses are bad feeders, and are the better for a little bran with their kooltie, say one or two measures a day; but it must not be given in sufficient quantity to affect the bowels unduly.

But whatever grain is given, it will not alone suffice to keep a horse in condition. Grass is also required—good grass and plenty of it. Many people are of opinion, that grass is the only kind of food which fattens horses, and that all the grain they eat only gives them strength; but I am not in a position to state whether this is strictly the case. To supply him with grass, each horse has, in India, a grasscutter, a woman employed solely for the purpose, attached to it.

The grass given to horses should not be too sappy or green, as it will then tend to act purgatively, and create windy colics, especially in cold wet weather. The description best suited, is that which is found creeping along the ground, and is fine, delicate, and crisp. It is found growing under hedges, in the jungle, and in sandy soils; or it may be cultivated, under the name of "hurriallie" grass, in one's own compound. It has to be grubbed up by the roots when very short, in dry weather, and the earth should, therefore, be well shaken out before it is given to the horses.

A little "guinea grass" may also be given daily, by way of a treat; it is certainly fattening, and gives a sleek coat, horses relishing it very much, especially in hot weather. These remarks also apply to an herb called "lucerne," which may be grown in the vegetable garden.

Hay is a very good food, but not always obtainable. It may be made by collecting a quantity of any fine sweet tender grass (such as "hurriallie" grass) at the end of the wet season, when it is generally extremely plentiful; drying and storing it in the stables or coach-house against the advent of the dry weather, during which grass is sometimes very difficult to get. Australian hay is sometimes obtainable at seaport towns, and being full of clover and corn, is an excellent and nutritious food. Of course, hay should not be entirely depended on in hot weather, and some green grass (such as guinea grass) should be combined with it; and if there is a supply of *both* on the spot, the grasscutter may be dispensed with for a time, and a small saving be thus effected.

About 30 lbs. weight of fresh grass is the quantity required for each animal daily, and it should be weighed occasionally, as the grass-women are very fond of shirking their work, and will every day bring a smaller and smaller quantity if not looked after.

Indian stables are seldom supplied with mangers, and as moreover in fine weather the horses should (as elsewhere advised) always be brought up and fed in front of the house, a light box or trough, raised upon legs, should be kept available for each to eat his food out of. The nosebag, which the natives are fond of using, is an uncomfortable arrangement, and soon gets rank and sour from food drainings and saliva.

Horses should be fed *punctually*, at stated hours every day.

In the stable they are usually tied up with heel-ropes, but this is quite unnecessary, unless the animal is given to rubbing himself against the sides of his stall; and it is an objectionable plan, often leading to severe rope cuts, or galls on the heels or pastern joints. It is much better to give well behaved animals a loose box, to move about in at will, and they should wear a headstall with a good fringe over the forehead, to keep the flies (which are very troublesome at certain seasons) away from their eyes.

The stables should be clean and cheerful, but not whitewashed inside, as the glare of white walls is apt to affect the horse's sight, and produce a tendency to shying. Grey or lavender is a good shade, and may be easily produced by mixing a little charcoal with the whitewash. The Indian stables are usually quite open on one side with a verandah; and it should be so arranged, that this side does not face towards the east wind, or in any exposed direction. Owing to the open character of the stables, a rug or blanket (jhool) should be put on the horses during the cold or wet season, especially at night; and it will be as well to see, now and then, that these are not taken by the horsekeepers to sleep in, such being one of their common tricks.

A farrier (generally a Mussulman) is in most cases retained, by a monthly fee of a rupee or so for each horse, to keep the animals in shoes and their hoofs in order.

It is most important to see that horses in India are supplied with a sufficiency of good water, as well as food; and as it seldom happens that there is a river or perennial stream in the neighbourhood, a supply of buckets should be provided.

Indian horses are usually very thin-skinned, at least all that are well-bred are; and, therefore, an ample quantity of straw should be laid down in the stalls every night, for bedding. Sufficient straw for the purpose can generally be obtained for a rupee a month, for each horse.

I shall now say a few words on a class of dumb favourites, more humble, but certainly not less faithful, than those last referred to.

People in England seem to labour under the impression that dogs, in India, have a tendency invariably to go mad, and frequently, in consequence, beg their friends not to keep such dangerous pets. This idea is partly a reasonable one, for of course the heat of the climate is inimical to English dogs, as it is to Englishmen; and the former do, without doubt, sometimes go mad when neglected; though hardly ever, if well cared for by kindly and intelligent owners. Masters frequently leave home for a month or two, to brace and refresh themselves on the hills, without choosing to remember, that Dash or Tan is as great an exotic as themselves; and that he too would be all the better for a run along the hill sides, and a ramble on the mountain tops. Indeed, he requires much to compensate him for the annoyances he suffers on the plains, what with the heat, the flies, the fleas, and that special enemy of dogs, the tic, or dog "poochey."

But his master thinks Dash will be a nuisance on the journey, an anxiety on the hills, or a worry at the hotel; and thus the poor animal comes to be left at home in charge of the domestics. These are not too assiduous in their attentions, once the master's eye is withdrawn; and though on the whole they are kind enough, and perhaps give him food enough, they do not prevent his ranging about during the burning heat of the day; instead of keeping him tied up during this time, and taking him out for a good run in the cool of the evening. They will scarcely be inclined to sit down with him in the verandah for a regular flea-hunt, or to give him his daily bath and combing, which are essential.

No wonder then, that, sad and dejected, Dash roams about the forsaken compound, careless of the scorching sun. No wonder that he mopes about the house, with his ears choke-full of tics; no wonder he misses his master's kind voice and cheery whistle, his morning or evening gallop after the horse; no wonder he becomes mangy and melancholy, and at last mad! Not long ago, a terrible case, in which the life of a young English doctor was sacrificed, occurred at Kurnool.

An officer from that station went away to the hills, leaving his dog at home in charge of the servants. After a time the animal became sullen, refused his food, and snapped at those who came near him. The servant, thereupon, took him to the doctor of the regiment for inspection. The latter, with a lamentable rashness, took the dog and attempted to open his mouth, but, while doing so, received a severe bite, and shortly afterwards died of hydrophobia.

For my part, I never could bring myself to contemplate going to the hills without being accompanied by my faithful little dogs. Ready to share with us every privation and discomfort, how ungrateful and selfish of us to grudge them the pleasures we can bestow by a little extra cost and trouble! And does not their delight repay us; their wild scampers and fantastic gambols when they find themselves among the long green grass, and on the open breezy moors? Then, what gay companions for our walks and strolls; what enthusiastic picnickers; what eager and excited playfellows in a game of ball; and how sleek and bumptious they grow with the cool air; and yet, how ready they are to return with us, when once again we are under weigh for the plains!

I should, indeed, strongly recommend no one to keep a dog in India, unless he is prepared to make some little sacrifice of time and trouble for its welfare; to see that it has its daily bath, a walk either with himself or with the dog-boy, and regular and wholesome food. None of the other servants will be prepared to perform these offices regularly, and the dog must, therefore, have its own proper attendant; which, however, will not cost more than three or four rupees a month.

I always kept two or three dogs in India, sometimes in the hottest parts; and owing to their being regularly attended to in the above particulars, they were always in excellent health and spirits. They were kept inside the cool sitting-room during the day, and had a rug to sleep upon at night, being regularly exercised every morning and evening. Two feeds a day—say boiled rice and milk in the morning, and rice and gravy in the evening—are sufficient; too much meat being apt to bring on mange and liver complaint. These animals should be washed every day in cold water, and then well dried and (if long-haired) well combed. Care should be taken also to keep them free from fleas and tics. The latter vermin get inside the ears and bury themselves in the skin. The only way of removing them is by using tweezers; and the only preventive against them that I know of, tobacco-juice squeezed inside the ear.

It is difficult to get pure English dogs in India, except from the captains or sailors of ships from home, who occasionally bring them out on speculation. The prices asked are often considerable; 60 or 70 rupees being sometimes refused for a very ordinary-looking English terrier. Once bought, care must be taken that they are not stolen, both natives and English soldiers being somewhat addicted to this branch of the dog-fancier's profession.

CHAPTER XII.

SOCIAL CUSTOMS.—*Calling.—Whom to call on.—"Griffins."- Clubs. —Government House.—Governor's levées, breakfasts.—Receptions.— "At homes."—Dinner parties.—Borrowing system.—Precedence.— Garden parties.—Ladies' lunches.—Bandstands. —"Social mourning."—Anglo-Indian hospitality fifty years ago and now.—Parvenu. —Advice to ladies.*

ONE of the first objects of the new-comer to an Indian station, who wishes to make for himself a comfortable social position, will be to become acquainted with some of the older residents. This is an easier matter than at home, where the stranger has to wait till the previous residents are pleased to make the first overtures; a rule which in India is reversed.

Within the first few days, therefore, after his arrival, the new-comer, if a bachelor, should call upon those whose acquaintance he wishes to make.

In the case of married people, the system to be followed is rather elaborate. The gentleman first goes round, by himself, to call upon the ladies of the station; the latter, with their husbands, then return the call; when, finally, the stranger makes a second round, being on this occasion accompanied by his wife. Bachelors, of course, always take the initiative by calling on any lady who comes to reside at their station, and whose acquaintance they wish to make, as ladies cannot call upon *them*.

People are of different opinions as to the limits to which a calling system should in general be extended. Some, on first coming to a station, call on every one in good society, without distinction. Others, if the truth were known, call only on those whom they consider likely to be turned to account in the way of balls, dinners, or other gaieties; while other people, equally business-like, call on every one whom they think it "the correct thing" to know. Some persons, again, more discriminating, limit their visiting list to a select few, including the families of their official superiors; admitting from time to time any one they may have met, and think likely to make an agreeable friend.

A young government civilian, on taking up his abode in a presidency town, will of course pay his respects at the houses of members of council, and the board of revenue, judges and other heads of civil departments; while a military officer will, with equal certainty, call on many of the former, and also upon the commander-in-chief, commandants, and heads of military departments.

In mofussil stations, the number of residents being often very limited, the best plan is to call on every one, so as to avoid the appearance of wishing to slight any; beginning, of course, with the chaplain, magistrate, judge, and military commandant.

No *absolute* rule can be laid down for general application, as each person in choosing his circle of acquaintances must necessarily, and will, be guided to some extent by his own tastes and circumstances. At the same time, in every small station, it is decidedly the proper thing for a gentleman to call on the chaplain, the magistrate, and the commandant; and in the principal towns, on the clergyman of the church he purposes attending, and a few of the leading people of his own special walk or calling; besides (in Calcutta, Madras, and Bombay) leaving his card at Government House and on the commander-in-chief.

Nothing can be more absurd than the plan adopted by some people, of making the Directory one's visiting list, in the large towns, and calling at every house up and down the road, indiscriminately. To expect that old residents, with already a large circle of friends and acquaintances, will extend it *ad infinitum*, and take up with enthusiasm any additional number of persons who may choose to present themselves, for no other reason than that the ten or twenty minutes' scrutiny, admitted of in a morning call, discloses no objectionable or disqualifying feature, is preposterous; and those who begin by making "a round of calls" on perfect strangers, with any such expectation, will inevitably meet with disappointment.

Officials, no doubt, consider it incumbent on them to show some attention to collectors in embryo; military officers to possibly incipient generals; or wealthy merchants to the young employé of some neighbouring firm or bank: but the obligation cannot be universal, or be extended in favour of every new-comer.

Of course, those who are the bearers of letters of introduction from mutual friends at home, presenting them on their arrival in the country, have every title to expect that some recognition will follow, even should this not extend beyond an invitation to dinner.

Apropos of indiscriminate visiting, an anecdote is told of a pair of "griffs," bent on calling *on every one*, who were justly punished for the attempt. Hunting in couple, and having first taken down the names of the people living in every house, from the Directory, off they set in a "gharry" one fine morning, and sent in their cards from house to house with the usual degree of success. By two o'clock p.m., the latest hour which etiquette permits for this occupation, they had made considerable progress; but were obliged to defer further operations till next day. At eleven o'clock next morning they set to work again; and driving up to the house which seemed to be the next on the list, were duly ushered into the drawing-room. In a few minutes the lady of the house entered the room, looking much surprised; when, to their horror, they realized the fact, that they had "done" this house the day before! The confusion arising from such a discovery may be more easily imagined than described; especially, as was soon the case, when the story became bruited over the whole presidency.

Instead of trying to have a large circle of acquaintances from the first, it is much wiser to wait till the circle has gradually extended itself, by the accession of friends made in society from time to time. There is no use hurrying in such matters; it being worthy of remembrance, that one friend is worth any number of mere acquaintances, and one pleasant acquaintance worth a dozen mere "bowing" ones.

Gentlemen residing in large towns, should try and join the principal club, where they will generally meet many of the agreeable men of local society. And even whether residing in the towns permanently or not, it is well to belong to a presidency club, since this ensures comfortable quarters always available when required. The Madras, Bengal, and Byculla clubs, in Madras, Calcutta, and Bombay respectively, are excellent institutions of their kind, and reciprocate the privileges of each other, to the extent of making a member of the one, an honorary member of the other while visiting its *localè*. The "Bombay Club," on the Esplanade, Bombay, is a rising establishment, and a great convenience to persons who have to frequent the Fort, as the business part of Bombay is called from its being at one time within the walls, of which very few parts now remain standing.

People who have been called upon by a stranger, and who desire to evince some inclination to make his acquaintance, will, within a short period, or, if in the presidency, at least within "the season" next following, invite him to their house to partake of some kind of hospitality. Should they omit to do this, it may be taken as a proof, either that they consider their list large enough already, or that, from some cause or other, his attention is not greatly appreciated. In such case, if there is no particular inducement to ignore or overlook the neglect, there can be no necessity for the visitor's continuing to bow when meeting such people on the road. Some persons, however, strange to say, like having a great many mere bowing acquaintances; and they, of course, will be satisfied to receive in return for their call, nothing more than the usual languid recognition, should carriages pass during the evening drive.

Wherever else calls are made, it is, as before remarked, in every case essential for gentlemen to pay their respects at Government House; and there are different facilities afforded by which this can be done.

Her Majesty's representative in each presidency ordinarily holds a levée at least once a year, at which all gentlemen are expected to attend. Then, public "breakfasts" are given once or twice a year, and gentlemen wishing to attend these, have merely to send their cards, the evening before, to the A. D. C. in waiting.

These "governor's breakfasts" are held in some large hall or room in Government House: long tables laden with cold viands, being arranged down either side, and a smaller one, on a dais, across the end, for the governor and his more particular friends. At nine or half-past, the hall begins to fill with gentlemen in morning dress, and a few minutes later His Excellency enters, followed by his staff, and bowing to the assembled guests. All now take their seats, and in half an hour or so the entertainment is at an end; the company dispersing, every one to his particular business. Gentlemen wishing to have a private interview with the governor, must state the wish on their cards (sent in the evening before), and His Excellency now remains to grant the desired interviews. The object of one, is perhaps to ask for a subscription to some charity; another is in quest of a post for himself; a third desires advancement for a friend, and so on; probably the majority being suppliants in one form or other. Attendance at a "breakfast" or levée, once a year, or oftener, is a proper mark of respect to the Queen's representative; and those who render it may look for an invitation to the annual public ball, given at Government House on the Queen's birthday.

A third mode of rendering homage to the representative of royalty is to call at Government House, and write one's name in a book kept for that purpose at the entrance.

Those who wish for the *entrée* to Government House on less general and public occasions, and all ladies, should take the first opportunity of paying their respects to the governor's lady, who ordinarily holds receptions in the afternoons, once a week or so during the cool season, as will be notified in the newspapers. Most people in society attend these receptions, such attendance being probably followed by the receipt shortly afterwards of a card of invitation to one of her ladyship's "at homes."

Before leaving this subject, I should mention, that every gentleman meeting the governor in public is expected to take off his hat and bow; a rule which must be more irksome to His Excellency than to the public, as it of course necessitates his saluting in return.

The principal social entertainment in Anglo-Indian society is the "dinner party;" the "evening" or "tea-party," so much in vogue in upper middle-class circles at home, being almost unknown. In India, nearly every one dines late as a matter of convenience, eight o'clock being the usual hour; and evening parties, distinct from the dinner could, therefore, hardly begin before nine or half-past, which would not be consistent with early rising.

There is little in the Indian dinner party different from that to which one is accustomed at home. At eight o'clock the guests are assembled in the drawing-room, and the ladies being each duly made over by the host to a male protector, the company pairs off to the dining-room. Here are troops of native servants; a large punkah sways, suspended over the table from end to end; the board is decked with flowers and fruit, *à la Russe*, and course succeeds course, from soup to dessert, with mathematical regularity. The *pièces de resistance*, consisting of roast sirloin or saddle of mutton, and turkey and ham, are carved on the sideboard, or in an ante-room ; and, as each guest has brought with him his own servant to assist in the general attendance, and to wait in particular on himself, operations are much facilitated.

A curious practice prevails in some not over well regulated households. The servants (whenever the supply of such articles is insufficient for the number of guests invited) freely borrow china, glass, cutlery, etc., from those of some other house, with or without the sanction of master or mistress in either case. It consequently happens, that a guest is sometimes disagreeably surprised, to find himself seated at a friend's table, eating off his own dinner service, or choice dessert set, borrowed and lent without his knowledge. Of course, hosts and hostesses are to blame in these cases, either for not seeing that they have a proper supply of what is required for the entertainment of the guests they invite ; or, when knowing they have not, for telling their servant to "get" the deficient articles, without taking the trouble to think how or where he is to do so. But sometimes a butler takes the onus upon himself, without the mistress's knowledge, to conceal his own carelessness and shortcomings, especially where undiscovered breakages, etc., have been going on. Such articles as lamps, extra china services, etc., can generally be hired for the evening from native dealers in such articles, and this way of getting an additional supply if required, is far preferable to the borrowing system.

There are, however, some people who look upon the latter as a very convenient arrangement ; and I remember one gentleman, a bachelor, relating in my hearing, evidently as what he considered a capital joke, that he had gone on for years, without more than enough plates, dishes, knives, etc., for two or three persons, leaving the butler, whenever a party was given, to overcome all difficulties and shortcomings as best he could. This somewhat loose system extends largely to flowers : at a house with hardly any garden, a splendid show of bouquets will some times appear on the table; and the host, on being complimented, and asked where they have come from, will probably say,—"I really don't know; I believe my gardener got them somewhere!" The truth being, that a few annas having been handed to his gardener, with a mandate to procure flowers "somewhere," a neighbour's flower-beds have been ravaged for the occasion. So common is this in some of the presidency towns, that people, when they find their compound more than ordinarily bare of flowers, naturally conclude that a series of festivities has been going on in the neighbourhood; though their gardener will stoutly deny that the beds have been robbed of a single bud, except what has been used in the house.

Rules of precedence in India are very minute and punctiliously regarded; a host sometimes finding it no easy matter to know which of the ladies he ought to give his arm to, or which of the gentlemen he should ask to support the mistress of the house to the dining-room. Then, at the end of the evening, the most important guests must leave first, and the rest of the company in due order: a grave offence being considered to have been committed by any one who, from whatever cause, is obliged to disregard the rule.

An Indian entertainment of a very pleasant kind, is the "garden party." This is held out of doors, in the afternoon; croquet, badminton, lawn-billiards or tennis engaging the attention of some, while others meet old friends or make new ones in an informal way, quietly chatting and strolling about the grounds, which are supplied with seats in well-shaded nooks; while refreshments, in the form of ices, coffee, cakes, etc., are handed round from time to time.

During the absence of their lords at business, ladies frequently invite each other to pleasant little tiffin parties, lasting from one or two till five o'clock; when the hour for the evening drive having come round, the *séance* is terminated. This is a much pleasanter and more healthful way of spending the afternoon than in sleeping.

In the mofussil, the "chota hazree," * or "early tea," at six o'clock in the morning, is often made the occasion of pleasant *réunions* among early risers, giving the opportunity of a morning walk or ride to all the guests at least.

In every station in which there is a military band, the evening band-stand is the unfailing *rendezvous* of English society, which makes it the object of walk, ride, or drive, according to taste or circumstances. Carriages containing parties of ladies are cynosures, round which the bachelorhood of the neighbourhood is irresistibly attracted; and, favoured by the sweet strains of Beethoven or Mozart, tender passages perhaps sometimes find expression for which occasion might otherwise be sought in vain.

The band-stand might indeed well be called the "ladies' levée," for great as are the charms of music, it may well be doubted whether they are half as potent with the majority of the stronger sex as those of female society, the local cream of which is always to be found at the Indian band-stand.

It has always been cause of wonderment to lovers of common sense and comfort in India, that it should be *de rigueur*, in such a climate, for gentlemen to wear exactly the same evening dress, no matter what the season, as is worn on similar occasions in London or Paris in the depth of winter. Why a host should think it necessary to exact from every guest, in tribute to his mahogany, so serious a sacrifice of comfort, and indeed of good taste, as is thus involved, is a question Anglo-Indians have long been asking themselves. A malicious person might, and no doubt occasionally does, feel a sort of grim satisfaction in claiming from others a penance he is reluctantly compelled to yield himself, for there can be little doubt he, as well as

* Literally, "little breakfast."

his guests, would gladly avail themselves of a common absolution from what is frequently a heavy price for social enjoyment.

Native gentlemen, when invited to English entertainments, come dressed in loose, floating muslins and silk, suited to the occasion in every way; and yet they are the only persons in the company who are accustomed to the temperature, and to whom it would cause but little inconvenience, merely on the score of warmth, to change costumes with their European friends: an arrangement which would *practically* be more reasonable than things as they are in this respect.

Ladies have, fortunately for themselves, been able to secure some latitude in these matters, and low dresses of muslin or grenadine are appropriate to a ballroom with the thermometer at 85° or 90°; but the other sex are apparently supposed to stand in need of no alleviation of the misery of broadcloth in the torrid zone.

The very hue of the civilian "full-dress" is suggestive of dyspepsia in a hot climate, and quite incompatible with gaiety or merry-making; and it is probably owing to the appearance of sombre gravity which it conveys, that the same costume has been uniformly adopted for waiters in hotels and *restaurants*. Formerly gentlemen in the East met each other in the evening in white jackets, white waistcoats, and white trousers; in fact, entirely in white, with the exception of a black silk necktie; and the effect, as might be expected, was a cool and cheerful aspect, and comparative comfort, in spite of a high temperature. But this excellent custom seems now to be going "out of fashion," even at bachelor parties, in the presidency towns; while the advent of a lady is the *never* failing signal for every gentleman to don ungallant mourning, Anglo-Indians being even more punctilious in such matters than the good people at home. Comfort and good sense will no doubt ultimately prevail; though some such encouragement as the Viceroy's appearance at a Government House ball in a suit of white, will probably be needed to bring about so practical, though apparently so trivial, a reform.

Some people complain of the quiet style of living adopted now-a-days by a proportion of the wealthier Anglo-Indian officials, who—the cavillers say—being largely paid, owe it to their position and to the public, to exercise a liberal hospitality.

Formerly, whatever may be the case at present, nothing could exceed the hospitality displayed by Englishmen in India. This was ever experienced by new arrivals, who seldom landed in the country without receiving, from some warm-hearted judge or collector, a cordial invitation to bed and board, until they should have been able to make some independent arrangements for themselves.

It cannot be supposed that Englishmen are really less warm-hearted now than they were fifty years ago, and therefore, if they have adopted a more sparing method of displaying this characteristic, it is probable that reasons are not lacking to account for the change. In the first place, civilized society all over the world has undergone a great change during the last fifty years; and formerly there was an amount of extravagance and jollification current among the Old Company's servants, corresponding with, if it did not exceed, the convivial habits of the "good Old English (or Irish) gentleman" at home, of the same period. Quiet manners have, however, taken the place of the old riotings, both at home and abroad.

It came to be discovered, even at home, that "fast" living did not answer, whether from a hygienic or pecuniary point of view, while the arguments against it are tenfold more potent in a tropical climate. Perhaps it has happened, that in the social revolution that has been proceeding, under the influence of a growing refinement, of late years, some features may have departed that would have been better retained; and it is not impossible, that from the indiscriminate hospitality and wasteful self-indulgence which characterised their manners in the early part of the present century, some Anglo-Indians of to-day are inclined to proceed too far in the opposite direction. It must, however, be borne in mind, that for one Englishman who then went out to India, twenty or thirty probably do so now; and while it was a trifling matter to entertain the one, it would become much more difficult to open one's house to the twenty. Ther the great advance which has taken place in the cost of all necessaries of life in India must not be lost sight of. Houses, servants, food, cost twice as much, in some places, as they did twenty years ago; and, therefore, incomes do not extend nearly so far as formerly.*

* The following on this point is taken from an article which appeared in the *Friend of India*:—

"A lady's bazaar-book of the last century! Such is the curiosity on which we have stumbled, at a time when all over the East—in Shang-hai and Hong-Kong, as well as in Calcutta and Bombay—a cry has gone up at the cost of living. The record begins on the 13th October, 1799, on which day the writer landed at Serampore, and began to keep house for what was then termed a 'Moravian Settlement,' of six missionaries, five wives, and eight children. The entries close with 29th October, 1803. In these four years . . . they lived within the common allowance of 240 rupees a month. They spent on themselves, exclusive of servants, in September, 1803, the sum of 202 rupees. . . . We may accept their expenditure as a fair representation of what the middle class of English residents in India paid for servants and food seventy years ago.

"The rent of their first house was 32 rupees per month. Though not in a good situation, it accommodated six families, and had a common room which for the time formed the church of the Danish Settlement. The moonshee was paid 15 rupees a month, and the mission sircar, 10 rupees. The khansamah received 8 rupees, and the cook 6 rupees. The bearer, gardener, doorkeeper, and sweeper, received each 4 rupees; the cook's boy, 3 rupees; and the common labourer in the garden, from 4 to 6 pice a-day (4 pice being equal to 1 anna or 1½*d.*) when only occasionally employed, or 2 rupees a month. The washerman was always paid at the rate of 14 rupees the thousand articles. . . . Turning to food, we find that mutton and tea were the only articles as dear then as they are now. The very first entries, which appear on the day the missionaries landed, were—pair of boots for Brother G., 1 rupee; four umbrellas, 1 rupee; boat hire to Calcutta, 8 annas

Again, more importance is now attached to early retirement; and attention, in a more calculating age, is turned with greater anxiety towards the means of providing for an unemployed future of some twenty years in England, after leaving the country.

Like that of other countries, the society of Anglo-India is not without its leaven of *parvenus*, who, by their would-be grandeur and small pretentiousness, afford a sort of study to the great bulk of society, and ample employment and anxiety to themselves. This class includes those who are really wealthy, and those who are not, but desire to appear so. I shall, however, deal principally with the latter section.

The object of these persons is to take by storm, or by fraud, a position in society which can only come spontaneously to those adjudged worthy by the community at large. Their shifts and manœuvres to attain their object are (albeit they imagine them known only to themselves) perfectly obvious to the keen eye of society. Ostentatious out of doors and before the world, in private their homes are scenes of discomfort and discontent; and money spent in carriages and dress would often be more beneficially bestowed in procuring wholesome food or drink, and other real home comforts. Let us peep into a household in which this foolish policy prevails:—

No guests are now expected, and the table is therefore stinted; the cooking, to say the least, uninviting; the wine (purchased at some cheap auction) will be found corked and unsound. On the table, covered with a soiled cloth, an imposing-looking butler solemnly places a dinner of messes he himself would despise; while master and mistress, with no attempt at neatness in their attire, sit down

(at present a boat for the fifteen miles would cost *three times* 8 annas.) Large fowls were purchased at 8 for the rupee; smaller ones at 11, and ducks at 6. Beef at 1 anna a seer ($\frac{3}{4}$*d.* per lb.). Eggs at 6 pice the dozen, loaves at 6 annas the dozen, etc."

with sour and dissatisfied looks, and—there being "nobody but themselves" to please—without the least intention of trying to please each other.

On the occasion of "a party," however, every effort is made to produce an effect; and, alas! many and grotesque are the mishaps which now take place. The extra cook hired for the occasion takes the opportunity to get drunk; the roast chanticleer, politely yclept "turkey," is underdone; "the ham," *alias* bacon, bought in the bazaar, rancid; the soup, half cold; while the wines give rise to *sotto voce* sneers and wry faces. Extra couches, lamps, dinner services, mirrors, and other fictitious finery, have been borrowed or hired for the occasion; and the whole entertainment, wretched as it is, has cost a great deal of money, much sacrifice, and more anxiety. And what is gained in return for all this? A childish display of "borrowed plumes"—ridiculous because obviously borrowed; a bad dinner, which some of the guests will not readily forget or forgive; unlimited subsequent detraction and ridicule; and, worse than all, a haunting suspicion of failure to gain the one object aimed at, of imposing upon society.

Such people, of course, seize with avidity every opportunity for outside gaiety, which the discomfort of home renders the more necessary; and, with this view, painful efforts are constantly made to court the favour of the rich and fashionable. People of this stamp are by no means addicted to indiscriminate affability. With those whom they look upon as superiors in wealth or position, their tone truly is all winning cordiality; but, on the other hand, towards those from whom little advancement in "society" is to be expected, they are extremely indifferent and brusque. In fact, nothing could be more strictly utilitarian than their principles in this direction.

This class, which is happily a small one, may be set down as being composed for the most part of persons who have left a questionable social position at home, and are consequently elated to find themselves suddenly hoisted into the temporary and fictitious aristocracy of Anglo-India. Like the young semi-savages brought home by a missionary from the swamps of Southern China, and who on being introduced into the magnificent drawing-room of a Scottish duke, showed no surprise at the grandeur and luxury with which they found themselves for the first time surrounded; so, among their acquaintances (they seldom have many friends) the constant endeavour of such persons is to conceal this elation, or any degree of pleasure in their new-found luxuries. Their conversation is continually made to turn on pseudo-reminiscences of home-life, which are intended to show that in coming to India they have not changed for the better: indeed that, on the contrary, everything is more or less intolerable and wretched by comparison. If a lady be the narrator, the ayah is not to be compared to "my maid" at home; the wretched tubs in India are so hard to put up with, after the "marble baths" one has been accustomed to; the Indian houses are so uncomfortable; and so on, to the end of the chapter.

But I need not dwell further on this subject. Should the reader come across any of the class, of whose distinguishing features I have endeavoured to convey some outline, he will not be long in recognising them, and can then shape his course accordingly. Their artifices are always evident, and one can therefore only entertain ultimately a feeling of pity for the poor impostors, who, sacrificing all the honesty and reality of life, after all succeed in duping only themselves.

Before concluding this chapter I must take the liberty of offering a few words of advice to Anglo-Indian ladies, dictated by personal observation of the principal causes which militate against their health and happiness, and often prevent their remaining abroad with their husbands and families more than a limited number of years; there being apparently no reason, were these causes fully recognised, and carefully guarded against, why life in India should be more irksome or less happy and enjoyable to them than to the stronger sex.

The grand panacea for the preservation of health of mind and body, wherever one's lot may be cast, is steady, useful, and interesting occupation, and extension of the sympathies beyond self, so that the mind may be prevented from, as it were, gnawing away its own vitals. Throughout life it will everywhere be seen, that those who make self their one preponderating object of solicitude, and who most study their own comfort, regardless of that of others, are the very people who are most dissatisfied with, and soonest tire of, life. Under such a system every little trouble, difficulty, or annoyance is dwelt upon and unduly magnified; the sufferer falls into a state of hypochondria, and becomes gloomy, fanciful, and desponding. The mind, like the body, requires constant supplies of fresh extraneous food to support, amuse, and keep it in health; the same is also the case with the heart and affections; and failing to find this, a mind at once begins to feed upon itself, and becomes weakly and diseased.

Useful occupation is an enemy to *ennui.* Few men in India are without it, their work being in great measure compulsory, and they are brought up so to regard it. But with ladies the danger is, that many of them regard household management and domestic duties as voluntary obligations, to be undertaken or neglected as they feel disposed. The consequence is, that when they begin to feel the heat of the climate, they refrain from exerting themselves, under the impression that they "need not do so unless they like;" and this being a self-created and very easy sort of absolution, they avail themselves of it ultimately as a permanency. One duty is dropped after another, until, having no healthy subjects of interest, they become hypped, listless, and depressed, and at last really *do* fall into ill-health. It is beyond dispute, that the inactive life which many ladies fall into the way of leading in India, is the true cause (or at least the principal one) of the belief that the climate is more inimical to them than to their countrymen.

Once let a lady in India get into the way of allowing her house to be managed by the butler, and from that moment she has begun to throw away her chances of health, contentment, and happiness. With no occupation to interest her during the long hours of her husband's absence at business, and at the head of a disorganised *ménage*, the climate for her assumes a terrible aspect. Every change of temperature is noted as a fresh torture and grievance, and everything connected with the country in time becomes abhorrent; until at last, broken in health and nerves, she is sent home to England, leaving the married widower, her husband, behind, to toil and sweat for the means of providing for her often heartless and self-indulgent extravagance —for heartless and self-indulgent she will by this time have become, however different her disposition originally.

This is no exaggerated picture, as will be admitted by many Anglo-Indians, and it is surely one the realization of which it is worth while earnestly to strive against.

For every cheerful, earnest-minded English lady in India, there is no lack of fitting occupation, or amusement either. To superintend an Indian household itself, is by no means a task for the successful prosecution of which either perseverance or tact can be dispensed with. Then, where there are children, how large a field is opened for the most interesting of feminine employments; while beyond the home, how much good may every one find to do, who is disposed to seek and undertake it.

In fact, ALL the ordinary objects which interest the English lady at home, equally present themselves for and claim her attention abroad.

CHAPTER XIII.

THE NATIVES.

THAT a moral influence over the natives of the country is an essential preliminary to success in an Indian career, must be obvious to all. Such an influence, however, will only be obtained by those who lay themselves out to cultivate the native's respect, or better still, though more difficult, his affection; and this is what every Anglo-Indian should do.

For such a task the European in India is very advantageously situated. At the outset, he will find the average native predisposed to respect him. His colour and nationality alike create this predisposition, and the *prestige* of belonging to the dominant race, at once gives him a position which he may pardonably regard as flattering, but which he should be careful to take advantage of in an intelligent and kindly spirit; and which, he should remember, lends a responsibility to his conduct and behaviour which elsewhere they could hardly possess.

The small or only mediocre mind, unaccustomed previously to find itself distinguished from the crowd, is apt to show signs of elation under such circumstances, and straightway to regard with contempt those who appear to recognise in it capabilities and merits which really do not exist; but persons so led away forget, that they are objects of a generic, rather than an individual regard, and that they are respected for their country's sake rather than their own.

Hence, probably, it is, that some Europeans treat the natives of India with such scant consideration. The great majority of these, however, it is to be borne in mind, are very young men when they enter upon an Indian career, and a certain levity at first is, therefore, the less inexcusable; the more so, that in all cases where a sound judgment, good principle, and benevolence (though dormant for the time) really exist, a worthier course of behaviour is not long in making its appearance.

And, as a matter of fact, it is generally found that the longer the European remains in India, the more conciliatory he becomes towards those of the natives with whom his avocations bring him into contact, and the more liberal an estimate does he come to form of native character at large.

The young Anglo-Indian arrives in the country, as a rule, burdened with prejudices and misconception regarding native character. One person has told him, that the natives of India are "great liars;" another, that they are "dreadful thieves;" and altogether, he has unconsciously drawn for himself a picture of the "mild Hindoo," in which the worst horrors of the mutiny, human sacrifice, suttee, infanticide, thuggism—to say nothing of sensualism and mendacity—are the prevailing colours.

Then, in addition to having written down the natives wholesale as liars, thieves, and murderers—grounds hardly sufficient to inspire contempt as well as repugnance, he supplements the imaginary portrait with such characteristics as cowardice, ingratitude, and absence of natural affection.

It is not then to be wondered at, that persons who take this view of the subject, even in a modified degree, should at first treat the Hindoo as a creature unworthy of consideration, and sum up their estimate of him in the epithet "nigger." And we find educated natives from time to time bitterly complaining, that too often the Englishman comes out to their country (as one of them said) "prepared to hate the native horribly." Baboo Keshub Chunder Sen and other thinking men have frequently protested against such a state of things; and I remember seeing it stated by one native writer, that "the young Anglo-Indian only looks upon the 'nigger' (to wit the native) as a creature to be beaten with a stick, and upon a stick in the light of its suitability for beating a 'nigger.'"

All this, as before remarked, arises from prejudice, ignorance, and want of thought; and prejudice, by those who would conciliate the esteem of the natives, by according to them a fair and enlightened treatment, must be at once and totally discarded.

Nothing can be more unfair than to prejudge a race unfavourably; and the results of such unfairness must prove most unsatisfactory in the end.

It is useless to expect the better qualities of men to be drawn out, where they find they are likely to receive no credit for possessing such qualities; and to manifest contempt, suspicion, and dislike, is certainly not the way to elicit confidence and candour, or to encourage the practice of morality.

Instead of trusting to hearsay—generally a most unreliable authority—let every one take some pains to obtain a *personal* and experimental knowledge of the people for himself. Commence by having a friendly chat every morning, after the vernacular lesson, with a respectable *moonshee,* on native manners and ideas. Show an interest in what concerns the happiness of the natives about you, and invite their confidence by a kind though, at the same time, dignified bearing; above all, give them credit for being *brother men,* and never imagine that they are destitute of ordinary sympathies, affections, and what little of natural goodness there is in humanity all the world over; avoid all appearance of distrust, while being as watchful as necessary; and suppress really, as unworthy, any mere dislike arising from pride of race or colour. By acting thus, you will find that the more you know of the natives, the more good qualities they possess for your discovery.

Notwithstanding many bad qualities, naturally resulting from time immemorial ignorance and superstition, they possess many attractive ones, for which perhaps they do not receive sufficient credit, even among those who know them best.

I must, however, go no further without remarking, that to discuss the character of the "natives of India," is to take in hand rather a large subject, as a glance at the map will show. From Cashmere to Cape Comorin, for instance, is "a far cry," and within such a space, no doubt, many distinctions of national character will be found; but the latter is everywhere so much shaped and moulded by religion, climate, and social manners and customs arising therefrom, that it will suffice, for my present purpose, merely to divide the subject so far as to consider separately the Mohammedans and the Hindoos.

These are the two most distinctively separate races or classes which make up the population of Hindostan, and it will be necessary to deal principally with the last-named.

With regard to the Mussulmans, I need hardly say more than that they are more bluff and independent in their bearing than the Hindoos, and hardly so well affected towards the English. This is to be accounted for partly on religious and political grounds, and partly by natural disposition and character. No doubt, the intolerant arrogance of Islamism has had much to do in forming Moslem character; but the political element also enters largely into the subject of our relations with the Mohammedans of India.

Over nearly the whole country, previous to British occupation, they were the dominant race; and all that we, and a great deal that the Hindoos, have gained, has been to them a loss; it is, therefore, natural they should regard us with less favour than the latter, who find themselves enfranchised by the change of rule.

As a class deriving almost infinite advantage from the British conquest of India, I would especially point to the Parsees of the west, who, before that event had been consummated, were literally the hewers of wood and drawers of water of their Mohammedan rulers; though they have since been enabled to become one of the most wealthy and enlightened races in the East.

Even Mussulman disaffection, however, will no doubt be overcome in time, by a policy of consistent firmness and moderation; and by a careful adherence to that policy of "non-annexation," which was inaugurated in 1858 by the "Queen's proclamation to the native princes and rulers of India."

Whatever their faults, it must be admitted that the Mussulmans of India are an energetic, persevering, and brave race, and probably capable of becoming a great one.

Perhaps in no other country in the world does the religious element exercise so supreme an influence over the character and customs of the people, as in India among the Hindoos. They not only marry religiously, but eat religiously, bathe religiously, bestow alms religiously, and perform almost every act religiously.

In analyzing the character of a people so influenced, it is, therefore, indispensable to have some idea of the aims, tendency, and character of their religion.

Hinduism is unfortunately a system corrupt, yet stern and uncompromising, and irreconcilably opposed to all progress or reform. Having only in view the interests of the class by whom it was originated, it has no lessons calculated to elevate or improve the masses, but actually works in the opposite direction. Consequently, we find its sacred records and traditions replete with vice glorified, and with obscenities that have no other tendency than to demoralize its votaries.

A common accusation brought against the Hindoos is want of natural affection; and this arises from acts into which they are driven by religious superstition. And did we not know the all-powerful tyranny of such superstitions, this accusation might very well be accepted as well founded.

For instance, fathers and brothers in former times would inaugurate with enthusiasm the *suttee* of their widowed daughter or sister; and sons, with apparent barbarity, would abandon to a wretched death their aged parents, on the river's banks. But these can hardly be taken as proofs of heartlessness, since we find Hindoos of all classes equally ready to immolate *themselves*, from similar motives; and it is a well-known fact, that not only in the annual celebration of the hoolee or swinging festival in different parts of India, have thousands of enthusiasts been ever eager to offer themselves up to voluntary torture; but that, were the vigilance of the police to be relaxed, thousands to this day would joyfully cast themselves to be crushed to death under the ghastly wheels of the Juggernauth cars which one sees in many a country village. Moreover, in their other relations of life we see no lack of affection; and it may even be said without hesitation, that the Hindoos make as good husbands and fathers as the people of other countries.

There is a great deal said about the seclusion and non-education of females in India; and the inference is consequently drawn, that these are habitually subjected to a treatment on a par with that recorded by Mrs. Beecher Stowe, some years back, as the fate of the American slave. But this is by no means the case; the sex, in fact, holding its own in Hindostan as in other parts of the world. An aged crone is often the ruler and dictator, and by no means a mild one, of the whole family; and if such a fact is no argument, I may add that cases of *husband beating* are not unknown among the lower classes.

While on this subject, I may take the opportunity of remarking, that the statistics of crime for India show, that in proportion to the population, there are actually rather fewer murders committed than in England and Wales, in spite of our boasted civilization. There is, however, no question that statistics can scarcely be relied upon to give an idea of the actual amount of crime committed in India. The apathy and want of energy, generally shown by a family, when one of its members disappears, the universal reliance on "kismet" (fate), the seclusion of the zenana in a well-ordered native household,—the fear of annoyance, expense, worry, and delay, entailed upon a witness at a distant court of justice, where he may reasonably expect to be made a victim to the extortions of its underlings, and, above all, "caste" and custom, are all causes of successful concealment of crime. The very existence of Thuggism, which is still practised, but on a vastly diminished scale, and for the detection and punishment of whose votaries separate administrative departments are established in Central India, in the province of Oude, and in the Punjab, was scarcely suspected till within the last thirty or forty years. Yet these half fanatics, half thieves and murderers, had for centuries carried on their horrible rites and practices, and sacrificed their thousands of victims to their own cupidity, their simple love of murder, and the presumed thirst of blood of their tutelary goddess, Kalee or Doorga. The late Colonel Sir William Sleeman was the first who discovered Thuggee, and by the judicious employment of other Thugs, who had turned queen's evidence, very nearly extirpated it. Being carried on under the guise of friendship to travellers and others into whose confidence they would insinuate themselves, their murders were committed with perfect safety to themselves and with scarcely any trace left of their deeds. Scarcely any European, however, ever succumbed to their wiles, and as there are no regular coroners' inquests anywhere but in the large towns of India, they were little suspected, even on the rare occasions when the bodies of their victims happened to be discovered.

The essential principle aimed at in Hindoo religious law, is *class preservation.* Every class of society, or caste, must preserve an unchangeable position with regard to the others. First we have the Brahmin, then the Kshetriya, the Vaisya, and the Sudra, with the innumerable subdivisions of each in similar order and sequence. And this system having the authority of great antiquity, being taught as the essence of religion, and being supported by the most extravagant denunciation (extending even to a future state) in case of infraction,—threats that would be ludicrous were it not that they have been carried into execution, as far as torture and disgrace in this world can go,—has taken hold of the native mind with extraordinary power.

For a breach of mere etiquette, or contact—even when it is involuntary—with cooked or animal food, or things proscribed by the laws of caste, a man often loses, even now, all that makes life desirable, and becomes an outcast from his people. This no doubt in some measure accounts for the extreme subordination and respect which are everywhere shown towards superiors; a fact which, however, is also induced by the natural inoffensiveness and placability of the Hindoo character.

Many persons are apt to suppose, that this quiet submissiveness, constantly met with, even under trying circumstances, arises from cowardice; but I think the above the more satisfactory explanation, especially when we remember the stubborn resistance our arms have encountered in every part of India at one time or other, studding the country with battle-fields, giving immortality to the names of many great and gallant Englishmen,—throwing a halo of glory round the history of the conquest of British India, and which further, I maintain, cannot be regarded as otherwise than suggestive of the existence of bravery among the inhabitants.

The natural courtesy of all classes, as above referred to, is a very marked feature of native character. Go where he will, the European is almost sure to meet with respectful civility and attention. The shikarree (sportsman), the ordinary traveller in want of a guide, will seldom be disappointed: a civil inquiry or request in every instance eliciting a like response; and a light for the smoker, a drink for the thirsty, or a resting-place for the jaded, will always be readily offered at the nearest hut.

The *empressé* hospitality of native princes to Europeans visiting their domains is notorious; and this I have myself experienced, from a Maharajah (Mysore) now deceased, who enjoyed a well-deserved popularity among the Europeans of Southern India.

Almsgiving and care for the poor is practised on a scale elsewhere unknown; and positively injurious, as tending to encourage mendicity to an intolerable extent. But it must always be remembered, to the credit of the natives of India, that poor-relief, which among ourselves is compulsorily levied by the state, is in India freely extended in universal voluntary contributions. Among the trading classes it is not an uncommon thing for one anna in the rupee to be devoted to charity.

This is also in great measure owing to the inculcation of almsgiving, as a religious duty in the laws of Menu; the Brahmins looking to mendicity as their principal means of support, and with this view actually laying it down in Menu as an *honourable* calling, proper and becoming for them to follow.

The marriage institution enjoys great honour in India, and every man and woman *must* be married at due age, on pain of loss of caste in this life and perdition in the next. A marriage ceremony is *the* great event of the Indian village; and the poorest families spend large sums on such occasions, though bankruptcy and ruin too often result. Cases are quite common, in which a man earning no more than six or seven rupees a month, has raised in one way or other, 200 or 300 rupees for the marriage of his son or daughter: this being done by mortgaging his hut and all the family jewels, of which even the poorest will possess some small supply. Of course, in marriage making, as in every other social institution, there is ample room for reforms, which is to be hoped will come in course of time, but on which I have not room to dwell here.

While opposing wholesale and exaggerated condemnation of the natives in these particulars, I cannot plead that morality or truthfulness are national characteristics. This it would be absurd to expect; and in all commercial dealings with them, the European will soon find there is a sad deficiency of what we should call honour or straightforwardness, and that there is every need of watchfulness and care on his part. This care may be exercised, however, without allowing suspicion or want of confidence to be apparent, on the principle that one is more likely to be cheated by those from whom we take no pains to conceal our distrust, than by those in whom we seem to repose confidence. We find, on the other hand, a special peculiarity in the natives that they are scrupulously exact with property entrusted to their safe keeping,—a fact which should always be taken advantage of where practicable.

A prominent native failing is a general disregard of punctuality, and this is constantly felt with annoyance by the prompt energetic man of business. It seems to arise from a want of appreciation of the value of time, and can only be guarded against by stringent agreements in every transaction.

In talking of "Asiatic insincerity," due allowance must always be made for Orientalism of manner and expression, which from time immemorial has been somewhat exaggerated and highflown.

It will be difficult to gain the confidence and friendship of the natives, especially of the upper classes, until some general idea has been obtained of their prejudices and customs, and of what we call etiquette. For this purpose, the best plan will be to retain the services of a *really* respectable moonshee; that is, a man of good caste and position, and one well recommended by respectable and experienced people; for there are a great number of disreputable natives in all the presidency towns, who call themselves "moonshees" and tout about for pupils, but whose instruction will be found practically worthless. Having secured such a guide, a good deal of useful information can be picked up in half an hour's chat, after the usual lesson in whichever language is being studied.

I have not space, nor is it necessary here to enter into the subject at length, but I may mention one or two particulars, just to give an idea of what I mean by "native etiquette."

You cannot, for instance, with propriety, offer a native gentleman a glass of wine in your house, much less invite him to dinner, because in doing so, you would invite him to incur the greatest of all misfortunes—loss of caste; while, at the same time, you cause him to commit what he considers breach of politeness, in declining your offers. For it is looked upon as bad taste to refuse any kindness, if such can be avoided, and this should always be remembered.

If a respectable man sends you a dinner, however loth you may be to partake of the viands (the cooking probably not being much to your liking), you should nevertheless have it brought in, and at least taste one or two of the dishes, to show that you appreciate the compliment intended.

On all great days, again, such as the New Year, or other festival, it is the practice for the natives of all classes to present each other, as well as their European friends, with some little token of amity; a bunch of flowers, a basket of fruit, sometimes a more substantial token, but as often as not nothing more than a single lime. In such case, to refuse acceptance would cause deep offence; and, therefore, if it be only your horsekeeper who offers you his lime with a smiling "salaam," the lime should be received, *i.e.* taken into the *hand.*

When a native gentleman calls upon you, he will expect

permission before he can retire ; and this should be known, to prevent awkwardness on such occasions.

Should you call on a native gentleman in his house or place of business, sitting without his turban, as will probably be the case in the hot weather, do not be surprised if he puts it on as soon as you enter, for this is a mark of respect and politeness, just as much as that which you are called upon to pay in taking *off* your hat. In the same way, a native takes off his sandals or slippers on entering your house, though he is not to be expected to do so should he wear *shoes and stockings* like a European, this having become the established rule.

It is not considered, as with us, a mark of politeness to inquire of a native after the female members of his family, all reference to whom must be avoided ; and it is also a rule never to speak to a female of her husband. Equally curious is the necessity of never praising a child's looks or conduct to its parents, to do so being looked upon as a very ill omen.

When a native gentleman invites his European friends to a nautch and supper, as a mark of courtesy, he is not to be expected to sit down to table with them, since this would involve a breach of caste, but he will remain in the room, superintend the hospitalities, and converse freely with his guests.

CHAPTER XIV.

CONCLUSION.—*Insect annoyances.—Ants.—White ants.—Fleas.—Bugs.—Musquitoes.—Jungle leeches.—Scorpions.—Musk-rats.—Dhobies.—Water filtering.—Postages.—Telegrams.—Learning the language.—Parting advice.*

IN the present chapter, I shall endeavour to touch upon a few points not already taken in hand, some information and advice regarding which seem to be necessary, to render my task complete.

INSECT ANNOYANCES.—*Ants* are extraordinarily numerous in India, and abound in every place, from the high road to the bedroom. They are principally annoying, however, in the storeroom and pantry, of all the contents of which they will insist on having a share, if particular pains are not taken to exclude them. Every jam-pot will be made either a barrack for living, or a cemetery for dead ants; the bread on being broken at table, will unexpectedly liberate a small community; the spoons which stir one's tea, will send to the surface some dozen victims to an over-fondness for sweets; and so on with everything. As to sweet preserves, it will be sometimes difficult to decide, whether fruit or ants enter the more largely into their composition; while the cold leg of mutton put on the breakfast table, will often require to be brushed free of these devouring legions. If a crumb of bread, or in fact any kind of edible, falls on the floor, it is soon black with ant life, the smaller objects being steadily carried off to colonies underground.

Ants are still more tormenting when their attacks become personal. One or two of the small red species will sometimes indulge in a trip down one's back, and begin to amuse themselves by trying the soil with their digging implements;

an operation producing sensations far from pleasant. I remember on several occasions being wakened up at night by finding my feet swollen and tingling with innumerable stings, from a regiment of ants which had taken up its quarters between the sheets at the bottom of my bed. The remedy is to rub the part affected with sweet oil, great relief being thus almost instantaneously produced. If the sting be very severe, and is caused by the large red kind, it may be worth while to apply a paste of ipecacuanha powder moistened with liquor ammoniæ.

The best way of keeping ants off is isolation by water; though it is supposed they will either jump, swim, or form a bridge across a (for them) fairly-sized canal. The legs of the sideboard, safe, or whatever the stores are kept in, should be set in vessels containing water; tin vessels being sold for the purpose in the bazaars. The same plan should be followed with beds. Pieces of rag soaked with margosa oil, and tied round the legs of the furniture, are also said by the natives to form an effectual bar to formic invasions.

White ants are extremely mischievous, as all the world knows, and precautions must always be taken against their depredations, except at a considerable elevation on the hills, where they are not likely to be met with. Boxes, etc., should never be allowed to rest with the bottom touching the ground, or some day unexpectedly, the whole bottom, and part of the contents, perhaps, as well, will be found to have been eaten away. Every box or case should, therefore, either have small pointed feet, at least 1½ or 2 inches high, to stand on; or should be raised on smooth stones, bricks, or empty glass bottles, either laid on their side or standing (the upper half having been cut off).

It is easy to cut bottles in halves for this purpose, by tying round them in the middle a piece of worsted soaked in turpentine; the latter should be ignited and allowed to burn for a few seconds, the bottles being then plunged into cold water, when the two halves will fall quietly apart.

Major H. T. Forbes took out a patent some years ago for preserving wood from the attacks of white ants. The process seems to be to paint the wood with a mixture of sulphate of copper (common "blue-stone") and some vegetable oil. Arsenic possesses a similarly protective power, but is more expensive than blue-stone.

Various kinds of floors have been from time to time recommended to resist the progress of white ants; but for my part, I have no faith in anything but asphalte (laid down in a pretty thick layer) or in common sand. For godowns and outbuildings where timber, or in fact anything, has to be stored, in localities infested by these insects, sand is perfectly suitable and efficacious, the floor being simply covered to a depth of from four to six inches. White ants can never work through this, for the simple reason that the sand, as soon as they have reached the under surface, falls in of its own accord, and cannot be excluded.

Many kinds of Indian timber are proof against white ants, among which are teak, black-wood, ebony, and halmalille.

Fleas are undoubtedly one of the plagues of India. Houses that have been recently vacated become filled in an incredibly short time, and persons entering will in a few minutes find themselves almost black with swarms of these vermin. Bad as fleas are on the plains, they are ten times worse on the hills, and always prove one of the most serious drawbacks to the enjoyment of Anglo-Indians in search of cool air. To free empty houses of these insects, I have heard of resort being had to two curious expedients, which I may mention, but neither of which I can recommend:—(1) Putting a layer of straw over the whole floor of the house, and then setting it (the straw) alight; and (2) driving a herd of cattle through the building, to carry the fleas with them on their exit. In the first case, however, the house will probably be burned down; and in the second, damaged, without any effectual remedy being obtained for the evil complained of.

In mofussil houses, which have very often mud floors, decidedly the best plan is to adopt the native system of plastering the whole with a cow-dung wash. Nothing can be more effective, and nothing is really cleaner than a floor so plastered, when dry, which it will be in an hour or two. If possible, the walls should be whitewashed simultaneously, to prevent the fleas taking refuge in chinks or cracks, which they will otherwise do.

Under circumstances where the above remedy cannot be adopted, the best alternative is to buy in the bazaar a drug called "batch" (Hindustani), or "wassamboo" (Tamil), which should be crushed into a mash, and then mixed with water till a wash is formed of the consistency of soapy water, the liquid being then sprinkled freely over the floor and walls.

Bugs are common enough in native dwellings, but can hardly be considered an annoyance to which Europeans are subjected. There is a green bug which flies into the house at night, attracted by the lamps. It emits a very disagreeable smell if touched.

Musquitoes are a great torment in some parts of the tropics, especially in hot steamy districts. They prevail in still, sheltered atmospheres night and day: but punkahs, which are in general use in such cases, are very efficient in driving them off, if pulled with sufficient vigour. Net curtains, of course, are a protection at night; and to be really so, they should be well shaken, let down and tightly tucked under the mattress all round, before darkness sets in in the evening. The framework, etc., of the bed should also be well beaten with a towel, to insure that none of these tormentors are lurking inside. One musquito is quite sufficient to destroy the night's rest of some people; even if it does not give many bites, its shrill, treble buzz having a most distracting effect on those who are nervous. It is, therefore, a pity that curtains and punkahs are not very compatible with each other, so that one or other is usually dispensed with; though I *have* seen a large "four poster" hung with curtains, and having the punkah (a small one of course) inside.

Musquitoes will take any refuge they can get during the day, especially in clothes, towels, or anything loose and hanging; all such articles should, therefore, be carefully excluded from the bedroom. On taking up a coat suddenly which had been hanging over the clothes horse, I have seen a perfect swarm of musquitoes fly angrily forth. Water always attracts, and possibly also generates, them; and this is why it is important to have the washing apparatus, as is generally the case, in a room distinct from the bedroom.

There is no immediate cure for the irritation, often excessive, arising from a musquito bite; limejuice rubbed in does good in some cases, eau-de-Cologne in others, and arnica lotion in others; but the best plan is generally to leave them alone, and avoid scratching, which often leads to festered sores. If the itchiness and irritation is so great that it is impossible to abstain from scratching or rubbing, a brush ought to be used for this purpose, so as to avoid breaking the skin.

Jungle Leeches have been referred to before; they abound in damp, jungly localities, principally on the hills, and fasten on the ankles and legs of the unwary pedestrian; the gaiters elsewhere mentioned, should, therefore, constantly be worn in districts much infested by them. Once bitten by jungle leeches, the best plan is to rub the part with salt, and then to sponge it with cold water; but the great thing is to refrain from scratching or irritating the bites (which is often difficult, owing to the acute itchiness they produce), as bad sores will otherwise be very apt to result.

Scorpions are very common, but people are not stung by them so often as might be imagined. These reptiles crawl into houses during or after heavy rains; they then take shelter under the furniture or mats, but under the bath-tubs they find their favourite retreat. This being the case, furniture, boxes, mats, and especially bath-tubs, should be moved from time to time, and the floor beneath them swept. A scorpion sting is exceedingly painful, and even sufficiently productive of inflammation to cause death in children. Immediate relief will in most cases result from the following treatment: slightly scarify the part with a lancet or penknife, and rub in ipecacuanha powder; or, apply a paste made of ipecacuanha powder and liquor ammoniæ.

Musk-rats are quite distinct from the ordinary rat or mouse. They are very numerous in many parts of India, and extremely objectionable vermin, emitting a sickening, musky odour, which taints immediately anything they may have passed over. Incredible as it may seem, I have known a whole shelf or tier of wine or beer, in the liquor godown, tainted by one of these creatures having *run over the bottles.* There is nothing to be done but to set traps, poison, etc., as in other countries.

DHOBIES.—The system of washing pursued in India is as follows: standing up to his knees near the bank of some river, tank, or canal, with a large flat stone coming just above the water's surface at his side, the dhobie or washerman plunges the garment to be operated upon into the water; then gathering it up by one end in both hands, he swings it vigorously round his head, and brings the loose end down with a bang upon the stone; the water by this means is literally shot through the web of the material. The process being continued for some time, ends are reversed, a fresh plunge is made in the stream, and perhaps a little soap applied, when the banging process begins again, until very soon all dirt is taken out of the cloth—and something more. This is a trying system to those who object strongly to have their clothes torn to pieces about once every fortnight, but there is nothing for it but resignation, there not being the slightest hope of ever inducing the dhobie to adopt the more tedious but less damaging process, of using a tub and "elbow grease." All the more delicate materials, however, can be given to the "silk dhobie," who charges more for washing, but is more careful and gentle in his operations. Laces, flannels, etc. should always be washed at home, but the silk dhobie is quite an expert at getting up shirts, waistcoats, ladies' dresses, etc.

Dhobies in general get the credit of hiring out to would-be "swells" of the lower East Indian community, the garments entrusted to them, and the best precaution against this is to leave the clothes in his hands for the shortest possible time; and, as European clothing is probably most in request among the class referred to, on Sundays, to have the washing always brought home on the Saturday night. The dhobie should then return for the soiled clothes on Monday morning.

Another reason for not allowing the clothes to remain too long in the dhobie's hands, is that he is very apt to throw them when damp into a corner, whence, if left "neglected half forgotten," they will emerge covered with iron-mould stains.

When giving the clothes to the dhobie a list should of course be taken; and if anything is found deficient when they are brought back, his pay should be stopped until the account is square again. Under such a system dhobies will be found extremely accurate in their accounts.

WATER FILTER.—The best and simplest arrangement for filtering water appears to be the following; the filter described is already in general use throughout India, but often so badly constructed, or so much neglected after its construction, as to be of comparatively little service:—Get an upright stand, with bars at convenient distances above each other, upon which to rest the successive chatties (or earthen vessels) through which the water is to pass. The top of the highest chatty should not be more than five feet from the ground, so that it can be easily filled by the waterman without assistance. Two chatties below this will suffice, but three can be used if desired, a space of three or four inches being left between each, *i.e.* between the top of the lower and the bottom of the upper one. These chatties can be got specially constructed, all but the lowest one having had a few holes punctured in the bottom, before being burnt,—or ordinary chatties can be got and bored in a similar manner to do equally well,—the object of course being to allow the water to percolate. The topmost vessel should now be half filled with tolerably fine gravel, previously sifted and washed; that next below should have an equal quantity of fine, clean sand, also washed, resting on a piece of strong, thick flannel; the next or third chatty should be half filled with charcoal (animal charcoal is the best) also resting on flannel. After having passed drop by drop through these three vessels, the water will have been rendered pure and wholesome, and may now pass into a fourth, from which it can be taken as required.

I should also mention, that flat earthen platters (also punctured) should be laid on the top of the chatties, to prevent the dust, etc., from being blown in.

The gravel, sand, charcoal, and flannel should be changed at least once a month; once a fortnight would be better still, as of course the longer they are used the fouler they must become; and, therefore, the less capable of answering the required purpose. It is also recommended, that *all* the vessels used (which cost only a few annas each) be broken, and new ones substituted, at least once every three months.

Too much importance cannot be attached to having at all times pure drinking water, as various loathsome and dangerous diseases, very common in India, especially among the natives (guinea-worm, elephantiasis, etc., not to mention fever, dysentery, and cholera), are supposed too often to owe their origin to bad water; and it will, therefore, be worth the while of every housekeeper to superintend the construction and renovation of his own filter, in person, instead of merely giving orders on the subject to a servant.

POSTAGES.—The rates of letter postage are as follows:—From any part of India to any other part, by dâk, not exceeding half tola (about one-fifth of an ounce) a half anna; from any part of India to any part of Great Britain, not exceeding half oz., *viâ* Southampton, 5 annas; *viâ* Brindisi, 6 annas.

TELEGRAMS.—From any part of India to any other part, for 10 words, 1 rupee; for 20 words, 2 rupees; from the same to Great Britain or Europe Rs. 2 As. 8 per word. Telegrams to or from any Stations east of Chittagong or in Ceylon are subject to a small extra charge.

In conclusion, I must strongly advise all my readers of the stronger sex (for I do not consider that the obligation necessarily extends to ladies), on arriving in India, at once to set about learning whichever of the vernacular languages may be most used in the province or district in which he finds himself located. In Bengâl or Northern India, he will find Hindustani, Hindi, and Bengali currently spoken; in Bombay and Western India, Hindustani, Marathi, and Guzerathi; in the southwest, Malayalim; in the south and southeast, Tamil; and along the east coast, north of Madras, Teloogoo. In the Mysore, and part of the Deccan, Canarese prevails; and elsewhere other languages, all more or less distinct from each other. The classical languages of the Indian Universities are Persian and Sanscrit.

Government servants, civil and military of course, will find languages prescribed, which it will be necessary to acquire, but for all other classes of Anglo-Indians, I would lay it down as a rule, that on the Bombay side of India, Marathi or Hindustani (or both) should be learned; in Bengal and Northern India, Bengali or Hindustani (or both); and in Madras or Southern India, Tamil or Teloogoo (or both). Of course no one can be expected to master *all* the tongues current even in only one part of India, since in some districts no less than four languages are currently spoken by the different classes of natives.* And the object clearly, therefore, should be to learn that one which will be most useful, or in other words, the one most generally understood.

It is quite useless for any ordinary man to hope to get on in a country while ignorant of the language of the people; such ignorance necessarily must lead to constant obstructions, annoyances, and misunderstandings, which no system of mere interpretation can ever entirely obviate.

The following brief set of rules, having for their object the *mens sana in corpore sano*, will be easily remembered by every one:—

1. Always sleep on an upper story, or as far from the ground as possible. Go to bed early, take plenty of sleep,—but rise early, so as to be out of doors by sunrise. Always have as much good air playing about your room as possible, and sleep cool, while carefully guarding against chills at night, as well as by day, especially those arising from exposure to land wind.

2. Take plenty of open-air exercise, but be careful to avoid over-exertion, or undue exposure to the sun.

3. Eat plenty of good wholesome food, but be at the same time moderate. Avoid stimulants, and things that are very heating, such as oatmeal, much coffee, etc. Smoke as little as possible, if at all.

* On the south-west borders of Mysore, Canarese, Malayalim, Tamil, and Hindustani are all in use.

4. Drink no water that has not been either well filtered or boiled, or such as the natives recommend and use themselves for drinking purposes.

5. Work as hard as you like while you are about it, but confine your work to certain hours—not after sunset; allowing due provision for relaxation and repose. Above all, avoid working by night as well as by day.

6. Preserve a calm and contented spirit, guarding as much as possible against needless worry and irritation, and never *magnify* small annoyances unduly.

7. To do this, it will be necessary to take a lenient and impartial view of native peccadilloes and peculiarities, which will lead to a bearing firm but courteous and conciliatory towards the natives generally, and such an attitude will make them more cautious of offending or annoying you.

MEDICAL GUIDE

FOR

ANGLO-INDIANS.

BY

R. S. MAIR, M.D.,

Fellow of Royal College of Surgeons, Edinburgh ; Deputy Coroner of Madras ;
Surgeon Infantry Volunteer Guards, Madras ;
Member of Royal Asiatic Society, etc.

INTRODUCTORY REMARKS.

THE first questions put by a European with an early prospect of Indian life before him, almost invariably refer to the climate, and to the mode of living he should adopt while under its influence.

The following pages have been written with the object of answering these questions, by pointing out what influence the climate does produce on the human constitution, and those principles of individual hygiene, embracing such subjects as food, drinks, exercise, etc., that must be attended to, in order to ensure a fair measure of health.

It cannot be too strongly impressed upon the minds of those who desire to maintain their health, that the influence of the climate may be materially modified or lessened, and that many of the diseases to which Europeans are liable, may be guarded against or prevented, by the exercise of no more than ordinary care ; and if the principles and rules here laid down are fairly carried out, as they easily may, the amount of health which the European will enjoy in the tropics, will amply reward him for any little trouble which attention to them will involve.

In addition to the chapters on climate and individual hygiene, others have been added, on the causes, symptoms, and treatment of those diseases and accidents that are most commonly met with.

The author must guard the reader against the idea that, in treating such subjects, he wishes every one to constitute himself his own doctor under all circumstances. On the contrary, he would earnestly impress upon all, seldom or never to rely upon their own judgment, when professional aid is within reach.

There is a large class of Europeans in India who live at such great distances from a doctor, that they are compelled to fall back upon their own resources, to treat, not only the members of their own household, but also those employed by them; and the author, while engaged for many years in an extensive practice, was frequently called upon to give such written directions, on the diseases herein discussed, to such of his patients as left the presidency town for remote or isolated districts in the Mofussil.

It is entirely for the benefit of this class, that the chapters on disease and accidents have been written, and it is hoped that they will prove of some value.

CLIMATE.

The influence of the climate of India upon European constitutions, has always been a fertile subject of controversy. Opinions, conflicting and diverse, have from time to time been expressed with all the weight and authority which individual experience was supposed to give. Some men, for example, have unhesitatingly asserted, that the climate of India is one of the finest in the world, and that Europeans can live there with as good a prospect of health and longevity as in their native land; while others with equal emphasis condemn the climate altogether, and regard it as pernicious and even fatal to the Anglo-Saxon. Those who formed the first of these opinions were probably men endowed with excellent constitutions, who were temperate in everything, and who were most careful to guard themselves against undue exposure. The second, on the contrary, probably numbered amongst them men far from cautious or prudent in their habits, injudicious in every respect, or triflers with their constitutions, but who when they broke down laid the whole blame on the climate, and on that alone. But the question is much too important to be decided in this narrow way, and a much wider view must therefore be taken than that afforded by individual experience.

For obvious reasons, no class of men are better qualified to take this comprehensive view, than members of the medical profession, and it is by the results of their experience that most people will after all be guided.

Not many years ago, the climate of India was looked upon as something to be dreaded. The young man proceeding to the East, was expected as a matter of course to return home, if he ever did return, a sallow, yellow coloured, emaciated invalid, with his liver sadly damaged, his mental energies and nervous system much enfeebled, and his constitution generally so shattered, as to render him unfit for any social intercourse or enjoyment. Nor was this altogether untrue, but in the majority of instances the climate was not entirely, sometimes even not at all, to blame.

In those days, and to no small extent even now, the habits and mode of life of the European were not conducive in any country, far less in India, to good health. He had no idea of the well known ordinary laws of health, and if he had, he despised or disregarded them; he indulged in vicious courses of all kinds; and when his health gave way or death overtook him, the climate was the ever-ready and never-failing cause to which all was attributed. It was the bugbear always convenient to cover a multitude of personal sins.

Medical men of any experience in India know full well, that even at the present day, in a very large, if not the greater number of cases, men whose constitutions have been so impaired as to necessitate a return to their native country, should assign the cause to their own imprudence and want of self-restraint, rather than to any direct influence of the climate. In fact, as Sir Charles Napier once pithily remarked, every evil from which the British have suffered has been laid to its door. The army medical reports afford abundant evidence of this, whilst "sanitary science has now reduced the question of climate to its proper dimensions, and shown that just as hot moist weather in England calls people to account for sanitary neglect so does the climate of India call to account people who are equally rash there." But it is not contended that the climate of India has no prejudicial influence whatever on the European constitution. It does produce an unmistakable impression on all, and the nature and degree of this impression depend in great measure on the sex, constitution, temperament, and habits of the individual, as well as on the age when he arrives in India.

Perhaps no race has such wonderful power of adapting itself, *for a time*, to almost any climate as the Anglo-Saxon. We occasionally see or hear of men who have lived on the plains of India for upwards of forty or fifty years, a residence unbroken by any change of climate whatever, and yet without any apparent effect being produced on their mental or physical health. But these are rare and exceptional cases, and only serve to illustrate the wonderful power which some constitutions (few in number they certainly are) possess, of resisting those agencies which influence health. As a rule, the climate does tell, sooner or later, on the European, if the residence is prolonged; and more especially, if uninterrupted by a run home, or a residence on some of the hill stations.

The newly arrived European has almost every function unduly stimulated, the circulation is increased, and there is not unfrequently a tendency, especially in those of plethoric habits, to acute inflammation or congestion of some of the abdominal organs. During the first year's residence the digestive powers are lessened, the appetite, particularly for animal food, is diminished, the skin acts freely, and a teasing, itching, and irritating eruption, called "prickly heat," soon convinces him that he is not now living in his own temperate climate. After a time, varying it may be from two or three, to twenty-five or thirty years, according to constitution, temperament, and habits, he begins to complain of lassitude and fatigue after the least exertion; the respiration is less deep and free, the circulation is enfeebled, he is more sensitive to heat than before, becomes sallow or pale, loses much of his mental vigour, passes restless nights, feels altogether unequal to the ordinary routine of duty, never ceases to abuse what he now calls the "abominable climate," and longs for the power, as he has the will, to quit the country at once.

If he cannot leave the country, the process of mental and physical deterioration, for such it unquestionably is, proceeds, and becomes still more marked in the generation which succeeds him. His children are, as a rule, comparatively feeble in mind as well as body; they are pale, flabby, and have an unhealthy appearance, whilst the prospects of another generation are very remote indeed, if the residence on the plains has continued uninterrupted by a change to a temperate climate. It is rare to find a third generation of pure Europeans in India, that is, of those of pure, unmixed blood, who have, since the first generation landed in India, never quitted the plains for a temperate climate. It is for this reason, and for this reason only, that it is idle to talk or think of colonizing the plains of India with Europeans.

The concurrent testimony of many distinguished medical men, attests most clearly, then, that the climate does deteriorate the human system; and further, that length of residence, so far from affording any guarantee or protection from the diseases peculiar to the climate, renders the European all the more liable to be attacked, and the diseases, when they are so attacked, more fatal. The health, mental as well as physical, becomes slowly, perhaps almost imperceptibly, affected; and this process of deterioration or degeneration goes on, and will go on, if not arrested by a change to another climate.

Much has been said and written about acclimatizing the European in India; but the idea, for the reasons just given, is scarcely ever seriously entertained now-a-days by those who have carefully studied the influence of the climate generally. The number of those who do return to Europe with their constitutions unimpaired, after a long residence in India, is but small; and in very few instances do those who can afford it think of rearing up their children entirely there. If they do, "parents soon mourn over the graves of their lost offspring, or sigh on beholding the sickly appearance of those who remain."

Females suffer perhaps even more than males. Their lives, especially those in affluent or easy circumstances, are generally torpid, and too little relieved by occupation. They have few necessities for exerting themselves; they take but little, often far too little, interest in domestic affairs; they become listless and apathetic, and they succumb to the climate sooner than men.

A woman's health is almost invariably so affected by the climate of India, after six or eight years' unbroken residence, that she is compelled to seek that change in her native land which can alone restore her. Great sacrifices and self-denial, financial as well as social, are often made and endured, by husbands, sending their wives and children "home," that they may be removed from the morbid influence of India, that their constitutions may become invigorated by a residence in England, and that the children may have that mental vigour imparted to them which it is believed they can only obtain there.

The prejudicial effects referred to are due to the long-continued action of heat on the body. A high temperature causing the atmosphere to be rarified, diminishes the amount of oxygen in a given bulk of air inspired, so that less oxygen is consumed in respiration as the temperature increases, while the amount of carbonic acid exhaled from the lungs is less also.

The blood, which passes through the lungs, for the purpose mainly of obtaining this oxygen from the atmosphere, in order to remove the carbon, in the form of carbonic acid, and thus to arterialize or vitalize it, receives a less amount than is necessary to render it fit for maintaining all the organs and functions of the body in a state of efficiency or good working order.

Respiration is imperfectly carried on,—the number and depth of the inspirations are diminished,—the heart's action becomes enfeebled, a considerable proportion of the carbon, which should be eliminated as carbonic acid from the lungs, is retained, and, circulating with the blood, is vicariously distributed in various organs of the body.

The lungs, heart, brain, and especially the liver, become embarrassed, their functions are more or less impaired, indeed, almost every organ of the body is to some extent affected by what may be called a semi-poisoned condition of the blood, due to the presence in it of superfluous unconsumed carbon.

This it is which causes that lassitude, debility, and disinclination for exercise, which are so commonly complained of during the continuance of the hottest weather, while it not unfrequently proves the proximate cause of serious organic disease.

The free but not immoderate action of the skin, by perspiration, relieves the blood of much of this superfluous carbon; exercise, moderate and systematic, produces a similar effect, and a carefully regulated diet, as will hereafter be shown, though exercising no direct influence in ridding the system of this excess of carbon, is of no small importance in preventing its increase, whilst indulgence in alcoholic beverages, beyond moderate allowances, tends directly to augment it.

But perhaps nothing produces such a beneficial effect, as

regular and periodic change to another climate with a lower temperature.

The European resident in India must, therefore, always bear in mind the fact, that the climate on the plains is exerting its influence on him, however little he may feel it. He may, as many do, confide too much in what he believes to be the inherent strength of his constitution, and remain there too long without any change. He may find out when too late that his vigour and energy suddenly leave him; and the change to a temperate climate, which would have reinvigorated him at the proper time, fails to produce the desired effect.

It is these *changes* which enable Europeans to prolong their residence in the East; and if taken periodically and systematically, the measure of health which the individual will enjoy, will far more than counterbalance any inconvenience and expense which these changes cause. They should, therefore, be taken advantage of regularly by those who can afford them, even although there is no apparent necessity for them, but for the purpose of obviating by anticipation the mischief to the constitution, which prolonged, unbroken residence on the plains is likely to produce. A residence for one month at least in every year, on some of the hill stations, and a thorough change to a European climate for twelve months after each ten years' residence in India, would do much to remove or remedy the deteriorating effects referred to.

For those especially who complain of lassitude, debility, and loss of appetite, who feel jaded and wearied, if not exhausted, after the least exertion, and who have not the usual physical or mental aptitude for the ordinary daily routine of duty, the climate of the hill sanitaria is particularly well adapted.

The appetite and digestion are much improved; respiration and circulation, previously oppressed, languid, and embarrassed, are stimulated and relieved; the vital energies generally are invigorated and braced up; and a sensation of buoyancy and vigour is experienced, which was not felt before.

In all cases some care is necessary in removing from the plains to the hills, to avoid the dangers or risks incidental to sudden transitions of temperature.

The effect of the rapid, sometimes abrupt, changes (as in the Madras presidency) from a temperature as high as 90° or 95° to one as low as 50° or 55°, must be carefully guarded against, by the necessary change of clothing. Inattention to this precaution (and it is one too often neglected) has been frequently followed by some illness, as fever, diarrhœa, dysentery, catarrh, rheumatism, etc., which has marred all the enjoyment or benefit that the change would otherwise have produced, while it not unfrequently results in still more disastrous consequences.

For those suffering from organic disease of the liver, kidneys, lungs, heart, brain, etc., the climate of the hills is as a rule not suited at all, certainly not for those in whom organic disease has considerably advanced. In all such cases, the judicious medical adviser ought to be consulted before such a change is taken.

The time of life when the European arrives in India exercises a greater power than many suppose in enabling him to *stand* the climate. Very young men, youths under twenty years of age, are less able to encounter the climate of the plains than those above twenty and under thirty years of age. They are generally less able to resist the influence of the continued high temperature; become during their first hot season predisposed to attacks of fever, dysentery, diarrhœa, cholera, or heat apoplexy; are more likely to fall victims to epidemic disease, and are not unfrequently so enervated and debilitated as to be obliged to leave the country before they have completed two or three years' residence. Newly arrived regiments generally suffer out of all proportion to those that have been some years in India, which is believed to be due to the circumstance, that these regiments almost invariably contain a larger number of young men under twenty years of age.

As a general rule the best age at which to arrive in India is not under twenty for males, and not under eighteen for females. After forty years of age, the European who proceeds to India for the first time, is certainly less fitted to bear up against the climate, than if he had been younger. He soon begins to complain of lassitude, deficient mental and physical energy, and debility generally. His habits, customs and inclinations have been fostered and matured under such different circumstances, that he now finds considerable difficulty in changing or accommodating them to his new position. He therefore easily becomes impatient, discontented, dyspeptic, perhaps has some organic disease lighted up, and seldom remains for more than a few years in the country.

Fortunate indeed are those who are able to retire from India in the prime of life, with constitutions sound, or but little impaired, by the climate. Many Europeans are too often tempted by the prospects of higher pensions or a larger fortune, to prolong their residence beyond the age when they will be capable of accommodating themselves easily to English habits and customs, and when they will enjoy their retirement; while not a few are induced to remain *the one year more*, which too often proves "the last straw that breaks the camel's back. Better far for the European to be satisfied, and retire with a moderate competency, at an age when the vigour and energy, if impaired by the climate, may soon be restored, and when he may resume his profession or embark in some congenial pursuit, with all the advantages of matured experience.

The state of health, and of the constitution generally, before going to India, is of no little importance as affecting the future capacity of withstanding the climate.

It is always advisable that every European before proceeding to the East should undergo a careful medical examination, in order to ascertain whether there is present any organic disease, latent or developed, or whether he possesses any idiosyncracy or peculiarity of constitution or temperament, which would render him unsuited for the tropics.

The plains of India are far from being a salubrious spot for the European to resort to, whose health is impaired or constitution damaged by organic disease originated in his native land. And yet many have gone there, those especially with affections of the lungs, in the hope that the climate, simply because *it is hot*, will arrest the progress of the disease. A vain and shadowy hope it too often proves, for the disease (consumption), if beyond the first stage, most commonly runs a rapid and fatal course.

Many Europeans, however, of a scrofulous constitution, or with only a *tendency* to consumption, or even with the disease in its first or curable stage, and having what is popularly called a "weak chest," enjoy good, perhaps better, health in India than in England, and have been known to outlive their brothers and sisters at home.

The European who arrives in India in a sound state of health, free from organic disease, and possessing a constitution vigorous and unimpaired by injudicious or bad habits previously acquired, has a much better prospect before him of resisting the influence of the climate, than if he were otherwise. He may remain in the country for a considerable number of years (as the author did) without any material injury to his constitution, and if he takes the periodic change to a hill sanitarium referred to, he may find that the climate of India is, after all, not quite so detrimental to his health, as he was, perhaps, led to imagine it would be, while he may be fortunate enough to retire to his native land with health but little damaged, and enjoy his *otium cum dignitate* with real zest and pleasure.

To enable him to do this, however, he must have some definite answers to the questions often asked, How am I to live in India? and what am I to eat, drink, and avoid? In other words, what measures should I adopt in order to preserve my health under the altered circumstances of climate? These questions are embraced in the comprehensive term of individual or personal hygiene, and include food, clothing, exercise, etc.

Individual Hygiene.

To ensure health in India, much the same care is necessary as is ordinarily required at home, with some differences suited to the climate. The old and familiar adage, that prevention is better than cure, is the foundation on which all hygiene, or laws regarding health, are based; and he who takes care to attend to these laws is more likely to preserve his health, than he who "cares for none of these things." It is neither necessary, nor is it desirable, that every unprofessional person should, for the sake of his own individual health, make a perfect study of these laws, for the simple reason, that if he did so, he would, perhaps, frustrate the very object he has in view, and probably end by becoming morbid, gloomy, fanciful, and hypochondriacal. It is enough for all practical purposes, that he should have some general principles and precepts to guide him in the management of his own health, that he may be able to "exercise that reasonable care, thought and prudence, which in a matter of such importance, every one is bound to take."

Many Europeans arrive in India, with the mistaken impression, that precisely the same habits and modes of living to which they have been accustomed can be continued with impunity. In every country in the world, the mode of living,—in other words, food, drink, clothing, exercise, etc.,—is and must necessarily be adapted to the nature of the climate, if health is to be maintained. All that the climate of India requires of the European then, is, that his habits and customs should be suitably modified, for the simple and obvious reason, that since he cannot get the climate to accommodate itself to him, he must endeavour to accommodate himself to the climate.

FOOD.

There is, perhaps, no subject of more importance to the Anglo-Indian than diet. The quantity, quality, and kind of food consumed, influence in no small degree our happiness, health, and longevity; and the normal performance of digestion is the most important of all the agencies which affect nutrition. The stomach is the great and wonderful laboratory, from which are sent forth those elements that are necessary to maintain all the organs of the body in a state of efficiency. It is, therefore, of no small importance, that every care and attention should be paid to supplying it with proper material for that purpose. The diseases connected with the organs of digestion are more numerous in India than any other, and it is no exaggeration to say that probably thirty per cent. of those who suffer these, owe their diseases in some way or other to food.

The European arrives in India generally full of life, vigour, and energy. His appetite is excellent, his digestion very good, and he probably consumes as much, if not more, food than he did in his own country. But the style of living in India is very different, some would say more luxurious than what he has been accustomed to. Instead of the three ordinary meals to which he has been used from childhood, he finds that custom in India has not only sanctioned four or five, but also made them very different. First of all, there is the little breakfast, or "chota-hazari," at six in the morning, which consists of tea or coffee and bread (with or without eggs) and fruit. Second, breakfast at nine or ten o'clock, composed of curry and rice, chops, cold meat, fish and eggs, with bread, tea or coffee, or claret. Third, tiffin at one or two p.m., consisting of a joint or fowl, curry and rice, pudding, and fruits. Fourth, dinner at seven or eight p.m., consisting of much the same as tiffin, with dessert, followed by coffee.

The new comer indulges his robust appetite heartily at all these meals, but as he cannot possibly have the same amount of active exercise as he had at home, his digestive powers become clogged and impaired, the "balance of power" is sooner or later destroyed, and he then finds out that he must (if he wishes to preserve his health) be more careful in reference to the amount of food, especially animal food, he consumes.

It is impossible to lay down precise rules sufficiently elastic to guide every individual as to the quantity and kind of food he should take. The nutrition of the body is so affected by individual peculiarities, as to cause a considerable variety in the kinds of food required by different persons, almost every one being pretty well aware of the exact diet which suits him best, and thus bearing out the truth of the familiar saying, that what is one man's meat is another man's poison. Perhaps no safer general rule can be given than that which experience as well as science has proved to be the best, and that is, "while conforming to the general principles of diet, not to encourage too great an attention either to quantity or to quality, but avoiding what experience has shown to be manifestly bad, either generally or for the particular individual, to allow a reasonable variety and change in amount from day to day according to appetite."

It should always be borne in mind that in India, as elsewhere, the amount and kind of food should be proportioned and suited to the nature of the climate, the demands of the system, to the expenditure or waste of tissue, in other words, "to the mechanical work done by the body, and to the equivalent of mechanical force, namely, animal heat."

In England and other temperate climates, people eat

more during the cold winter than during the hot summer weather, while it is well known that the Esquimaux and Laplanders, in their frigid climate, consume enormous quantities of food. The natives of India, again, live almost entirely on rice, wheat, and farinaceous substances generally. Nature indeed dictates what food is really required in each climate, and science tells us that in cold regions or during cold weather, more animal and fatty, or heat-producing, food is necessary than in the tropics or during hot weather.

Europeans in India, as a rule, consume more animal food than is necessary for the nutrition of the body, perhaps absolutely more than they were accustomed to take before their arrival in the tropics; whereas less is actually required because the metamorphosis or waste of tissue is not so rapid in high as in temperate climates. The human body loses less in a high temperature than in a cold one, and the need of food to supply temperature is lessened by the heat.

It is a great though common mistake to suppose that there is a greater actual waste of the human body continually going on in India than in temperate climates, and that, therefore, more food or nutriment is necessary to supply the waste. The skin is the only part which acts more freely, as evidenced by abundant perspiration. But this does not imply waste of tissue, as the amount of perspiration is in proportion to the diminished action of the kidneys, and to the consumption of fluids, which is considerably increased by the high temperature. On the contrary, the solid organs of the body undergo less rapid changes, or metamorphoses, than in the temperate latitudes. There is greater or less tendency to congestion or stagnation, and the consumption of large quantities of animal food (if more than sufficient for the ordinary requirements of the system) will only increase this tendency, and eventually prove a source of weakness rather than of strength, by causing organic disease or functional disorder.

The European has, before reaching India, been accustomed to animal food, and if he suddenly discontinued it, he would almost to a certainty render himself unusually liable to be seriously and early influenced by the climate. But as it is unreasonable to expect the digestive organs to prove as active, and the demand for animal food to continue as great, in India as in England, it is of no use, nay it is very wrong, attempting to pamper the system with such food in a climate where much exercise cannot be taken, and where the high temperature interferes with its rapid assimilation. It has over and over again been remarked, that those who eat largely of animal food in the tropics, are less healthy than those in whose diet vegetable food predominates.

It has been supposed by some, that Europeans should imitate the natives in the matter of food, but it must be remembered that the Hindus have not the same constitutions as Europeans, and the use of ages has accustomed the former to the habit of taking large quantities of such grains as form their diet; whereas if the European were to attempt to do the same, his digestive powers would not be equal to the work thus imposed upon them, and mischief in the liver or some disorder of the stomach would soon be caused. The wiser plan dictated by common sense, as well as by experience, is to take an intermediate course.

Under these circumstances, what every European should endeavour to do, is to conform in some measure to the native system; that is, adapt their diet as far as is possible to the European constitution. In other words, eat sparingly of animal food; and let the diet consist in large measure of farinaceous and vegetable substances and fruits. There is no occasion systematically to deny oneself any kind of such food as fancy or taste dictates. Variety is necessary in order to keep the digestive system in a healthy condition. Dyspepsia, with all its attendant evils, is often caused by the uninterrupted continuance, for a long time, of one unvarying article of food. Individual experience will therefore prove the best guide in the selection of the most appropriate or most digestible substances.

The maxim inculcated by Canaro, "take in moderation that which agrees with you best," is about the safest that can be adopted, but before it can be carried out, every one must find out by experience what does agree with him best, and what is moderation. For those who believe in no rules unless supported by figures, it may here be stated that according to the calculation of competent authorities, an adult in health, of average weight (140 lbs), and height (5 feet 7 inches), requires one-twentieth part of his weight in food during the twenty-four hours; that is, 7 or 7½ lbs. food, including solids and liquids; 1 to 1½ lbs. (16 to 24 ozs.) being solid, the rest water.*

The diet table which long usage has sanctioned in India, need not be altered so far as the number of meals is concerned, but there is much room for improvement as regards the nature of these meals. The early morning tea or coffee should be taken with bread and fruit only. Breakfast should consist of the same, with curry and rice, or fish, or a little cold meat or fruit, and one or two eggs. Tiffin, if not made the principal meal of the day, should invariably be light, and consist only of bread or biscuit, fruits, and a glass of sherry or claret. Some people make tiffin an excuse for a double dinner, but any one who eats largely at both these meals, eats more than is necessary. Heavy tiffins make men heavy, sleepy, and interfere with the due performance of active work in the after-part of the day. Either take a substantial tiffin and a light dinner, or a substantial dinner and a light tiffin.

At all meals select what is most agreeable to the palate, but be careful, at the same time, not to let that liberty lead to excess, but rather always bear in mind the often laid down and well-known rule of leaving off with an appetite. Beware of eating too quickly. Proper

* Parkes.

and slow mastication of the food and its mixture with the saliva, form the first steps in healthy digestion. By the first, the food is broken into small pieces, upon which the gastric juice can sooner act; and when well mixed or moistened with the saliva, digestion is greatly facilitated.

Dyspepsia, indigestion, and many other affections of the stomach, arise from defective mastication and swallowing too rapidly. If the food is introduced into the stomach too quickly, or in too large quantity, or washed down with large doses of fluid, that organ soon rebels; it becomes so distended, that the gastric juice is not properly secreted, and flatulence and heartburn, with all the evils of indigestion, sooner or later result.

Some persons are often thin, because they eat chiefly meat, and eat it too rapidly; whereas they ought to consume a larger proportion of farinaceous substance, as bread, arrowroot, cornflour, and such-like. Fat persons should adopt the opposite course, reduce the amount of bread, etc., and take more exercise. Some persons are, however, naturally fat, and some naturally thin, though even in their cases, a properly regulated diet may be found useful.

The importance of tea and coffee as articles of diet, though now well recognised, is not appreciated by many who affect to despise them, as a convenient excuse for the use of alcoholic beverages as substitutes. Experience, says Dr. Letheby, has shown that there are certain articles of food, which are not particularly nourishing in themselves, but which serve some important purpose in the animal economy. This is the case with tea and coffee; in fact, the use of a vegetable infusion containing astringent matter, and an active principle rich in nitrogen, has been almost universal amongst mankind from the earliest times. The physiological action of these beverages appears to be of a somewhat singular kind; for while they excite the brain, they calm the nervous system generally, and though they produce a state of wakefulness and activity, yet they also induce a species of languor and repose. Lehman has ascertained by experience that coffee greatly diminishes the wear and tear of the system ; it oils the machinery as it were, and checks the waste of function ; for those who use it find that during active exercise the destruction of tissue is prevented, and that there is less demand for food ; in fact with a maximum of work to perform, and a minimum of food to accomplish it, he will best sustain his solid powers who resorts now and then to a cup of tea or coffee.

Dr. Waring, in his "Tropical Resident at Home," thus pithily sums up the rules that should be observed in regard to food.

"There is an old saying, 'A good master makes a good servant,' and if this be true, as it undoubtedly is, in domestic life, no less true is it with reference to the relation between you and your stomach in the matter of dietetics. Regard it as your servant, remember its delicate organization, treat it fairly; do not overtax its powers; do not throw upon it more work than it is in its province or power to fulfil ; supply its wants regularly, without pampering or over stimulating it ; and in its turn it will serve you well and faithfully, and will contribute essentially to your health, comfort, and happiness. Abuse its powers, and treat it on principles opposed to those just advised, and it will turn upon you, and wreak its vengeance by saddling you with dyspepsia and all its attendant evils.

"There is a point in which the above analogy ceases to hold good, you can always get rid of a bad servant by the payment of a month's wages ; you cannot get rid of a bad digestion on the same terms, even if you succeed in doing so at all."

Alcoholic Beverages.

The newly arrived European in India *requires* no alcoholic beverage whatever; that is, if he comes to India, as he certainly ought, full of life, vigour, and energy. If he does require stimulants, he has assuredly made a mistake in going out to India at all. The idea that beer, wine, brandy, or some alcoholic stimulant, is necessary to counteract, as is fancied, the depressing effects of the climate, is a delusion, and too often a snare. It is the rock on which more lives have been sacrificed in India than from any other cause. Our best Indian medical authorities, including such men as Johnstone, Sir Ranald Martin, Parkes, and many others, have all written in the strongest terms to the same effect, and yet nothing is more common than to hear the remark that the climate demands the use of these stimulants.

The climate demands no such thing. Alcohol heats the system, lessens the perspiration (which is the method adopted by nature to keep it cool), and causes congestion of internal organs. It is astonishing how long and how well one can go on in India without any stimulant whatever. Complete abstinence is not at all inconsistent with vigour, health, and longevity. Water, iced if it can be had, or mixed occasionally with limejuice, should form the only beverage of the European, for some time after his arrival in India; indeed, it need never be changed for beer, wine, brandy, etc, if he finds his health keep good, as it probably will.

The young man who has acquired temperate habits at home, and maintains them in India, has a good prospect before him of enjoying a fair measure of health, and of being much less influenced by the climate, than he would if he were otherwise. The man in vigorous health then, who has been unaccustomed to any alcoholic beverage, must therefore not allow himself to be deluded with the idea, that such stimulants are necessary, nor let him be tempted by others to partake of these beverages, merely because he finds many around him indulge in them. In by far the majority of instances, custom and not necessity has been the origin of the habit of taking stimulants. In that, as in other matters, custom is the god before which many fall down and worship, never perhaps for one moment troubling themselves with the question, why should they do so?

These beverages, however, in some form or other, are almost universally used by Europeans in India as elsewhere; and as no amount of preaching will convince many that they are not absolutely necessary for those in health, the question comes to be, in what form and in what quantity may they be taken with the least danger, or with the least injury to health.

Sound vigorous health, as already mentioned, requires no alcoholic stimulant at all, and this is the condition in which all young Europeans are supposed to be on arrival in India. But after a residence there of two or three, or perhaps more years, when digestion begins to flag, a spur may be needed; a glass of beer or good dry sherry, or half a pint of good claret may then be taken once or at most twice every day with advantage. These quantities are quite sufficient, as a rule, to stimulate the appetite and perhaps improve nutrition. It is, however, impossible to fix the precise quantities that may be taken in all cases, as so much depends on sex, age, constitution, and temperament, as well as on the amount of exercise taken, of the mechanical work done, and on the amount of exposure to the open air. Much, therefore, must be left to individual experience. Some men, however, have such elastic consciences as to argue themselves into the belief, that almost any amount of these beverages is necessary, and they measure the quantity more by their inclinations than by their requirements. Most persons in these days, as a rule, take too much; and, indeed, it is almost incredible the quantity of beer, wine, and brandy that some men do consume in India. If it were always borne in mind that these beverages should be taken, not so much for their positively stimulating action as for their purely tonic effects, there would be little chance of the habit becoming a vice. The moment they produce excitement or flushing of the face, injurious effects are produced, and a bad habit engendered.

No beer or wine should on any account be taken at any time except at meals, unless prescribed medically. Beer drinking between meals is pernicious in the extreme. Those who thus indulge, soonest need a change, and blame the climate of India for compelling them to go. Beer should not be taken before tiffin ; if taken at breakfast, as many do take it, the system is at first excited, then depressed, when a stimulant is again demanded to enable the individual to go on with his work.

This is simply forcing the human machinery to do by artificial means, what ought to be done by purely natural ones, and the result is, as any one with any forethought might expect, functional or organic disease, or damaged health generally

Brandy, whiskey, gin, arrack, or any other ardent spirit, must be shunned as poison, and like all other poison, should be taken only under medical advice. Medical experience condemns them as totally unnecessary to any one in health, and yet, next to beer, if not equal to it, the most common alcoholic stimulant used in India is brandy. In some districts the Englishman is marked out by the natives from every other race, by the fact that "he eats beef, *drinks brandy*, and has no religion."

No one ever begins to drink brandy from choice. He is in his younger days tempted by his seniors to partake merely for social enjoyment, and he has not the moral courage to resist ; nay further, he may even be, and too often is, deluded with the idea that a little—only a little—brandy and water is necessary to obviate or remove the depressing influence of the climate upon him. The habit once commenced, gradually, almost imperceptibly grows, and the small quantity which was originally taken perhaps with a shudder and to please others, is now increased, and felt to be needed to supply the fancied want or craving, which has been caused by the very stimulant itself. So insidiously does this habit grow, that the victim is too frequently not aware of the enemy he is nursing within him, and when he perceives his error, when his health has suffered from it, with the singular inconsistency of human nature, he will conceal it from his medical adviser, to whom he is professing perfect openness.

Every medical man of any experience in India, can tell how very frequently the brightest hopes and prospects, as well as the finest constitutions, have been blighted, impaired, and sometimes utterly ruined by this indulgence. In the daily routine of professional duty, he often meets with men who are suffering from symptoms produced by brandy drinking and by nothing else, but who have yet no idea that they are intemperate in their habits, and can with difficulty be made to believe that their bad state of health is caused by these habits.

Occasionally a dialogue something like the following takes place.

Patient.—Well, doctor, I have not been feeling at all well.

Doctor.—What symptoms do you complain of?

Patient.—Well, I can hardly tell, but I really feel good for nothing, and [here passing his hand in a confused, tremulous manner over his forehead] I don't sleep well at night, get up uncommonly "seedy" in the morning, have little or no appetite for breakfast, or indeed for any meal.

Doctor.—Do you attribute these symptoms to anything you have been eating or drinking?

Patient.—Oh dear no! My food is simple in the extreme, and I eat very little of that. It is this abominable climate which I think is the cause of all, and I wish I could quit it.

Doctor.—You said just now that you were worse in the morning; do you take anything to relieve the lassitude and discomfort you feel at that time?

Patient.—Well, yes. I do generally take a bottle of sodawater, with some brandy, only to cover the taste of the soda, and this appears at the time to do me good.

Doctor.—And you take this before breakfast?

Patient.—Yes. I am obliged to do so, as I feel so shaky, though there is nothing I detest so much as brandy. I have really been feeling so "out of sorts" lately, and as it is the only thing which does me good, I sometimes take another dose before breakfast, just to relieve a depression which comes on:

Doctor.—And what do you take for breakfast,—tea or coffee?

Patient.—Oh dear no. I can't stand tea or coffee; they make me more nervous than ever, and give me heart-burn; indeed the only thing I can take which does not disagree with me is brandy and soda, or a bottle of beer.

And so on; the doctor thus finding on prosecuting the enquiry still further, that the details of the entire day's programme reveal a fact which the patient is slow to admit—that he has been consuming by these repeated doses, very nearly one bottle of brandy daily; thus: one or two glasses before breakfast, one at breakfast, one or two before or at tiffin; the same in the afternoon; and one, two, or even three in the evening. No human constitution in any country, far less in India, could stand out against such excessive indulgence; and nothing will save it from disease and premature death, but complete abstinence from the liquor which has been acting as a poison, and which has produced all the symptoms described.

Nor is this intemperate indulgence confined to men only Many women, educated, refined, and in easy circumstances, take such quantities of alcohol in some form or other, at different times during the day, openly or secretly, as to cause the very symptoms just described,—precisely those, in short, of chronic or permanent alcoholization. The convenient and favourite excuse, that they are taken by the "doctor's orders," is too often put forth to cover the infirmity. Medical men are sometimes, it must be confessed, much too careless in prescribing these stimulants for ladies; they too often take for granted that their patient is too sensible or strong-minded to exceed the quantity ordered, or to fail to discontinue it when no longer absolutely necessary. Some ladies do religiously adhere to the orders given, while others allow themselves a latitude and licence to suit their own inclinations or wishes. In women, owing to physiological differences, and a more susceptible nervous system, intemperate habits paralyse the will earlier than in men; they become sooner the creatures of impulse, and less able to resist the seductive influence of alcohol, while its effects upon them are more ruinous to mind, character, and health.

All physiologists agree that alcohol becomes a poison to the nervous system, when it blunts perception, weakens the will, and causes tremulousness, and the quantity required to produce these effects, may be at once seen from the following:—"One and a half ounces of pure alcohol, or two in the case of unusual exercise of body or mind, is about the maximum standard of allowance for adult men; and the recent researches of Dr. Parkes confirm this belief, at least so far as showing that indubitably evil results follow, when this quantity is exceeded. If such be the proper allowance for a man weighing 160 lbs. (mostly bone and muscle), and always engaged in either powerfully exerting his muscles or his brain, or both, it would surely seem reasonable to say that a woman, weighing say 120 lbs., (much of it fat), and hardly ever using either her muscles or her brain vigorously and continuously, ought, at the outside, not to exceed the daily quantity of three-quarters of an ounce of pure alcohol, which would represent about two ordinary glasses (two ounces each) of the usual highly fortified sherry or port which many prefer,—two such glasses in the entire day mind, or say (to put the matter in a still more intelligible form) one glass of port or one fair tumbler of Bass's ale at each of the principal meals,—any quantity beyond this being injurious,—as injurious as a slight nervous shock per diem would prove."*

If a simple rule could be made to suit every one, male as well as female, the following might be considered a safe one to meet the requirements of the greater number. One glass of wine or one pint bottle of beer at tiffin, and the same at dinner; or, better still, substitute half a pint of claret for the beer or wine. Claret is the safest of all beverages for Europeans in India: it is cooling, has an agreeable acidity, yet causes no acidity in the stomach, and perhaps more important still, it contains a small proportion of iron, which is the very ingredient that the blood most needs in India. Other French and German wines may be used in preference to the highly fortified port and sherry *manufactured* nowadays. But after all, experience will be the best guide as to the suitability of a particular wine in individual cases. "The only real test for wine," says Dr. Druitt, "is the empirical one. It is impossible to dogmatize on it *à priori*; to say that such and such a wine must be good in such and such cases, because it contains certain ingredients. The only questions needful to ask are, not what is the chemical composition, but do you like it, or does it agree with you, and do you no harm? The stomach is the real test-tube for wine, and if that quarrels with it, no certificate of Liebig and no analysis are worth a rush."

One word about mixing wines at the same meal. This is a common cause of dyspepsia, more especially if champagne and port, or the former and beer are mixed. Few stomachs

* "The Practitioner."

will stand out against these obnoxious mixtures; and the morning headaches which almost invariably follow such indiscretion, fully attest the importance of caution in this respect.

EXERCISE.

Moderate and systematic exercise is one of the most important means of maintaining health in India. The healthiest persons there, are those who take open-air exercise regularly; and few things predispose the system to be materially and early influenced by the climate more than indolence and inactivity. The pale complexions, the torpid secretions, the languid movements, and disordered functions attest the truth of this. The languor and listlessness, so often complained of, after even a short residence in the tropics, are quite as frequently due to inaction, as to the climate itself, and should be resisted and overcome, not by alcoholic stimulants, but by regular exercise. This equalizes the circulation and checks the tendency to congestion, which is the cause of the languid feeling referred to.

The greater number of Anglo-Indians lead sedentary lives, and take far too little exercise, some scarcely any at all; and, although the climate on the plains does not offer many inducements or facilities for active exercise, yet there are times and seasons when such exercise can and ought to be taken. Every one has the power and the opportunity to engage in it, in some form or other, if he will only summon resolution to make the experiment, and where there is a will, there will generally be found the way.

The best time for exercise is in the early morning, about sunrise, when the air is fresh and cool, and the body and mind in a much better condition to enjoy it than in the evening, after the fatigue and labour of the day. It is always advisable, and notably in malarious districts, never to go out in the morning without first partaking of a cup of tea or coffee. A moderately active walk for about one hour every morning will be found soon to produce keenness of appetite, lightness of digestion, and buoyancy of spirits, which will themselves be the best of all encouragements to persevere.

The nature and amount of exercise depend on individual constitutions, and must therefore be ascertained by experience. Those who have been unaccustomed to morning exercise will soon train themselves to it if they only make an effort to begin, and though the first attempts may accomplish but a small amount, perseverance, gradual and persistent, will soon enable them to increase it. It is best then to begin with a minimum, to go on gradually, to increase the amount according to the pleasurable sensations it induces, and to be especially careful to avoid such active exercise, either as to quantity or manner, as causes fatigue.

Gardening offers inducements to some, riding to others, while walking is open to all, and rowing, cricketing, shooting, are all means of open-air exercise suited to special tastes. Walking exercise has many advantages, inasmuch as it is most natural, is generally practicable, is attended with no trouble, and is the most independent and free. Riding on horseback is perhaps the most efficacious of all modes of healthy exercise, involving neither labour nor fatigue, while the rapid movement causes such a constant current of pure air, as to impart a tone and vigour to the system, as well as such a keenness and relish for food, which many will scarcely credit until they try.

Exercise in such games as cricket, boating, and rackets, must on no account exceed the limits of moderation, otherwise more harm than good will result. These games, when contested, involve much too great a strain on the whole body, and those who engage in them must always bear in mind that they cannot without prejudice to the health, expend the same amount of mechanical force on them in India, as they were accustomed to do in Europe. The great rule to be observed in regard to exercise of whatever kind, is never to permit it to cause fatigue or exhaustion; never to begin or end violently, but to begin moderately, and continue so long as pleasurable sensations are felt.

Ladies in India, as a rule, stand much more in need of exercise than men, and perhaps nothing sooner causes them to succumb to the influence of the climate, than the want of it. Confined, as they mostly are to their houses, during nearly the entire day, leading generally very sedentary lives, having little or no mental or physical occupation, they soon droop, become listless, languid, and apathetic, and eventually are incapable of any exertion at all. The evening drive does but little to rouse or invigorate them, and is beneficial only in diverting the mind, and enabling them to get some fresh air; but exercise, worthy of the name, it cannot be called. Yet these ladies could take proper exercise, to prevent or counteract many of the evil influences of the climate if they would only summon resolution enough to begin. The amount of exertion which some will undergo night after night in ballrooms during the cool season in India, would, if directed in another way, namely walking or riding in the open air in the early morning, do much to preserve their health, and enable them to prolong their residence beyond the seven or eight years which is at present about the average duration of their stay in India.

SLEEP.

Health depends much on the quantity and kind of sleep. The habit of early rising is very soon acquired by Europeans in India, and late hours are early abandoned. Eight hours' sleep are, as a rule, quite sufficient for all the requirements of the system, but the quantity depends much on habit, state of constitution, and mode of living. To have one good sound sleep is the rule, and to ensure this, attention must be paid to diet, exercise, and regular and temperate habits, as well as to the state of the mind, which should, on retiring to rest, be free from anxiety or care. The custom adopted by many, and especially by ladies, of indulging in a *siesta* for one or two hours daily, after tiffin, has nothing to recommend it. On the contrary, the sleep thus taken is generally unrefreshing, and is followed frequently by depression, languor, and listlessness, which perhaps only the evening drive may remove. Sleep is not called for then, and it has moreover the further objection that it commonly interferes with the sound sleep during the night. It is no excuse to say that the heat of the climate causes an overpowering drowsiness, which cannot be resisted. It is precisely by the very opposite, viz., exercise or occupation, that this can be and should be overcome. Those who give in to this habit of indolence and inactivity, soon complain of the enervating effects of the climate, and require a change.

If ladies would take more active interest in their domestic affairs generally than very many do at present, the inclination for this afternoon's sleep would not be felt, while they would probably find their health much better, and themselves in every respect much happier.

During the hottest months of the year, when the air is close and still, the nights are often passed in restless slumber; the system is depressed, and the body bathed in perspiration. The night punkah is invaluable then, and those who can afford it, should sleep under it during such weather, for it will make all the difference between sound refreshing sleep and the reverse. Restless nights unhinge the nervous system, affect the general health, and render one unfit for the ordinary duties of the day. When night after night is passed in unrefreshing rest, as they often are by those who have long lived an unbroken residence in India, even although they have been temperate in their habits, a change to the hills or some cool station must be taken. Nothing short of this will probably be of the least avail, and nothing more will generally be required. These restless nights are not unfrequently the earliest indications that the climate is exerting its baneful influence on the constitution, and ought not to be disregarded.

Sleeping during the night in the open air at any time during the year is most objectionable, and particularly so when the person is exposed to the rays of the moon, as blindness has sometimes resulted from such exposure; while paralysis is occasionally produced by the direct action of the land winds, which set in early in the morning.

Tatties, or mats made of kuskus-fibre or other material, placed in front of doors and windows, and kept constantly wet with water, are used in many parts of India to cool the air in the sleeping room. They answer the purpose very well, when used with proper precautions. They should always be so placed that the air in passing through them, cools the room generally, and is not allowed to play directly on the person; and they ought to be constantly wet, otherwise the apartment becomes oppressive, from the closeness and heat of the atmosphere. Fever, rheumatism, and a feeling of malaise, not unfrequently result from inattention to these precautions.

BATHING.

As the skin is the great safety-valve in the tropics, it is of the utmost importance that it be kept in a sound, healthy state. Free perspiration regulates the temperature of the body, and carries away from the blood not merely water, but also a large amount of animal matter, acids, alkalies, salts, gases, etc., which otherwise would embarrass and eventually cause disease in the lungs, kidneys, liver, etc.

The perspiration is secreted by small glands under the true skin, and is conveyed by means of extremely minute capillary tubes, terminating in what are familiarly known as the "pores" on the surface. The number of these pores on every square inch of skin, is calculated to amount to 2800, and the total number of pores in a man of ordinary size (five feet seven inches) amounts to no less than 7,000,000. Further, as each of these small perspiratory tubes measures a quarter of an inch, their total length amounts to 1,750,000 inches, or 145,833 feet, or 48,600 yards, or nearly twenty-eight miles. But besides these little tubes, there are large numbers of small glands, which secrete an oily substance, conveyed through other minute chambers to the surface of the skin. The object of this oily matter, is to lubricate the skin, to protect it from external influences, and to facilitate the elimination of noxious principles, secreted by the perspiratory glands. But there is always a certain amount of perspiration and oily secretion, deposited on the skin, and if this is not removed, or if it is left undisturbed, for some time, the pores become more or less blocked up, the safety-valve is closed, and derangement of the health sooner or later follows.

In India there is at all times greater action of the skin than the European was accustomed to at home, and if as little attention is paid to it there as in England, the health will very soon suffer. The bath becomes, then, an essential part of the ordinary daily routine of life, for the sake of cleanliness. But it is not merely as a local cleanser that the bath is useful, but also as a general tonic, imparting, or at all events maintaining, vigour and energy, and in no small degree fortifying the system against the influences of the climate.

The best time for bathing is early in the morning, immediately or a few minutes after getting out of bed; most, however, prefer it after the morning ride or walk, when it ought to be taken at once, and not after allowing the body to cool. A good bath after the morning exercise has a wonderful effect in sharpening the appetite for breakfast, and it is pleasant to sit down to that meal with a sense of being clean and fresh, and prepared for the avocations of the day. There is no necessity, indeed there is not unfrequently positive harm, caused by remaining in the bath more than five or ten minutes. The body should then be well rubbed down with a good rough dry towel, or even the hair glove. The *shower-bath* is especially useful, in those whose nervous system has become depressed by long exposure to tropical heat, and this in a modified form, or by the "douche," can at all times be adopted, by the use of earthen pots full of water, that have been exposed outside, during the night.

As a rule cold water is best for bathing, but this must be decided by individual experience. If a pleasurable glow and feeling of warmth and comfort are felt after the cold bath, it is the best of all proofs that it agrees, but if a feeling of discomfort, or a chilly and unrefreshed sensation, is experienced, the cold bath must be discontinued, and tepid water substituted. Every one whose liver is affected should bathe in tepid water.

The *wet sheet packing*, as adopted by the hydropathists, is one of the very best means of imparting tone to the nervous system, when depressed by the influence of tropical heat, and may be applied as follows:—Place a double folded large sheet, soaked in cold water, on a couple of blankets, on an ordinary cot; let the person, divested of all clothing, be laid on the surface of the wet sheet, then have the latter wrapped round the entire body, taking care to tuck it well in, covering every inch of surface, except the face and head. The blankets must then be made to surround the body in the same way, and the person allowed to remain thus enveloped for at least one hour. All the coverings should then be removed, and the body plunged into cold water for one minute immediately afterwards or it may be briskly sponged over with cold or tepid water, and then rubbed with a rough dry towel.

The *sitz bath* is also of great value in remedying a tendency to constipation so commonly complained of in India.

FRUIT.

Fruit as an article of diet is probably more useful in a hot than in a temperate climate, having no small influence in cooling the system, as well as in aiding digestion. The plantain or banana, the pine-apple, mango, pummalo, and mangosteen, with a few others, are those most commonly used in India, and if taken in moderation and in good condition, are most useful as well as grateful. The plantain is the safest and the most wholesome of all; it is procurable at any time during the whole year, and is so universally used that its absence from any meal would be conspicuous. Plantains may be eaten plain, or beat up with milk and sugar, forming an agreeable imitation of strawberries and cream; or they may be made into fritters. The pine-apple, carefully divested of its seeds and seed cases, and in a ripe juicy state, should be taken in moderation, either plain, or soaked in simple syrup or claret. The mango is *par excellence* the fruit which is most relished, and is indulged in freely during the few months it is in season. All fruits should be taken fresh early in the morning, and as a rule, seldom, if ever, at night.

The new comer, tempted by the novelty of fruits he has not before tasted, too frequently indulges to such an extent as to cause diarrhœa, dysentery, or indigestion, and not unfrequently eruptions of the skin, which become sometimes troublesome and persistent. They should therefore be partaken of sparingly at first, and too much care cannot be taken to see that the fruit is good and ripe.

Whenever diarrhœa or dysentery, or any other symptoms indicating irritation in the stomach or bowels are present, fruit as a rule should not be taken.

WATER.

The free action of the skin, which when not excessive

is most salutary, causes a great demand for fluids, and no fluid will fulfil the requirements of the system better than pure water, and it need scarcely be added, that no other fluid will better allay the feeling of thirst. Water then may be taken freely at all times of the day, except during or immediately before and after meals, when more moderation is necessary, as large quantities would then dilute the gastric juice and interfere with digestion. The habit of drinking large draughts of iced water, so common in India, when the body is heated, or during meals, is often attended with mischief, and always with risk to the stomach or other of the abdominal organs. Such water should be taken in small quantities at a time, or even slowly sipped; and if the water can be so cooled as to render it palatable by exposing it in earthen vessels covered with wet straw or cloths, no ice need be used at all.

Water used for drinking or cooking purposes should always be filtered through sand or charcoal, or both combined, to remove organic impurities, which in various forms are more frequently the cause of dyspepsia, fever, cholera, diarrhœa, skin eruptions, and other diseases than many suppose. Well-water may be unexceptionably clear and tasteless, and yet contain ingredients deleterious to health, if not removed by filtration. In some districts, notably where malaria abounds, the natives have a rooted and well grounded aversion to particular wells, and will on no account use the water in them for any purpose whatever.

Europeans of any experience, fully aware as they are of the uncertain condition of well-water, invariably carry with them while travelling filtered water, or they use one of those small portable carbon filters, which are so convenient as well as inexpensive. Boiling the water before using it, has some influence in destroying organic impurities, and may be adopted when no other means are available. Brandy has no such effect, and its use under such circumstances, is probably but an apology for the sake of the stimulant. Two or three drops of Condy's fluid to each gallon of water will be found most useful in purifying it, when no filters are procurable.

Soda, Seltzer, and other aërated waters, when taken in moderation, are not objectionable, but when largely consumed, that is to the extent of five or six bottles a day, they produce a depressing effect, and occasionally dyspeptic symptoms.

SMOKING.

The excessive use of tobacco, in which many Anglo-Indians indulge, has a much greater influence on the health than they imagine. By interfering with the natural secretion of saliva from the mouth, and by its direct action on the nervous system, digestion is generally impaired, and the nutrition of the several structures materially interfered with. Not unfrequently the heart's action is enfeebled, the nervous system injured, and the whole constitution so depressed as to render it more readily influenced by the climate than otherwise. Medical men in India often meet with cases of persistent dyspepsia or indigestion, accompanied with distressing nervous symptoms, which are mainly, if not entirely, due to the excessive use of tobacco. Smoking early in the morning, or immediately before meals, cannot be too strongly condemned, as the healthy appetite is not only thereby considerably affected, but the digestion of the food, and the elaboration of the chyle and blood seriously interfered with.

But as smokers will smoke, in spite of all that is said against it, they ought at all events to confine their indulgence within moderate limits, and not smoke, like some men in India, with little or no intermission from morning till night. It is difficult to define what is moderation in smoking, as so much depends on individual constitutions, but it may be safely stated that three or four ordinary cigars a day should be the *utmost limit.* If men will smoke, let them do so with some regard to their health, and never on any account persist in the habit, when the mouth and throat become dry, when digestion is impaired, or when the nervous system becomes in the slightest degree affected.

DISEASES.

DYSPEPSIA.

Few Europeans in India escape this troublesome complaint in one form or other, and yet it may often be prevented by the exercise of no more than ordinary care. The digestive organs are exposed more directly than any others, the lungs excepted, to the contact and agency of external matters, and it is wonderful what we put into them, and what work we expect them to do. In robust, vigorous health, the digestive power of the stomach is something marvellous, but when tampered with (as too many in India do) by over-feeding or over-drinking, the function of digestion, which hitherto proceeded without our consciousness, is now attended with discomfort or even pain.

Causes.—The European is only too ready to blame the climate, the moment the first indications of dyspepsia appear. Dyspepsia is sometimes connected with the debility of the nervous system which is induced by prolonged residence in the tropics, but in by far the greater number of instances, the cause is due to errors in diet, to the use of indigestible food, over-feeding, the free indulgence in alcoholic beverages, excessive smoking, want of physical exercise, and irregular meals. Dyspepsia is sometimes also merely a symptom, and a very important one, of organic disease of the liver, kidneys, brain, etc.

Symptoms.—Want of appetite, flatulent distension of the

stomach, protracted digestion, heartburn, sour eructations, headache, nausea, and diarrhœa or constipation. These symptoms may be sooner or later followed by others more mental than physical. The nervous system suffers, the mind becomes despondent, gloomy, depressed, sometimes almost distracted. The victim is too often haunted with the idea that some serious organic disease exists within him, or he is in constant dread of some impending calamity; indeed there is scarcely any limit to the morbid fancies or delusions which add to the miseries of the hypochondriac.

Treatment.—No patients are more difficult to treat, or rather to manage, than those suffering from dyspepsia. They are often so wedded to habits, customs, and pet indulgences, of a nature totally opposed to sound digestion, that they cannot easily be induced to change or modify them, nor can they sometimes be made to believe that these are the cause of all their symptoms.

The dyspeptic must bear in mind, that medicine will, as a rule, prove of far less avail in relieving him (if the affection is unconnected with any organic cause), than the practice of some little self-denial. Obvious errors in diet must be corrected; the food should be of the simplest and most easily digestible nature, and ought to be taken at regular and stated times, as referred to at page 233. Over-indulgence in alcoholic beverages, or even the moderate use of such beverages, as are not suited to the individual, is a common cause of dyspepsia, and must be corrected and modified. Excess in smoking and other indulgences must be abstained from, and overtaxing the mental powers must be guarded against. The bowels should be regulated, by good systematic walking or riding exercise, assisted by the sitz bath and wet bandage as recommended at page 249; and failing these, by the occasional use of a simple gentle aperient, while the tone of the stomach may be improved by cordial tonics, if the above hygienic measures fail to produce this effect.

But avoid drugging by all means if possible. Dyspeptics rely too often on medicines, to relieve their symptoms, instead of trying what a little care, caution, and self-denial would do for them. The remark by a celebrated physician of a bygone age, that "physic is the art of amusing the patient while nature cures the disease," finds its best illustration in the treatment of dyspeptics; and the sage advice of Dr. Abernethy to the same class of patients, to "live on sixpence a day and earn it," is about the most comprehensive prescription that was ever given for dyspepsia.

DIARRHŒA.

This is one of the most common diseases in India, and it is perhaps the very first from which the European will suffer after his arrival. The ordinary symptoms of a simple attack are repeated large evacuations of a more or less watery consistence, dark in colour and of a bad smell, flatulence, uneasy sensations, sometimes amounting to severe griping pain, especially in the lower part of the abdomen, occasionally nausea and vomiting, and generally a white-coated tongue and foul breath.

Diarrhœa is distinguished from dysentery by the absence of blood and mucus in the stools, by being unattended with straining, or by inflammation, or fever.

Causes.—Indigestible food, unripe fruits, or ripe fruits in excess, badly cooked vegetables, some particular kinds of fish, and notably shellfish, such as crabs, prawns, oysters. It is also not unfrequently caused by previous constipation, the abuse of purgatives, by suppressed perspiration, by liver disease, or by the presence of worms in the intestines. It is also the premonitory symptom or first stage of cholera, and in such cases immediate attention is imperatively called for.

Europeans on their first arrival in India, cannot be too careful to avoid indulging freely in fruits, vegetables, and articles of food to which they were not accustomed, as an attack of diarrhœa is almost certain to result.

Treatment.—When the diarrhœa is caused by indigestible food, the purging is nature's own remedy to rid the stomach and bowels of substances which are offending them, and no treatment is required beyond simple diluent drinks, as barley or rice water, and such food as beef tea or chicken broth, arrowroot or sago, with or without milk, and tea and toast. If the diarrhœa is troublesome and annoying, a simple purgative may be given to facilitate recovery, by removing the irritating cause. A teaspoonful of castor oil, alone or with eight or ten drops of laudanum, or the same quantity of Gregory's powder, in plain or peppermint water, will be found speedily beneficial. If the purging continue beyond one day, or if the evacuations are so frequent and so copious during the first day as to cause depression and faintness, thirty drops of chlorodyne, or twenty drops of laudanum, with half a wineglass of brandy, or a glass of port wine, may be taken, and repeated in three or four hours after; or an astringent mixture may be prepared and kept ready for use, thus ;—

Take of	Powdered prepared chalk	one dram.
	Powdered cinnamon	one scruple.
	Laudanum	one dram.
	Tincture of catechu	four drams.
	Peppermint or plain water . . .	three ounces.

Mix, and take a tablespoonful after each loose motion.

Or the following ;—

Take of	Tincture of rhubarb	two drams.
	Tincture of catechu	four drams.
	Laudanum	half dram.
	Peppermint water	three ounces.

Mix, and take in the same way as the last.

If there is much griping or pain, or nausea, apply a good sized mustard poultice, or one made with bran or linseed meal, or a turpentine fomentation over the abdomen.

Irritability of the stomach, if present, may be relieved by small and repeated draughts of soda-water, or other effervescing drinks, or by small quantities of crushed ice.

The diet should be simple and light, and consist of tea and toast, arrowroot, sago, tapioca, or cornflour, beef tea, or chicken broth.

When the diarrhœa is caused by worms in the intestines, or by liver disease, or by any other causes than those mentioned, the symptoms do not come on so suddenly, nor progress so rapidly, and require special remedies suited to the case. If in these cases the symptoms do prove severe, before professional assistance can be had, the treatment above recommended may, with perfect safety, be adopted as a temporary measure to obtain relief.

The diarrhœa which is so often complained of by Europeans on going to the hill stations, is most commonly caused by sudden change of temperature, by cold and moisture, and very frequently by bad water. The treatment is the same as that already given; but much might be done to prevent these attacks, if more attention were paid to the change of clothing necessary for the colder climate, and if a flannel binder were worn round the stomach.

Diarrhœa in young children is commonly caused by teething, by irritating substances in the bowels, such as undigested food, or worms, and as a rule should not be suddenly checked. In either case, the best and safest treatment at the outset is to give half a teaspoonful of castor oil or Gregory's powder, if the child is about one year old. If the purging continues after this, a teaspoonful of either of the astringent mixtures already prescribed (p. 256) should be given every three or four hours, or one of the following powders as frequently.

Take of	Grey powder	one grain.
	Dover's powder . . .	one grain.
	Bicarbonate of soda . .	three grains.
	Ipecacuanha	half a grain.

Or eight to ten grains of the compound chalk powder may be given alone, or with twenty drops of tincture of catechu and one drop of laudanum. One drop for each year of age, is the ordinary dose of laudanum for children, but none should be given to infants, unless under medical advice.

If the purging still continues in spite of the above treatment, and the age be that when teething is likely to be the cause, the gums should be first lanced freely over the most prominent points, or where they are full and swollen, and then if necessary the above treatment.

When the diarrhœa is caused by worms, give to the child (if one year old) two grains of santonine, with a little sugar and water at bedtime, and the same dose early in the morning (fasting), followed one hour afterwards by a teaspoonful of castor oil.

In the case of very young infants, diarrhœa is almost invariably caused by errors in feeding, or injudicious nursing. The fault may lie either in feeding the infant too often, or there may be something wrong with the nurse herself. No infant should, as a rule, be nursed oftener than once every two hours at first; and the interval should be gradually lengthened, as the age of the child increases. Over-feeding, by frequent nursing, is a most prolific source of mischief, and no small amount of infantile mortality is due to this cause alone. Fresh milk taken into the stomach, while the previous supply is there being digested, materially interferes with, if it does not entirely arrest the digestive process altogether, and the food thus partially digested, proving a source of irritation in the bowels, causes diarrhœa.

Another common cause of infantile diarrhœa is the injudicious and premature administration of farinaceous food, as arrowroot, cornflour, etc., and these should therefore rarely be given to very young infants. When the fault lies with the nurse, she must either have some medical treatment, or another nurse must be substituted; but whether the fault lies with the nurse or with the management of the feeding, no medicine will prove of any avail until the cause is removed.

It may be mentioned here, and it cannot be too well remembered, that during the prevalence of cholera in a district, the slightest diarrhœa should be attended to without any delay.

CHOLERA.

Cholera is, without exception, the most dreaded of all diseases. Its invasion is so sudden, its course so rapid, and its fatality so great, that it is little wonder its appearance in any district should excite more or less fear and consternation. In some parts of India it is scarcely ever absent, and with very few exceptions no spot in the whole peninsula escapes its ravages during the year.

In large cities and densely populated villages, where ordinary sanitary laws are disregarded,—in other words, where drainage and ventilation are bad,—the disease every now and then breaks out and spreads with great rapidity.

No particular season of the year appears to be exempt from this disease, though it is more prevalent in some places at particular times than at others. The commencement of the rainy season, especially if the rain is not abundant at the outset, is generally believed to be the most common, or at all events the most likely, time for its appearance. Although little or no advance has been made in regard to the treatment of this disease, much has been accomplished during the past few years to arrest its progress, when once it appears in any spot. Sanitary reformers have probably directed more attention to this malady and its causes than to any other; and the result of their labours has been unquestionably favourable. The preventive measures suggested by them, irrespective of any theory regarding the contagiousness or non-contagiousness of the disease, are now adopted wherever the epidemic appears, and in many instances its ravages have been cut short, when there was reason to believe they would have spread rapidly and destroyed thousands if no such precautions had been taken.

These preventive measures may be expressed in one word, *cleanliness*. As soon as it is evident that cholera threatens a district, the drains should be attended to, not on any account opened merely for the purpose of stirring them up, but thoroughly flushed with water, alone or containing a quantity of Condy's fluid, or chloride of lime, or some equally good disinfectant. All houses should be whitewashed, and in the case of those in which even one single person has been attacked, the place should be vacated for a time, and the inmates sent elsewhere at the very earliest possible opportunity, for the purpose of having the house thoroughly cleaned and purified by disinfectants.

Further, as it is now almost universally believed by medical men, that the matters discharged from the stomach and bowels of a cholera patient, contain the germs or infectious principles of the disease, it is evident that these discharges may prove a prolific source of communicating the disease to many others. It is a matter of the first importance then, that these discharges should not only have some disinfectant mixed with them before they are cast away, but also that they should be buried in the ground at some spot distant from any well or tank, from which water for cooking or drinking purposes is obtained, otherwise they may impart infection to the water, and so cause the disease to be widespread.

Bedding, clothes, towels, and such-like articles, defiled with these choleraic discharges, may prove a powerful medium of infection, if not thoroughly washed and disinfected, or destroyed; so that a single case may exert a terrible influencing power on large masses of population, local circumstances and individual carelessness co-operating.

It is by adopting, and most rigorously carrying out, these preventive and precautionary measures, that infinitely more good can be accomplished, than by any known treatment of the disease, when once it has been allowed to proceed unchecked.

But these measures also prove most beneficial in removing or allaying the nervous fears of the people, which frequently so depress the system as to predispose it readily to an attack. The Hindus appear to be well aware of the influence of fear in predisposing the system to attacks, not only of cholera, but of other epidemic diseases; for during the prevalence of any pestilence, they offer up propitiatory sacrifices to the particular divinity which in their opinion presides over the disease, one of the effects of which is to inspire them with confidence and courage.

Whatever obscurity may overhang the actual or exciting causes of cholera, there can scarcely be any regarding the circumstances which exercise such a predisposing influence on the human body, as to make it more than usually susceptible of the disease. Depression of spirits, fatigue, scarcity of food, exposure to a hot sun by day and to cold dews at night, incautious use of unripe fruit or badly cooked vegetables, intemperance, overcrowding of inhabitants in badly ventilated places, saline purgatives, etc., all exercise a debilitating effect on the system, and thus render it a more easy prey to the malady.

Symptoms.—The symptoms of an ordinary attack of epidemic cholera, are as follows; a feeling of distension and uncomfortable rumbling in the stomach and bowels, followed soon after by nausea, vomiting, and purging. The discharges are at first commonly bilious in appearance, followed shortly by copious evacuations, resembling rice (congee) water, cramps in the fingers, toes, calves, thighs, muscles of the abdomen, and loins. The skin is covered with cold, clammy perspiration, the eyes are sunken, and have a dark circle round their orbits, the voice is reduced to a whisper, the features are sharpened and contracted, the expression of the countenance is apathetic and indifferent. The whole surface of the body, and more especially the fingers and nails, assumes a shrunken leaden blue or purple hue, the thirst is intense, and the pulse is thready, or imperceptible at the wrist. The patient is exceedingly restless, constantly throwing his arms about and casting the bed-clothes off him; the respiration becomes laboured and oppressed, and the breath cold; the secretion of urine is suppressed, and in the worst cases the whole body exhales a peculiar earthy, sometimes urinous, odour, followed soon after by coma and death.

The duration of these symptoms, from their commencement till death, varies from one or two to twenty-four hours. The first fa ourable indication of reaction generally takes place from twelve to fifteen hours after the first symptoms have set in. The pulse is felt at the wrist, the bowels are less freely purged, urine is passed, the features improve, the skin assumes a more natural colour, loses its cold, damp, clammy feeling, and becomes warm; and the patient, from being restless, is inclined to sleep. In some cases, however, dangerous and most serious symptoms set in after reaction has commenced, and the patient may sink under some disease of the head, liver, or other organ.

Treatment.—There is scarcely a medicine in the Pharmacopœia that has not been tried, and yet no certain remedy has hitherto been discovered for this disease when fully developed. But although the grand arcanum has yet to be found, especially for the stage of collapse, many lives may be saved by careful nursing, and by assisting nature in the effort of reaction by the judicious administration of remedies for that purpose. It is in the premonitory stage, or that of diarrhœa, that most good can be done. When cholera threatens, or is prevailing in a district, the slightest form of diarrhœa should be at once attended to, otherwise it is almost certain to run into well-marked and uncontrollable cholera. Saline purgatives should be religiously avoided at such a time. Immediately on the first symptom of derangement of the bowels appearing, the patient should take twenty-five drops of laudanum, or thirty drops of chlorodyne, with half a wineglassful of brandy, and the same quantity of plain or omum water, repeating the dose in two or three hours, if necessary. The above dose is for adults, but in children the proportionate dose of laudanum and of chlorodyne is one drop for every year of the child's age. If purging still continue, give the following astringent mixture, which should be always kept ready for use.

Take of	Powdered prepared chalk	one dram.
	Cinnamon powder	half a dram.
	Sugar	half an ounce.
	Tincture of catechu	six drams.
	Spirits of sal volatile	two drams.
	Chloric ether	two drams.
	Tincture of opium (laudanum) . .	two drams.
	Peppermint or omum water . .	six ounces.

Mix, and give a tablespoonful every two hours.

If there is much nausea or vomiting, a mustard poultice should be applied for twenty-five or thirty minutes over the pit of the stomach, and the following effervescing draught given, if ordinary soda-water is not procurable: dissolve a saltspoonful of carbonate of soda in a wineglassful of water, then add a teaspoonful of limejuice, and drink while effervescing, repeating this as often as it is called for. The patient should keep perfectly tranquil, in the recumbent position, and take as food, simple toast and tea, arrowroot or sago, or plain mutton or chicken broth, avoiding all solid food till the diarrhœa is checked.

This treatment, if adopted at the very outset, will in very many cases arrest the progress of the disease. If the purging and vomiting continue in spite of, or without any treatment, the patient will rapidly fall into a state of collapse. In this stage no medicines containing opium, such as laudanum, chlorodyne. etc., must on any account be given. It is in this stage of the disease that most harm is likely to be done by the injudicious administration of drugs. A struggle is going on between the inherent powers of the patient's constitution and the cholera poison within him; and although no medicine has hitherto proved of any certain use in collapse, the case need not be despaired of. Every effort must now be made to rouse the flagging energies of the system. Good nourishing broth should be given in small quantities every few minutes, and this can easily be made at any time by using Liebig's extract of meat, a teaspoonful to a cup of hot or even cold water, giving the patient a spoonful of this repeatedly. Small doses (a dessert-spoonful) of brandy, diluted with half a glass of water, or small quantities of champagne, may be given every hour or half-hour, until the pulse becomes perceptible at the wrist, or till the skin becomes slightly warm. If these stimulants fail to rouse the patient from his profound collapse, the following is recommended.

Take of	Spirits sal volatile	four drams.
	Chloric ether	two drams.
	Camphor water	five ounces.

Mix, and give a table-spoonful of this every half-hour.

Or the following, which has proved most successful in apparently hopeless cases :—Mix the white of four eggs, four teaspoonfuls of table salt, and, if procurable, two drams of chlorate of potass, in half a pint of water, and give the patient half a wineglassful every few minutes.

Cramps may be relieved by the application of hot bran, sand, or ashes, by mustard poultices, and by smart friction with or without turpentine.

The following mixture has been recommended to promote reaction, and is considered of so much importance that it is ordered in the "Medical Field Companion" to be kept always ready by surgeons in charge of troops on the march. Take oil of aniseed, oil of juniper, and oil of cajeput, of each half a dram ; ether, half an ounce ; tincture of cinnamon, two ounces ; strong sulphuric acid, eight drops ; spirits of wine, twenty-four drops ; mix, and give ten drops in a tablespoonful of water every quarter of an hour.

When, in the stage of collapse, vomiting is not present or has suddenly ceased, the case is a very serious one indeed. The pulse may not be perceptible at the wrist, the voice may be scarcely audible, the surface of the body may be cold and clammy and blue, and the urine may be suppressed, but if there be still occasional vomiting, the case need not be looked on as beyond hope. Vomiting, when repeated five or six times under these circumstances, is often followed by an increase in the frequency of the pulse, and a warmth coming over the surface of the skin. Pure cold water may be given freely. The patient calls for it and drinks it eagerly, and it fills the stomach, and produces vomiting, immediately after which he again demands more. The act of vomiting rouses the patient, and is a means, not to be despised, of restoring what alone is needed for recovery, viz. circulation and heat.

When reaction has fairly set in, little or nothing need be done beyond continuing the nourishing diet referred to ; and it is astonishing how rapidly recovery takes place when once the case has taken a favourable turn. Occasionally, however, this reaction is so severe as to involve such organs as the brain, liver, or even the blood itself. But as such cases require treatment suited to their individual peculiarities, medical aid should be called in, if not already there.

DYSENTERY.

This disease is much more prevalent in India and other tropical regions than elsewhere, and is considered, with good reason, one of the pests of hot climates. It is more commonly met with and more destructive when there is a fall of rain after a long continued drought, as at the change in the monsoon, and a high temperature long continued predisposes to an attack.

Exposure to heat and cold, sudden variations in temperature, intemperance, a malarious atmosphere, unwholesome food, etc., are among the ordinary exciting causes, while not unfrequently it is the result of previous persistent constipation or of organic disease of the liver.

Symptoms.—Severe griping pain, especially in the lower part of the bowels, increased on pressure; frequent evacuation of the bowels, with great straining, the stools being composed of mucus, or slime, and blood, or both together; the tongue is coated and foul, there is depression and generally some fever, and subsequently great prostration.

Treatment.—A teaspoonful of castor oil with twenty drops of laudanum will, in many cases, if attended to at the outset, be found sufficient to arrest the disease. If this fails, the following course must at once be adopted. Give the patient thirty drops of laudanum in a tablespoonful of water; fifteen or twenty minutes afterwards give thirty grains of powdered ipecacuanha, mixed with a small wineglassful of water, and immediately after, apply a good-sized mustard poultice over the stomach for about half an hour. The patient must now lie down, keep perfectly quiet, and be undisturbed by any food or drink. This treatment will cause intense nausea, and perhaps great depression, but if vomiting occur within one hour afterwards, the very same course must be adopted about three or four hours subsequently. This is now considered to be the specific treatment of dysentery; as it has proved more successful than any other hitherto tried, and the cases are rare and exceptional indeed in which it fails. The above treatment may require to be repeated three or four times during the course of two or three days, but it would be injudicious to push it any further if no benefit results, owing to the great depression produced by the ipecacuanha. If it fail, thirty drops of laudanum in one wineglassful of water or thin arrowroot may be injected into the bowels, and repeated two or three times in the course of the day.

Warm poultices of bran, linseed meal, or rice flour, should be applied over the abdomen constantly, and the patient kept quiet in a well-ventilated apartment. The food should be of the simplest kind, and such as is least likely to disturb the stomach. Good broths, beef tea, arrowroot, sago, corn-flour, or other farinaceous substances, with milk, should be given frequently in small quantities.

The above treatment is chiefly applicable to dysentery in its acute stage, though it is frequently most successful when the disease has been long standing. When the disease assumes a chronic form, that is, when all the symptoms are less severe, the treatment must be modified according to the probable cause.

Few diseases can boast of so many reputed remedies as chronic dysentery. In nearly every household, native as well as European, prescriptions for it are to be found, which are often held sacred as infallible and specific. These prescriptions, though occasionally containing a formidable array of ingredients, are not always to be despised or contemptuously thrust aside. They are generally and principally composed of astringent and aromatic substances, and while they may not unfrequently do great good, they very seldom do much harm. The natives of Southern India, however, often give large doses of mercurials, such as calomel and corrosive sublimate; the results of which are most disastrous.

It would be superfluous here to enter into the details of the treatment of chronic dysentery, as each case must be studied and treated according to its originating cause, and there is generally ample time for professional aid to be called in. If, however, the doctor resides far distant, and may not be able to see the case for one, two, or more days after being sent for, the patient, if suffering much, may take ten grains of Dover's powder three times a day; or a *third* of a *teaspoonful* of castor oil, with eight or ten drops of laudanum and a little water, three times a day. Pomegranate peel, dried, is sometimes also of great use, and is usually given in the form of decoction, made by boiling half an ounce of the dried peel in two teacupfuls of water down to one cup, and drank in the evening or morning instead of tea or coffee. Bael fruit, also, sometimes proves successful when all other remedies have failed. It may be taken in the form of extract, conserve, decoction, sherbet, or syrup. The latter. being the most convenient form, is prepared by adding half a wineglassful of water and a teaspoonful of sugar to half a moderate-sized bael, divested of its stringy part. This may be taken as one dose, and repeated two or three times a day. If the patient is living in a malarious district, probably no treatment will prove of any benefit, unless he be removed from the morbid influence of the place. Indeed some cases of dysentery resist all treatment, and a thorough change, such as a sea voyage, affords the only chance of recovery.

Dysentery in children is frequently most obstinate and intractable. At the outset of the disease, the best thing to be done, is to give a small teaspoonful of castor oil; and this failing, the following mixture may be given for a child one year old:—

Take of Castor oil	one dram.
Powdered gum arabic	half a dram.
Sugar	two drams.
Laudanum	five drops.
Aniseed or peppermint water . .	one ounce.

Mix, and give a teaspoonful every four hours.

If the symptoms still persist, give the following powder three times a day:—

Dover's powder	one grain.
Ipecacuanha	quarter of a grain.
Quinine	quarter of a grain.
Rhubarb	one grain.

A thin linseed-meal poultice should also be applied over the abdomen; and if the child has much straining, or is very restless, inject one drop (for each year of age) of laudanum with a dessert-spoonful of cold water into the bowels two or three times a day, if necessary.

The bael fruit, as already recommended, is sometimes of the greatest benefit in these obstinate cases.

If the teeth are suspected to be causing irritation, the gums must be scarified; and if worms are supposed to be the cause, as they often are of dysentery, santonine should be given, as already directed when treating of diarrhœa.

If the infant is at the breast, changing the nurse alone may effect a cure; while for those who are beyond that age, no food should be allowed except arrowroot, sago, bread and milk, beef-tea, or chicken and mutton broth, and tea and toast. A flannel binder should in all cases be worn round the abdomen.

FEVERS.

The ordinary fevers met with in India are Continued, Intermittent, and Remittent. There are several degrees of the first, their duration extending from one or two days to several weeks; while the symptoms vary from the mildest to the most severe and fatal, often involving important vital organs in their course.

The ordinary symptoms which usher in an attack of simple fever are, a chill sensation, sometimes amounting to shivering; pain in the head and back, languor, weakness, loss of appetite, quick pulse, foul tongue, and increased heat of skin. All these symptoms may be caused by exposure to cold or wet, by indigestion, or over-fatigue; and they may disappear within twenty-four hours without any treatment at all, beyond rest, a simple warm footbath, a warm drink at bedtime, light farinaceous food, and, if necessary, a mild purgative in the morning, such as castor oil, Gregory's powder, or a couple of compound colocynth pills.

If the fever continues twenty-four hours without any intermission, active treatment is required to subdue it, as well as to anticipate or prevent serious organic complications, which are so apt to come on during its course. An emetic, composed of one grain tartar emetic, and fifteen to twenty grains of ipecacuanha, in half a tumbler of water, should be given; or a convenient substitute will be found in two or three teaspoonfuls of common table-salt dissolved in a tumbler of tepid water. When the stomach has quieted after the vomiting, give a simple purgative, such as either of those above mentioned for simple fever; and after the bowels have been well moved, give the patient the following powder, if the fever still continue :—

Dover's powder	five grains.
James' powder	four grains.

To be repeated three times a day

Or the following fever mixture :—

Take of	Sweet spirits of nitre	half an ounce.
	Nitrate of potass	one dram.
	Mindereris spirit (aq. acet. ammon.)	three ounces.
	Water	two ounces.

Mix, and give a tablespoonful every three hours.

The entire surface of the body should be frequently sponged (portions at a time) with tepid water and vinegar, as this cools the system, is most agreeable to the patient, and has no small influence in subduing the fever. The head should be kept cool by applying cloths soaked in cold water, with ice if procurable, or in vinegar and water. If the fever continues two days, in spite of the above treatment, and if no medical aid is at hand, the following may be given.

Take of	Quinine	ten grains.
	Calomel	six grains.
	Rhubarb	fifteen grains.
	Jalap	fifteen grains.

Mix, and make into a mass with syrup or honey, and divide into ten pills.

Two to be given every four or five hours. If pain in the abdomen, chest, or back is complained of, warm water fomentations or bran or linseed meal poultices should be applied.

The turpentine stupe is of great value in such cases, and its mode of application is as follows:—Soak a piece of cloth of the size required in spirits of turpentine, place this over the part where pain is complained of, and while it is allowed to remain there twenty minutes, hot water (flannel) fomentations should be constantly applied.

In children, perhaps no remedy is so effectual and so speedy in producing and promoting perspiration as the wet sheet; and it is quite safe. It is applied thus:—Soak a double-folded sheet in water quite cold, or with the chill taken off; spread this on the floor, and on it lay the little patient stripped, quickly enveloping every part of the body (head and face excepted) with the wet sheet, and tucking it well into every hollow space; over this wrap one or more blankets, and place the child in bed, when it will soon fall asleep. Let it remain thus for one hour, or even longer; afterwards remove the coverings, sponge rapidly the surface of the body with tepid water, and after drying it, let him have some sleep, if so inclined. This treatment may be repeated two or three times in the course of the day.

The administration of food in fever, forms one of the most important elements in its treatment, and too much care cannot therefore be taken in regulating both the quality and the quantity of nutriment to be taken.

Fever is such a consuming disease, that the vital powers early become much enfeebled, and the whole body emaciated by a severe or prolonged attack. The patient cannot eat, and if he did, he could not digest, solid food. The diet must, therefore, be almost entirely liquid. Beef-tea, soups, plain or thickened with arrowroot, sago, or ground rice, should be given in small quantities repeatedly; and during convalescence, a light pudding may be taken in addition. Half a glass of port or sherry wine may be given to adults two or three times a day, if much weakness is complained of.

If the fever continue *uninterrupted and severe* for two or three days, every effort must be made to obtain professional aid, for the simple reason that the persistency of the fever may be due to the existence of serious mischief in some organ of the body. Inflammation may thus occur, and may make some progress before it is discovered, in consequence of the diminished sensibility of the patient to internal as well as external sensations.

It is in these cases that the judgment, skill, and experience of the medical adviser are tested, for he must trust, not to the sensations of the patient, but to his own tact in interpreting other signs and symptoms, in order to discover the cause of the obstinacy of the fever.

It may be here mentioned, that as fevers of a continued type are not unfrequently caused and kept up by bad drainage, bad ventilation, and uncleanliness generally, every care should be taken to remedy these by measures which are obvious to any one.

INTERMITTENT FEVER, AGUE, OR JUNGLE FEVER.

The primary cause of this disease, as it is indeed of many others in India, is *malaria*, of the precise nature of which nothing is known beyond the fact that it is a specific poison which produces a specified effect on the human system. Malaria is most likely to prevail about the end of the hot and dry weather, and its development is in proportion to the temperature and humidity of the previous hot season. It is most active from sunset to sunrise, and it is during this period that the body is most predisposed to receive it. It is heavier than the atmosphere, becomes entangled in fogs, and keeps close to the ground; hence the danger of sleeping in the open air at night on the ground. It adheres to the foliage of high, wide-spreading trees, and this facility of attracting and, as it were, arresting the miasma, should be taken advantage of, by planting such trees round dwellings and districts where it is reputed to exist.

The time which elapses between exposure to malaria and an attack of ague is very variable. Some persons suffer immediately, while long periods may elapse before any symptom appears in others. Strangers visiting malarious districts are generally more susceptible than natives or Europeans who have long lived there; indeed many of the latter do not suffer at all till they remove to the plains.

Varieties of Ague.—1st, *Quotidian*, when the attack comes on once every twenty-four hours; 2nd, *Tertian*, in which the paroxysm occurs once in forty-eight hours; and 3rd, *Quartan*, when it comes on once in seventy-two hours, the symptoms being the same in all, though differing in degree.

Symptoms.—A fit of ague consists of a cold, a hot, and a sweating stage. The usual symptoms which usher in the first, are languor, debility, listlessness, yawning, stretching, and a sense of oppression about the stomach; a chilly sensation is complained of all over the body, especially along the course of the spine; the features shrink, and the skin becomes dry and rough. These are soon after followed by violent shivering and chattering of the teeth; the lips, cheeks, ears, and nose become blueish, the breathing quick and anxious, the pulse frequent, and occasionally feeble, the tongue dry and white, and severe pains are sometimes felt in the back, loins, and head. The shivering and cold sensations gradually go off, and the second, or hot stage commences. Heat gradually returns, at first in alternate flushes about the neck and face, followed by a burning, pungent, dry heat of the whole body; the features lose their pale shrunken aspect, and become more natural, or more red and flushed, the pulse is quick, full and strong; throbbing of the temples is much complained of, the pain in the head being sometimes intense, and the patient is very restless. These symptoms are again followed by others which constitute the third, or sweating, stage. Moisture appears on the face and neck, bursting out afterwards in profuse perspiration all over the body, the burning heat and thirst disappear, the pulse becomes natural, the sweating soon goes off, and the patient begins to feel in his usual health.

The period which intervenes between one fit and another is called an *intermission*, and if these intermissions are complete, that is, if the usual health is resumed, the fever is called intermittent. If, however, the patient does not entirely recover, if he continues uneasy, unwell, and perhaps slightly feverish, the disease is called remittent fever.

The duration of an attack from its commencement till its close, varies from one to two or more hours. A fit may come on at any moment unexpectedly while the individual is employed at his ordinary occupation, or during meals, or whilst engaged in some amusement or recreation. The causes which predispose the system to an attack, are debility, however produced, and intemperance.

Treatment.—In the first or cold stage, the great object is to shorten it, and this is to be done by warmth. The patient should at once be put to bed, covered with blankets, and have hot bran, sand, salt, or water-bottles, applied all round him; he should drink freely of warm tea or rice water, and take a glass of wine or spirits with warm water. A pot containing hot charcoal, placed under the bed, is an excellent means of warming the patient.

Emetics are sometimes of great use in abridging this

stage, but they should not be administered unless there is nausea, a foul tongue, or other indications of a loaded stomach, and in such case twenty grains of ipecacuanha, mixed with half a grain of tartar emetic, in a tumbler of tepid water, may be given at the outset.

In the second or hot stage, all the treatment adopted during the cold stage must be discontinued; the patient should drink freely of cold or iced water, or soda-water; the whole body should be sponged with tepid water, and the head kept cool with cold-water cloths. A grain of opium, or twenty drops of laudanum, is sometimes of great benefit in subduing the fever, relieving the throbbing at the temples, and promoting perspiration. During the third, or sweating stage, nothing need be done except to encourage the perspiration (if not already too free) by keeping the patient covered with one or two blankets, and giving him some warm tea or rice-water to drink. He must afterwards be well wiped with dry towels, have his clothes changed, and get out of bed, or go to sleep if so inclined. If much weakness is complained of, a little brandy or wine and water may be administered.

It is not so much during the paroxysm, as during the intermission, that the treatment is most important. One attack predisposes the system to another at a more or less distant interval, while repeated attacks render the system still more prone to their recurrence, and as the patient soon begins to know by experience when the next attack may be expected, he should anticipate it by appropriate treatment. A simple purgative pill, composed of eight or ten grains of the compound extract of colocynth, with or without a quarter of a grain of podophyllin, should be taken at first, if the bowels have been, as they commonly are, confined; and immediately after the purgative has ceased to operate, specific remedies must be used.

Of all the medicines that have hitherto been recommended as specifics for ague, none has stood the test of experience so well as quinine; and this drug (the sheet anchor in ague) has the further advantage that it can be safely trusted in the hands of unprofessional persons, which is more than can be said of such remedies as arsenic. The dose of quinine to be taken after the above purgative, if a paroxysm is threatening, is from ten to fifteen grains; indeed, in malarious districts, experienced hands in ague do not think of measuring or weighing the dose at all, but unhesitatingly take from their bottle (always with them) a flat teaspoonful of quinine powder, which probably contains about twenty grains. If this treatment is adopted at the very outset, the attack may be prevented. But further treatment is necessary, as the paroxysm may return at any moment. The quinine must, therefore, be continued, in smaller doses however, say two or three grains, two or three times a day; and if the bowels are confined, and urine scanty, it may be combined with other medicines as follows.

Take of	Epsom salts	one ounce.
	Nitre	one dram.
	Quinine	two scruples.
	Diluted sulphuric acid .	one dram.
	Or the juice of one lime.	
	Water	one quart.

Mix, and take a wineglassful two or three times a day.

A practice commonly exists in malarious districts, of taking one grain of quinine immediately before breakfast and dinner, under the supposition that it prevents the action of malaria on the system. As this small dose may really produce the desired effect, and can do no harm, the practice may be adopted. The only caution to be observed in giving quinine, is to *suspend* its use, after it has caused deafness or frontal headache.

If attacks of ague continue to recur in spite of all treatment, the only course left is, for the patient (if his health has been much damaged) to quit the malarious district, for some more salubrious locality, or to take a sea voyage.

When this is impracticable, persons exposed to a malarious atmosphere, or who have had an attack of fever, would find it worth their while to attend to the following cautions. First, beware of sudden exposure to cold, and of damp or wet feet. Second, avoid over-fatigue and exhaustion, however produced. Third, never sleep in the open air during the night, and never close to the surface of the ground. Fourth, go early to bed, but do not get out of doors too early in the morning. Fifth, never leave the house in the morning with an empty stomach. Sixth, be temperate in habits.

Heat Apoplexy, or Sunstroke.

Coup-de-soleil was the name which formerly distinguished all cases of sunstroke, from the mistaken notion, that they were necessarily the result of direct exposure to the beams of a hot sun. Such exposure, however, is by no means necessary to an attack. On the contrary, in a large number, if not the majority of cases that have been reported, the patient has *not* been so exposed. During the hottest months of the year, it is not at all uncommon for men who have gone to bed apparently well, to be seized during the night. A high temperature, with a close still atmosphere, overcrowding and bad ventilation, are the conditions under which attacks of heat apoplexy are most likely to occur. The predisposing causes are bodily fatigue and exertion, suppressed perspiration, intemperance, existing disease, and indeed anything likely to lower the system.

Symptoms.—These may be classed under two forms. In the first they come on slowly, and gradually increase; while in the second, they are sudden and severe. In the first, the patient complains of swimming in the head, drowsiness, faintness, and languor, confusion of ideas and great depression, mental as well as physical. These symptoms, if not attended to, are soon followed by others of a still graver nature. The headache is intense; a feeling of weight, tightness, and heat at the back of the head is complained of; the breathing becomes laboured, oppressed, and sighing; the skin is hot and burning, the face is sometimes flushed, the thirst intense, bowels generally confined, and the urine suppressed. There is also generally nausea, and a disposition to vomit, with a sense of anxiety, weight, and uneasiness about the pit of the stomach; the patient is frequently distressed and agitated, and is possessed by a feeling of horror or of some impending calamity. These symptoms, if allowed to continue, are followed by violent convulsions, terminating in coma, or deep stupor, and death.

In the second or sudden and severe form, the patient, after perhaps a little staggering unsteadiness in walking, is at once seized with violent convulsions, ending in deep stupor, from which he cannot be roused; the breathing is sonorous and puffing, the skin intensely hot and dry, the pulse is at first full, quick, and bounding, shortly after it becomes soft and feeble; the convulsions sometimes return, the respiration becomes more and more laboured, froth appears at the mouth and nostrils, and death soon follows. The duration of an attack may be from a few minutes to several hours. Some recover rapidly (if treated at the outset) from the symptoms, which are more immediately dangerous, but even these persons are liable to future attacks, and can ill stand a high temperature with a still, close atmosphere. The least exposure causes in them intense pain and tightness at the back of the head, with a feeling of fulness in the head generally.

The severe headache, burning heat of the skin, great thirst, and uneasy sensations about the region of the stomach, so often complained of by Europeans travelling by rail in India during some of the hottest months of the year, are the premonitory symptoms of an attack of heat apoplexy. Few therefore, caring to expose themselves to such risks, travel during the day, but prefer journeying by night, taking care even then to be well provided with water and ice.

Treatment must be prompt, active, and persistent, since much good may be done before medical assistance can be obtained. The patient should be placed in a recumbent position, in a cool, well-ventilated place, with his head and shoulders raised and supported, and his upper garments removed. Water, iced, or as cold as it can be had, must be steadily poured from a height, and in a small stream, on the head, face, and chest, and most resolutely persevered with as long as the preternatural heat of the skin continues,—in fact, almost as long as there is life. As some encouragement, it may be mentioned, that cases of heat apoplexy have occurred, in which this determined affusion had been used for five hours, before they were restored from perfect insensibility to consciousness. Mustard poultices should also be applied to the chest, abdomen, calves of the legs, and spine, and an enema administered, composed of one or two table-spoonfuls of turpentine, three or four table-spoonfuls of castor oil, and a pint of tepid water. When the patient is able to swallow, a dessert-spoonful of brandy, or a teaspoonful of sal volatile in water should be given every hour till reaction sets in. He must then be kept quiet, and have simple milk diet or broth, and a purgative if necessary.

Preventive measures ought always to be taken by those travelling by rail during the hot weather. The head may be kept constantly wet, either by occasionally pouring cold water on it, or by keeping a handkerchief, soaked in water, on the top and back part of the head, and even on the face, by means of which latter, *the hot air passing to the lungs is considerably reduced in temperature.*

DISEASE OF THE LIVER.

Most disorders of the liver are characterized by an

uneasy, dull, heavy, aching sensation in the right side, a pain at the top of the right shoulder, loss of appetite, sluggishness of the bowels, occasionally diarrhœa or dysentery, and great general weakness. If not early attended to, these symptoms are sooner or later followed by others more serious, when medical aid is indispensably necessary.

Treatment.—The application of a mustard poultice or a turpentine fomentation, and a couple of compound colocynth pills, may, and very often will, remove all the above symptoms. A full dose of ipecacuanha powder (25 to 30 grains) is often most useful in this stage also.

If the symptoms continue, however, the right side should be sponged every morning with nitro-muriatic acid lotion (made by mixing a quarter of an ounce each of strong nitric and muriatic acid, with a pint and a half of water), and one of the following pills taken once or twice a day.

Take of Podophyllin	three grains.
Compound extract of colocynth .	two and a half scruples.
Ipecacuanha	four grains.

And sufficient extract of taraxacum to make the ingredients into a mass, which is to be divided into twelve pills.*

Should the symptoms continue after one week's treatment as above, the right side should be painted over with a solution of iodine (iodine ten grains, iodide of potass twenty grains, and water half-ounce); or a fly blister may be applied for eight or ten hours, and the same pills as above, continued, or the following mixture, taken:—

Podophyllin	four grains.
Diluted nitro-muriatic acid .	half an ounce.
Fluid extract of taraxacum .	three and a half ounces.

Mix, and take a teaspoonful in half a glass of water three times a day.†

* The above will be found particularly useful as a simple anti-bilious pill.

† The podophyllin may be omitted if there is diarrhœa or a tendency to it.

The diet should be light, and easily digestible, and no alcoholic drink should be taken, unless there is a great prostration of strength, when a glass of good dry sherry, or of claret, two or three times a day, may be allowed. The water used for bathing should always be made tepid, even during the hottest weather. Torpidity of the liver is so very frequently caused by sedentary habits, that often nothing further is required to remedy it beyond good, active, systematic exercise. If Europeans would only take more active exercise, eat less animal food, and be more temperate in the use of alcoholic beverages, the risk of suffering from liver disease would be materially diminished. Indeed, it may be safely asserted, that a very large, if not the larger, number of those who suffer from "liver," owe their diseases more to their own imprudent habits, than to the climate pure and simple.

Prickly Heat.

Few escape this troublesome complaint. It is perhaps the first that the new comer to India suffers from, and though unattended with danger, it is sometimes so teasing as to render the victim unfit for anything. The symptoms are, itching, tingling, pricking, and a sensation of heat accompanied with that popularly known as "needles and pins;" and the skin is covered with a bright red eruption, resembling pimples or freckles. It may be confined to one part of the body, but it may also extend rapidly over every inch of surface. The irritation may disappear while the body is at rest, but it reappears with intensity when the skin acts freely, as during exertion, or after taking a glass of water, or tea, or anything likely to cause perspiration.

Prickly heat is rather salutary than otherwise; that is, it is a symptom indicating the free action of the skin rather than a *cause* of good health.

Many remedies have been recommended, but few prove

of much, if any, use. Sponging the parts affected with toilet vinegar and water or Eau de Cologne, washing with carbolic soap, or dusting with ordinary violet powder, are among the remedies which will probably be found most beneficial.

New comers who suffer much from prickly heat, should be temperate in eating and drinking; avoid exercise during the heat of the day; keep the bowels regular; wear light cotton clothing; and abstain from cold bathing when the eruption is abundant

Boils.

These are very troublesome in India, and may come on at any period of the year, though the most common time for their appearance is about the commencement of the wet and cool weather. In some parts of India, especially in the north-west and upper provinces, they are so large and so abundant as to prove sometimes very serious.

Ordinarily, however, they are not attended with danger, but they always prove a source of much discomfort and pain, and in the case of ladies, of disfigurement. They sometimes appear single and solitary; at other times in crops and clusters, and occasionally, though rarely, the whole body may be studded with them.

Treatment.—When large, solitary, and hard, an attempt must be made to promote their absorption, in other words, to prevent them from suppurating. This may be done by painting them over with tincture or solution of iodine (see page 280) once or twice a day; or by the application of a plaster, composed of four parts of galbanum plaster, and one part of camphor, spread on leather or cloth; or better still, by an ointment composed of one dram extract of belladonna, half a dram powdered opium, and one ounce of basilicon ointment.

This boil ointment, spread on leather, and applied to

the boil, has proved more successful than anything else in relieving pain, promoting absorption, and dispersing the swelling, When this fails, and when the boil becomes red, painful, enlarged, and soft, apply hot water fomentations, or linseed meal or rice poultices, or a cream composed of equal parts of honey and goulard water; or the simple benzoated lard only, till they burst or are ready for opening. These large boils should in all cases be opened when they are soft and fluctuating, or when there is no tendency to absorption. This should be done by a simple *puncture* with a lancet, and the above belladonna ointment afterwards applied.

When the boils appear in clusters all over the body, constitutional treatment is required. A tablespoonful of the following mixture should be taken every morning or oftener, provided the bowels are not already too freely moved:—

Take of Epsom salts	two ounces.
Cream of tartar . . .	one ounce.
Water	one quart.

If the sulphate of potass with sulphur (as one drug) can be procured, half an ounce of it may be added to the above mixture. The following mixture, taken in the same dose, will be found beneficial when the appetite and health generally are below par:—

Epsom salts	one ounce.
Sulphate of iron . . .	half dram.
Quinine	one scruple.
Diluted sulphuric acid . .	two drams.
Water	eight ounces.

For persons who are liable to crops of boils, a full dose of quinine (ten grains) taken immediately on their threatening to appear may arrest their progress.

The system is sometimes so depressed when the boils are abundant, that a glass of good dry sherry or of claret, two or three times a day, besides good nourishing food, may be absolutely necessary. A complete change of air, a trip to sea, removal to some more bracing climate, or even from the locality in which the patient lives, is sometimes indispensable, and will be found beneficial, when all other remedies have failed.

CONSTIPATION.

Habitual constipation is a complaint to which Europeans are frequently subject after their arrival in India, and arises as much from want of exercise as from any other cause. Medicine will prove far less effectual to remedy it, than a well regulated system of diet and regimen. Good active walking exercise, the use of bran bread, fruits, and plenty of good fresh drinking water will, if persevered with, probably effect all the good desired.

The so-called hydropathic treatment is most beneficial in these cases. The patient should sit in a small quantity of cold water every morning, for about a quarter of an hour, at the same time rubbing the abdomen gently with the hand or sponging it with cold water; or a wineglassful of cold water may be injected into the bowels, and retained there while a brisk walk is being taken. A wet bandage round the abdomen is also sometimes of the greatest benefit, and the mode of applying it is as follows:—Soak a double piece of American drill, twelve inches square, in cold water; place this over the stomach, covering it with waterproof sheeting one inch larger all round than the wet cloth; and then apply a dry bandage round the body, fastening it with tape, or buckles and straps.

This should be applied early in the morning, and kept on for about two hours, during which time active exercise ought to be taken, and one or two tumblers of fresh water drunk, with or without some simple fruit, as the plantain or mango.

Purgative medicines must be avoided if possible, for they not only interfere with digestion, but they also often aggravate the disease they are intended to cure. Enemas, if used copiously and warm, impair the tone of the bowels, and eventually do more harm than good. When a purgative is absolutely necessary, the simpler it is the better; and there is perhaps none safer than castor oil or Gregory's powder. The effervescing citrate of magnesia is a mild, agreeable, and cooling purgative, and is well suited for Europeans in India.

It should always be borne in mind, however, that it is much better to allow a certain amount of constipation than to fall into the bad habit of taking purgatives often.

Colic

May be caused by indigestible food, by drinking bad water, or by exposure to cold and damp. The symptoms are, severe twisting pain in the abdomen, which is generally relieved by pressure, accompanied sometimes by nausea and vomiting.

Treatment.—Thirty drops chlorodyne, or twenty drops of laudanum, with half a glass of brandy and water; and repeated in two or three hours if the pain continues severe. The abdomen to be fomented with flannels wrung out of hot water, or covered with a large bran or linseed-meal poultice, or a mustard plaster may be applied. If the bowels have been much constipated, give an enema composed of two or three table-spoonfuls of castor oil and one table-spoonful of turpentine in a quart of warm rice-water. The bowels should afterwards be freely moved by a full dose of castor oil, taken by the mouth.

In *children* and *young infants*, colic or "gripes" is almost invariably caused by indigestible food, and is usually quickest relieved with a teaspoonful of aniseed, peppermint, or dill water, with or without laudanum (one drop for every year). If this fail, and the child is crying much, put it into a warm bath, rub the belly with warm salad oil, and, if much puffed, apply over the surface a paste made of burnt sweet flag and water. An enema of warm water, with one table-spoonful of castor oil, may also be given.

When the attacks of colic are frequent in infants, there must be some fault in the nursing, or in the nurse herself. Too frequent and irregular nursing is a very common cause, and nothing will prove of the least use in relieving the child of its pain, until a proper course is adopted. No infant above one month old should be nursed oftener than once every two hours. When griping is frequent, the following mixture will be found very useful:—

Take of Magnesia	one dram.
Sugar	two drams.
Gum powder	one dram.
Tincture of asafœtida . .	half dram.
Essence of aniseed . . .	twenty drops.
Dill water	two ounces.

Mix, and give a teaspoonful as a dose, three or four times a day if necessary.

CONVULSIONS

May occur at any moment when medical aid is far distant, and if no means are adopted to arrest them, a life may be lost. Convulsions may be caused by teething, by irritating substances, such as indigestible food, worms, etc., in the stomach and bowels, and they may also come on during the course of other diseases.

The symptoms which usually usher in a fit, are turning in of the thumbs towards the palms of the hands, squinting, twitching at the mouth, starting or jerking of the arms or legs, and violent screaming. The whole or part of the body suddenly becomes rigid, the back is bent in the form of a bow, and the entire body is much agitated and sometimes distorted from the violence of the spasm, while froth escapes from the mouth, and the breathing is hurried and laboured.

Treatment.—Put the child at once into a hot bath, immersing the entire body (except the head); and while it is in the bath, pour cold water out of the spout of a teapot from a height on to the top of the head. The child should remain in the bath for at least ten minutes, but the cold water must be continued to the head for at least half an hour longer, if the fit persists, or the head be still hot. If the child is able to swallow after its removal from the bath, give it (if one year old) five grains of ipecacuanha in a little tepid water, or a small teaspoonful of ipecacuanha wine, and repeat either of these, two or three times within half an hour, so as to make the child vomit. In all cases an injection should be given, consisting of one teaspoonful of turpentine, two teaspoonfuls of castor oil, and about a wineglassful of tepid water. Mustard poultices should be applied to the feet, calves, or thighs, and to the spine, and kept on eight or ten minutes. If any teeth are suspected to be causing irritation, the swollen gums over them must be freely scarified with a gum lancet. If worms are suspected to be the cause, give two grains of santonine after the fit is over, repeating the dose in two hours afterwards, followed one hour subsequently by a teaspoonful of castor oil.

Convulsive fits may last from only a few minutes to many hours. In the latter case, the hot baths may be repeated at intervals of one or two hours, according to the strength of the little patient; but the head must be kept constantly cool by cold water poured over it, or by the continuous application of ice or cloths soaked in cold water.

As these fits are very liable to recur, every care and attention should be paid to the state of the bowels and teeth, and indeed to anything that is at all likely to cause the least irritation.

CROUP.

This is another of those diseases for which the treatment must be prompt and active. The symptoms come on so suddenly and advance so rapidly, that much good may be done, danger averted, perhaps life itself saved, long before medical aid is available.

Symptoms.—A harsh crowing sound in the breathing, a dry metallic (brassy) cough, quick pulse, and difficult respiration. The disease sometimes passes away quickly, while at other times it runs its fatal course in a few hours.

Causes.—Exposure to cold or damp, indigestible food or other irritant in the bowels, and teething.

Treatment.—Give (to a child one year old) a teaspoonful, every ten minutes, of the following mixture, till vomiting is produced :—

Take of	Ipecacuanha	twenty grains.
	Tartrate of antimony (tartar emetic)	two grains.
	Water	two ounces.

The seriousness of the case is in proportion to the difficulty of exciting vomiting; if vomiting is early and freely induced, the chances of recovery are more favourable. Put the child into a hot bath, which will assist the emetic; and after its removal from the bath, continue the emetic, if there has been no vomiting. Apply a mustard poultice to the throat and upper part of the chest, or a thin bag of hot salt, or sand, or bran. After free vomiting has occurred, the child should have a quarter of a grain of calomel with two grains James' powder every two hours, until twelve such powders have been taken. The bowels should be moved by castor oil or an enema.

In those mild cases where the child has simply a croupy cough, and in those severe ones, after the urgent symptoms have disappeared, the same emetic mixture as above should be given, in doses of a quarter of a teaspoonful, or the same quantity of ipecacuanha wine, every three or four hours. The throat and chest should be rubbed with warm oil or mustard oil, and hartshorn in the proportion of one part of the latter to four parts of the former, and covered over with a piece of soft flannel.

Children, in whom there is a tendency to croup, should never be allowed to remain out exposed to the night air or damp.

Intestinal Worms.

Three kinds of worms infest the human body, viz. the tape, the round, and the thread worm, and the treatment varies with each.

For tapeworm, the best known and most certain remedies are spirits of turpentine, kousso, and the oil of male fern. The dose of the first is one teaspoonful; of the second, two drams; and of the third, from half to one dram. In either case, the dose should be taken on an empty stomach, followed four or five hours afterwards by a dessert-spoonful of castor oil; and this treatment should be repeated once or twice a week, until the whole of the tapeworm has been passed.

For round worms, five grains (for an adult) of santonine powder should be taken at bedtime; the same quantity early next morning, and one hour afterwards a dessert-spoonful of castor oil. If this fails, one teaspoonful of turpentine with two teaspoonfuls of castor oil should be taken early in the morning, fasting.

Thread Worms almost invariably infest the lower part of the bowels, and are best treated by injecting some bitter infusion as that of quassia, gall-nut, or chiretta, or a solution of santonine, five grains to one ounce of water.

Worms are a common cause of diarrhœa, dysentery, convulsions, and wasting in children. The symptoms that usually indicate their presence are itching and picking at the nose, grinding of the teeth, a sallow pasty complexion, with often a darkish ring round the eyes. The appetite is capricious and fanciful, the child loses flesh, and perhaps has its stomach distended and sometimes hard. Worms may be suspected and treated for in those cases of diarrhœa and dysentery which resist the ordinary remedies. The dose of santonine for a child two years old is two grains.

Accidents.

Wounds are incised, contused or ragged, punctured, and gunshot.

Incised or clean-cut wounds should first be cleansed of all dust or other matter, and after bleeding has stopped or been controlled, the edges should be brought close together by strips of adhesive plaster, then covered with dry lint and a light bandage. If the wound is large and gaping, a fine needle and thread may be passed through the edges at different parts, according to the size, and tied in a simple or reef knot, the lint and bandage being then applied as above. In the case of wounds on the head, the hair must be shaved off all round the injured part, before the above treatment is adopted.

In *ragged* wounds it is no use attempting to bring the edges together. Apply in the first instance, plain cold-water dressing and a light bandage. If there is much pain, a light poultice or warm-water dressing may be used, to be replaced by the original dressing when the pain has subsided, and this treatment should be continued till the wound is healed.

In *punctured and gunshot wounds*, the danger is often very great, as important organs and vessels may have been injured. In all cases, it is best, if no particular symptom indicating serious internal injury is present, to apply lint soaked in cold water over the wound, to keep the patient lying on the wounded side, so as to facilitate the escape of any matter, and to keep him at perfect rest and on low diet. If the wound begins to throb, and is hot and painful, warm-water dressing or a poultice should be applied, and frequently repeated. If there be any fever, a simple purgative must be given, followed by the fever mixture (see page 270).

As punctured and gunshot wounds are often attended at first with great shock to the nervous system, it may be necessary to give the patient a glass of brandy to rally him. If a bullet, or broken part of a knife, or other instrument, can be felt or seen at or near the surface of the wound, it must be gently and cautiously removed with a pair of forceps or clean blunt pliers.

BRUISES.

These are simple or compound, according as they involve the superficial textures only, or those deep seated, with the tissues destroyed.

In the simple form, the treatment is rest, fomentations at first, and afterward gentle friction with soap liniment or oil, with or without camphor. Cloths soaked in tincture of arnica diluted with four parts more of water, or in vinegar, or a garlic or onion poultice, will be found useful in removing the discoloration due to extravasated blood.

Leeches and friction generally do more harm than good at the outset, and should therefore never then be used. The first are only necessary if inflammation sets in, which it sometimes does as a secondary result of the injury. Friction, if adopted at the first, may so irritate as to *cause* this inflammation, and should therefore only be adopted after all excitement has passed, and even then cautiously and gently.

In more severe bruises, where the tissues are torn, the best treatment in the first instance is to apply fomentations, by soaking a double piece of cloth in warm water, and covering it over with oil-silk or waterproof sheeting larger than the cloth applied. This should be changed two or three times a day, and continued till the surface become clean, after which *cold* water dressing and a light bandage will be found sufficient to effect a cure. Loose skin or other tissue, not falling off spontaneously, may be removed by scissors. If proud flesh (granulations) appear abundant, a simple astringent lotion composed of two grains of sulphate of zinc in one ounce of water may be used, instead of the plain water dressing, or the surface may be dusted over once every day with finely pounded alum in a muslin bag before applying the simple water dressing.

If the discharge is very offensive, and the part looks dark coloured and unhealthy, a poultice made with charcoal and linseed meal or grated carrots, and plain water or yeast (Indian toddy fermented), should be applied; or a lotion of carbolic acid, one part to twenty of oil may be used.

If insects appear, they may be destroyed by dusting in a small quantity of a powder composed of equal parts of calomel and camphor.

It must always be borne in mind that bruises of the simplest nature in natives of India may be followed by the most serious, even fatal, results, from tetanus or lockjaw supervening. It is therefore necessary that care should be bestowed even upon what may appear to be only a trivial accident.

SPRAINS.

The limb must be kept at perfect rest, and cold water continuously applied. If after this there is much pain, a few leeches may be applied, and when all inflammatory symptoms have passed away, gentle friction with the hand or with soap liniment, followed by bandaging, may be employed. When the swelling and the uneasy sensations have abated, the joint may be moved in different directions, in order to restore the natural movements. Tincture of arnica, diluted with four parts of water, sometimes gives relief in sprains, after the immediate excitement has passed. Occasionally, the sprain may be so severe as to require the application of one or two splints, in order to ensure perfect immobility. In almost all cases, the more perfectly the limb is kept at rest *at the outset*, the sooner will the symptoms disappear. Sprains of the ankle are best treated by the careful application of strapping to the injured part, and the immediate but cautious use of the limb.

Bleeding, or Hæmorrhage.

This may occur to such an extent from a wound as to prove in itself a source of danger, if not arrested. In ordinary cases, as in incised wounds, exposure to the air or a moderately tight bandage, with a small compress of dry lint or cloth, will be found sufficient to stop the bleeding. If these fail, a firm pad about half an inch thick, made of several layers of lint or rag, should be applied over the bleeding part, firmly kept on by a bandage or by pieces of adhesive plaster and a stream of cold water poured over all. When pressure cannot be employed, as when the bleeding comes from the nose or mouth, or from large surfaces, astringents must then be used along with cold applications (ice if it can be had). Powdered alum, tannin, matico, pernitrate of iron, turpentine, caustic, or even a hot iron, may each and all be tried.

Hæmorrhage caused by a wound in an artery is recognised by its bright red colour, as well as by its jerking and spouting character. If the artery so wounded is small, the bleeding may be stopped by the means above recommended; but if large, a ligature must be applied at once, as even in these cases the flow of blood may be arrested till medical aid arrives. If it is the leg or arm, a good-sized firm pad should be placed *above* the wound, over the principal artery, on the inside of the limb, where the artery can usually be felt pulsating, and tightened with a bandage until the bleeding ceases. The limb should be kept well raised up, and the patient perfectly quiet.

If a vein is wounded, the blood is blueish or black, and the bleeding is always easily stopped by the pressure of a pad; but the pad must be applied *below* or beyond the wound, on the side most distant from the heart. Pressure applied above the wound, would in this case increase or encourage the flow of blood. In all cases where the bleeding has been arrested, the pad, bandage, and dressings generally, must not be disturbed for at least three or four days, otherwise there is great risk of the bleeding returning.

Burns and Scalds.

A slight burn should be treated as an ordinary blister, viz., by the application of lint or cloth soaked in salad or sweet oil; or the part may be covered only with a layer of cotton wool and a light bandage. The leaf of the plantain-tree, smeared on its smooth side with castor or salad oil, is also one of the simplest and best applications for simple burns and blisters.

When the burn is extensive and severe, the same treatment as above should be adopted; or the parts may be freely covered with flour, or finely powdered chalk, or violet powder with cotton wool above, and a bandage over all. The dressings should not be disturbed for at least two or three days, when they are to be cautiously removed, assisting their removal, if necessary, by a bread or rice poultice or by soaking them with simple tepid water. This treatment must be continued until the parts assume a healthy appearance, or until all the blisters have disappeared. If the surface then looks clean, nothing will heal it up more rapidly than water-dressing covered with oil-silk.

In no case should the wrinkled skin be cut off or removed, but if the blister is large, it may be pricked with a needle before any application is used.

Burns of the face are best treated by applying salad oil with a feather or soft brush.

Extensive burns cause such an amount of depression as well as pain, that small quantities of wine or brandy must be given to keep up the strength. One grain of opium or twenty drops of laudanum (in the case of an adult) may be necessary to soothe and procure sleep. Beef-tea, chicken broth, and bread and milk should constitute the diet.

Caution.—When the fingers or toes are burnt, they should be so dressed as to prevent the contact of one with the other, otherwise firm cicatrices (bands of skin) will form between each finger or toe during the process of healing.

Snake Bites.

Venomous snakes abound in almost every part of India; and the fatal casualties that result from their bite are greater than from any other single cause of unnatural death, except drowning. In the Madras presidency alone, between eighteen and nineteen hundred deaths are annually reported as due to snake bite; while throughout the whole of India the number of deaths, from this one cause alone, is estimated at upwards of twenty thousand a year.

It is a common idea that venomous snakes will not bite unless themselves meddled with; but this is a mistake, for in by far the larger number of deaths recorded, the victims were known to have been bitten, while asleep during the night.

The parts most frequently bitten are the fingers, toes, and ankles; and the person bitten, if asleep, is at once aroused by the pain of the bite.

The pain is not severe at first, but increases in intensity afterwards, and extends rapidly upwards, the patient meanwhile complaining of extreme depression and faintness; the skin is covered with perspiration, a tightness in the chest and great difficulty in breathing are felt, and he gradually becomes comatose, and dies. Death usually takes place from one to six hours after the bite has been inflicted.

Although no antidote has yet been discovered for snake poison, yet some measures may be tried to save the life of persons under its influence. First apply a tight bandage or ligature a few inches above the wound; cut out the bitten part mercilessly, or freely scarify it with a lancet or penknife by small incisions all round. There need be no fear of the bleeding if the part cut out is on the fingers or toes; but if it continue too profuse, steady firm pressure with the thumb will arrest it. A red-hot iron, or nitric or carbolic acid may now be pressed into the bitten part, or applied at first if the patient will not submit to excision or incision. Sucking the wound should also be tried, but care must be taken that the party performing this operation has no broken surface on his mouth or lips.

Twenty drops of the strongest liquor ammoniæ, or eau de luce, diluted with water; or half a glass of brandy or rum, should be given at once, and repeated every fifteen minutes till reaction sets in. Mustard poultices, or a cloth soaked in liquor ammoniæ, should be applied over the stomach and heart; and the patient should be encouraged to walk about a little in order to combat the drowsiness which so commonly comes on.

It may be mentioned, that cases not unfrequently occur in which symptoms like those described are present when the person has been bitten by a snake *free from venom.* These cases soon recover if treated as above, and even with no treatment at all.

Scorpion and *centipede stings* are best treated by applying to the part, a paste made of ipecacuanha powder and liquor ammoniæ, or by the saturated solution of iodide of potassium in liquor potassæ. The juice of a fresh onion or garlic, and the bruised leaves of the jack-tree, applied as a poultice on the wound, till the smarting has ceased, are all remedies, which experience has proved to be successful.

In some parts of the West Indies these stings are treated as follows: two or three scorpions or centipedes are kept in a small bottle of rum; and when any one is bitten or stung, some of this rum is rubbed into the wound, and the cure is said to be almost instantaneous.

The pain of the scorpion sting, though most intense, seldom lasts longer than one hour. Children have died from it.

FRACTURES.

These are simple or compound, as they have an external wound leading to the broken bone or not.

Symptoms.—Pain, swelling, grating of the bones, and inability to move the limb.

In all cases, much good may, with care, be done by unprofessional persons until medical aid (which ought always to be sought) can be obtained. The treatment is comprised in *rest*, *position*, and *patience*.

Fracture of the Leg.—Straighten the limb by steady pulling, until it is brought, as nearly as possible, into the natural position; then apply splints (with moderately thick pads) extending, one on each side of the limb, from the knee to the heel, and retain them by a bandage from the foot upwards, or by two or three straps.

Fracture of Thigh.—Extend and straighten the limb as above, apply a padded splint from the armpit to a little beyond the heel, and another from the top of the thigh, inside to the heel, securing them both round the waist, thigh, and leg by bandages or straps.

Fracture of the Lower Arm.—Extend and straighten the limb as before, then bend the elbow at right angles; apply one padded splint on the inside of the arm, extending from the elbow to the ends of the fingers, and one on the outside from the elbow to the back of the hand, securing all with a bandage or straps.

Fracture of Upper Arm.—First treat as already described, then apply padded splints in front and behind, with a bandage or strap all over, then place the arm in a sling, allowing the elbow slightly to drop.

Fracture of Collar-bone.—In this injury the patient cannot raise his arm upwards to the head, the shoulder is flattened, and the broken bone is prominent.

Treatment.—A long cone-shaped firm pad should be placed well up in the armpit, the elbow should be pressed firmly down to the side of the body, and a bandage must then be applied over both shoulders, crossing in front and behind, and lastly round the chest, the whole arm being rendered immovable.

Fracture of Ribs.—The patient complains of a severe catch in drawing his breath, and also a grating sensation of one or more bones, which indeed may be felt by applying the hand over the part complained of.

Apply a bandage at least eight or ten inches wide, and about six or seven feet long, tightly round the chest from the pit of the stomach to the armpits, and keep the patient at perfect rest for at least one or two weeks afterwards.

Compound Fractures, or those with external wound.—Endeavour by gently extending the limb to replace or put back the broken ends of the bone, if they project externally; apply a piece of wetted lint or cloth, or a paste made with one part carbolic acid, twenty parts of sweet oil, and sufficient chalk; over either of these place a piece of oil-silk or waterproof sheeting, and then apply the splints and bandage as already described.

In all cases of fracture, care should be taken not to apply the splints too tightly, but with just sufficient firmness to keep the broken bones from grating or moving one upon the other.

The limb, when once set, and in good position, should not be disturbed unless there is much pain, or unless the bandage has loosened and the splints have shifted. If there is much pain and swelling, it is advisable to reduce them by cold water applications before applying the splints and bandages.

All splints and bandages should as a rule be kept on for five or six weeks.*

When the bones of the head are fractured, apply cold water cloths to the part, keep the patient perfectly quiet and on low diet, and lose no time in sending for medical aid, as these cases prove most serious.

DISLOCATIONS.

These accidents, if discovered and attended to at once, especially those of the shoulder, elbow, and hip-joint, may be repaired by unprofessional persons, although it is always advisable to obtain medical aid if within reach.

Dislocation of Shoulder.—The head of the bone is most frequently displaced into the armpit, the shoulder is flattened, the motions of the arm are abridged, its shape and contour are altered, and the elbow sticks out from the side. The patient also complains of great pain, and not unfrequently of numbness in the fingers. On raising the arm, the head of the bone can easily be felt as a hard round lump or ball in the armpit.

Treatment.—Place the patient on his back on the ground, and seat yourself by his side; then plant your unbooted heel firmly in the armpit; grasp the hand and wrist of the injured limb, pulling steadily towards you, while

* The ordinary bamboo split up, or thick millboard, forms an excellent substitute for the regular splint, and can be made of any size.

your heel is pushing in the opposite direction, and the head of the bone will glide into its socket with an audible snap.

Another method is to have your patient seated on a chair, and while pressing your bent knee (with the foot resting on the chair) well into the armpit, steadily depress the limb, when the head of the bone will glide into its place.

Dislocation of Elbow.—In this case there is much deformity, the joint is bent almost at a right angle, and is immovable, or nearly so.

Treatment.—Let one person take firm hold of the upper arm, and another of the wrist; then let each pull steadily against the other, while a third manipulates the joint by grasping it with his hands (the forefingers in front and thumbs behind). While this is being done, let the arm be bent suddenly (if possible unknown to the patient), and the bones will resume their natural position.

Dislocation of Wrist.—Apply extension and counter extension as above, till the contour and shape of the wrist are restored.

Dislocation of Fingers.—Apply round the upper part of the finger a loop of tape attached to a handkerchief, and pull steadily till the bone slips into its place.

Dislocation of Hip.—The limb is one and a half or two inches shorter than the other, the foot is turned inwards, the knee is slightly bent on the opposite thigh, and can with difficulty be moved from that position, and the hip is flattened.

Treatment.—Place the patient on his back on the floor, and whilst he is firmly held by the shoulders, grasp the foot and ankle firmly, and by gradual extension, parallel with the body, and rotation of the limb at the same time, the head of the bone will slip into its place, if the case is attended to immediately after the accident. But if some time has elapsed, more powerful measures must be adopted, and these can only be satisfactorily managed by a skilful surgeon, who should be called in without delay.

Dislocation of Jaw is generally produced by yawning; the mouth is open and cannot be shut, the chin projects and is depressed, saliva trickles over, and articulation is more or less affected or impossible.

Treatment.—Place both thumbs, well protected by cloth, far back on the last lower grinders, and press them firmly down, while the rest of the fingers outside raise the chin upwards and forwards, and the jaw will slip into its place.

In all cases of dislocation, after the bone is replaced, a bandage should be applied and retained for a few days, otherwise there is risk of displacement again occurring.

Extraction of Foreign Bodies.

From the Skin.—Needles, splinters of wood, etc., are frequently imbedded in the skin, and cause so much irritation and pain as to necessitate their removal. A very small incision or puncture will be quite sufficient to reach one end of the foreign body, which can then be pushed through the opening by pressure on the opposite end, and extracted or removed with the fingers or a small pair of pliers. Needles, if unbroken, are easily extracted by pressing the head (if detected) so as to push the point through the skin opposite.

From the Eye.—By keeping the eye still, and blowing the nose vigorously, foreign matter, such as sand or dust, may be washed away by the tears. If this fails, open the eyelids as wide as possible and examine the eye; if any foreign substance can be seen, it may be removed with a camel's hair pencil, or with the folded point of a soft handkerchief; or it may be washed away by gently injecting a small quantity of tepid water, or by placing an eye-cup with water over the open eye. But sometimes the foreign substance is lodged inside of the upper eyelid, and in that case this eyelid must be everted by placing a probe or bodkin on its edge, and drawing with the thumb and fingers the eyelashes upwards and backwards. The irritating body if there, can then be easily seen and removed in the manner described.

In the absence of any assistance, these foreign substances may be dislodged by raising the upper eyelid with the finger of one hand, then drawing it downwards and forwards over the under lid, afterwards removing the fingers, and thus allowing the lids to separate themselves.

From the Nostrils.—Breathing forcibly through the stuffed nostril, while the opposite one is compressed, will often succeed in dislodging the foreign body; syringing the nose with tepid water, or irritating it with snuff, will often produce the same effect. Failing these, introduce a small bent scoop, or the bent end of a hair pin, up the nostril, behind the offending substance, and, raising the handle, gently withdraw it, when the foreign body will pass out at the same time. These substances should never be pushed upwards and backwards into the throat.

From the Ears.—The same treatment as that last recommended for the nostrils may be here adopted, but more care is necessary to avoid injuring the drum of the ear. Simply syringing the ear will in most cases answer; the extrusion of the foreign body being assisted by keeping the affected side downwards. Insects may be dislodged by pouring a little oil into the ear.

From the Gullet.—Fish bones, needles, pins, and other small, sharp substances are frequently entangled at the back of the throat, while large solid bodies, such as portions of food, etc., are arrested and lodged in the passage further down. In both situations, and especially in the first, the fingers can usually reach the offending body to extract it. A sudden effort of swallowing water, or a good sized bolus of bread or rice, will sometimes dislodge the substance;

tickling the throat with a feather, so as to excite vomiting, may prove equally successful. If these measures fail, as they probably will when the foreign body is lodged down in the gullet, an instrument must be used to push it down. This may be made by securely fastening a bit of sponge to the end of a long piece of whalebone or thin rattan. The patient should be seated with his head thrown well backwards, so as to make the channel from mouth to stomach almost a straight line; the above instrument must then be pushed gently over the back of the tongue (during an effort at swallowing) into the gullet, until it comes into contact with the foreign body, which should then be cautiously pushed downwards into the stomach.

A painful sensation frequently continues for some time after a foreign substance has been dislodged from the throat or gullet, leading the patient to believe that the offending substance is still there. This sensation may be so great as to require the application of fomentations or a mustard poultice to relieve it.

Buttons, coins, brads, marbles, and other hard substances are often swallowed by children, and cause much alarm to the patient; but they generally pass through the bowels without doing any harm, and all that is required is a dose of castor oil to expedite their expulsion. When pins, needles, or other sharp-pointed bodies have been swallowed, the bowels *must not* be disturbed by purgatives.

From the Windpipe.—Foreign bodies here, if they are not dislodged quickly by the violent efforts nature herself exerts by coughing, cause serious and alarming symptoms. If they are not far down, they may be caught hold of, and removed by the fingers, or by a blunt hook. If this fails, and urgent symptoms, such as threatening suffocation, are present, the patient should be placed, face downwards, on a board placed on a table; the board should then be suddenly tilted forwards, the patient's back being at the same moment smartly tapped. This was the method which proved so successful, even after the windpipe was opened, in the well-known case of Brunel, the celebrated engineer, who inadvertently allowed a gold coin to drop into his windpipe. In all these cases professional aid should be instantly called in, as a surgical operation may be necessary to save life.

DROWNING.

This is the most common of all accidents in India, and in the list of deaths from unnatural causes, it occupies the first position. Wells and tanks are, with rare exceptions, the places in which this accident occurs, and every house and garden has one or more of these wells.

It not unfrequently happens that a body is removed from the well or tank within such a short time after immersion as to render it almost certain that life would be saved, if proper measures to restore animation were promptly adopted. These measures are simple, and the directions of the National Life Boat Association will be found most valuable if thoroughly carried out, as follows :—

To Restore Breathing.

To Clear the Throat.—Place the patient on the floor or ground with the face downwards, and one of the arms under the forehead, in which position all fluids will more readily escape by the mouth, and the tongue itself will fall forward, leaving the entrance into the windpipe free. Assist the operation by wiping and cleansing the mouth.

If satisfactory breathing commences, proceed to induce circulation and warmth. Rub the limbs upwards with firm grasping pressure and with energy, using handkerchiefs, etc. Wrap the whole body in blankets or other warm covering. Put bottles of hot water or heated bricks to the pit of the stomach, the armpits, between the thighs, and to the soles of the feet, the patient meanwhile being placed on his side, but not on his back. If there be only slight breathing, or no breathing, or if the breathing fail, then

To Excite Breathing, Turn the patient well and instantly on the side, supporting the head, and exciting the nostrils with snuff, hartshorn, or smelling salts, or tickle the throat with a feather, etc., if they are at hand. Rub the chest and face warm, and dash cold water, or cold and hot water alternately on them. If there be no success, lose not a moment, but instantly

To Imitate Breathing, Replace the patient on the face, raising and supporting the chest well on a folded coat, or other article of dress. Turn the body very gently on the side, and a little beyond, and then briskly on the face again, repeating these measures, cautiously, efficiently, and perseveringly, about fifteen times to the minute, or once every four or five seconds, occasionally varying the side.

By placing the patient on the chest, the weight of the body forces the air out; when turned on the side, this pressure is removed, and air enters the chest.

On each occasion that the body is replaced on the face, make uniform but efficient pressure, with brisk movement, on the back, between and below the shoulder blades, or bones, on each side, removing the pressure immediately before turning the body on the side.

During the whole of the operation, let one person attend solely to the movements of the head and of the arm placed beneath it.

The first measure increases the expiration, the second commences inspiration.

Should these efforts not prove successful in the course of four or five minutes, proceed to imitate breathing by Dr. Sylvester's method, as follows :—

Place the patient on the back on a flat surface, inclined a little upwards from the feet; raise and support the head and shoulders on a small firm cushion, or folded article of dress, placed under the shoulder blade.

Draw forward the patient's tongue and keep it projecting beyond the lips; an elastic band over the tongue and under the chin will answer the purpose, or a piece of string or tape may be tied round them, or by raising the lower jaw the teeth may be made to retain the tongue in that position. Remove all tight clothing from about the neck and chest, especially the braces.

To Imitate the Movements of Breathing.—Standing at the patient's head, grasp the arms just above the elbows, and draw the arms gently and steadily upwards above the head, and keep them stretched upwards for two seconds.

(*By this means air is drawn into the lungs.*)

Then turn down the patient's arms and press them gently and firmly for two seconds against the sides of the chest.

(*By this means air is pressed out of the lungs.*)

Repeat these measures alternately, deliberately, and perseveringly, about fifteen times in a minute, until a spontaneous effort to respire is perceived; immediately upon which, cease to imitate the movement of breathing, and proceed to *induce circulation and warmth.*

The above treatment should be persevered in for some hours, as it is an erroneous opinion that persons are irrecoverable, because life does not make its appearance, persons having been restored after persevering for many hours.

Cautions.—Prevent unnecessary crowding of persons round the body, especially if in an apartment. Avoid rough usage, and do not allow the body to remain on the back, unless the tongue is secured.

Under no circumstances hold the body up by the feet.

When consciousness returns, give the patient light fluid

food, with a little wine, and let him rest completely for at least twenty-four hours, as he may have a severe fever, and will then be confined to bed for some weeks.

POISONING.

In almost every case of poisoning the symptoms generally come on suddenly after eating or drinking, and they run their course so rapidly that prompt and active measures must be at once applied, even by unprofessional persons, while no time is lost in obtaining efficient medical assistance.

When poison is suspected, the stomach should be cleared out, without delay, by either of the following

Emetics.

Take of	Common salt . . .	one tablespoonful.	Mix.
	Mustard	one teaspoonful.	
or,			
	Powdered ipecacuanha .	twenty grains.	Mix.
	Tartar emetic . . .	one grain.	
or,			
	Sulphate of zinc . . .	twenty grains.	

The emetic should be mixed with a tumblerful of warm water, and repeated three times at intervals of ten minutes, till free vomiting is induced, assisting or exciting this act if necessary, by tickling the throat with a feather or the fingers.

OPIUM POISONING.

Opium, either solid or liquid, as in laudanum, morphia, chlorodyne, etc., causes, in poisonous doses, great drowsiness, deep stupor, quick breathing, rapid small pulse, and contraction of the pupil of the eye.

Treatment.—If the patient can be made to swallow, give

him one of the emetics recommended above, or if practicable, use the stomach pump; and after the stomach has been cleared out, give a tablespoonful of animal charcoal, mixed with water, every ten or fifteen minutes. Every possible effort must be made to keep the patient awake by trotting him about, splashing cold water over his head and shoulders, syringing the ears with water, applying snuff or ammonia to the nostrils, shaking and pinching him, and having tomtoms or other equally noisy instruments, sounded close to his ears. These measures must be persevered with until all symptoms of profound drowsiness have disappeared.

He may then have some strong coffee in small quantities; he should be kept warm, and allowed to have a short sleep of *about half an hour only*. A small quantity of brandy or sal volatile may be given during recovery, if the patient complains of much exhaustion, and a purgative of castor oil may be necessary afterwards.

Poisoning by stramonium, henbane, hemlock, and indeed almost all vegetable drugs, is treated in much the same way as the above.

Arsenic.

This poison produces symptoms very like those of cholera,—vomiting, purging, burning sensation in throat, great thirst, pain in stomach and bowels, cramp, and coldness of the extremities.

Treatment.—Give either of the above emetics at once; raw eggs and milk, or milk alone, should be given in frequent draughts, both before and after the vomiting, followed by large quantities of magnesia mixed with water. The best known antidote for arsenic is *hydrated sesquioxide* of iron, a preparation somewhat similar in composition to the yellow-coloured rust, which forms when iron is fully exposed to water and to air.

Corrosive sublimate, sugar of lead, copper, and some other common mineral poisons, produce symptoms more or less like those of arsenic, and are to be treated in the same way.

When vitriol or any other concentrated mineral acid has been taken in poisonous doses, the best antidotes are chalk, soda, or soapsuds.

In poisoning by prussic acid, a teaspoonful of sal volatile in a glass of water should be given immediately.

List of Medicines.

The following list includes almost every medicine or remedy that is referred to in the previous pages, or likely to be required for ordinary use.

Ammonia, Liquor
Aniseed, Oil of
Arnica, Tincture
Asafœtida, Tincture
Basilicon Ointment
Belladonna, Extract of
Blister Liquid
Calomel
Camphor
Carbolic Acid
Carbolic Soap
Castor Oil
Catechu, Tincture of
Caustic, Lunar
Chalk, Prepared Powdered
Chlorodyne
Cinnamon Powder
Cinnamon Tincture
Colocynth, Compound
Condy's Fluid
Cotton Wool
Cream of Tartar
Dover's Powder
Epsom Salts
Ether, Sulphuric or Chloric
Galbanum Plaster
Ginger, Essence of
Goulard Water
Gregory's Powder
Grey Powder
Hartshorn
Iodine, Tincture of
Ipecacuanha
Jalap
James's Powder
Juniper, Oil of
Kousso
Laudanum
Lint
Magnesia
Magnesia, Effervescing Citrate of
Mindereris Spirit
Nitre, Sweet Spirit of
Oil Silk
Opium, Powdered
Paregoric
Peppermint, Essence of
Plaster, Adhesive
Podophyllin
Potass, Chlorate of
Quinine Powder
Rhubarb
Saltpetre
Sal Volatile
Santonine
Soda, Carbonate of
Spirit of Wine
Sugar of Lead
Sulphate of Iron
Sulphate of Zinc
Sulphuric Acid
Taraxacum, Extract of
Tartar Emetic
Turpentine
Violet Powder

TABLE OF THE DOSES OF MEDICINES REQUIRED FOR DIFFERENT AGES.

AGE.	COMMON DOSE ONE DRAM.	PROPORTIONATE DOSE.
Under 3 months	$\frac{1}{15}$ of a dram.	4 grains.
6 „	$\frac{1}{12}$ „	5 „
1 year	$\frac{1}{8}$ „	$7\frac{1}{2}$ „
2 „	$\frac{1}{6}$ „	10 „
3 „	$\frac{1}{4}$ „	15 „
5 „	$\frac{1}{3}$ „	1 scruple.
10 „	$\frac{1}{2}$ „	$\frac{1}{2}$ dram.
15 „	„	2 scruples.
20 „	Common dose.	1 dram.
60 „	$\frac{11}{12}$ „	55 grains.
75 „	„	45 „

ILLUSTRATION.

Suppose the ordinary adult dose of the medicine (rhubarb for example) to be twenty grains, the proportionate dose for a child above two and under three years of age would be five grains, or one fourth.

DIRECTIONS FOR ADMINISTERING THE MEDICINES.*

Liquor Ammoniæ.

A powerful diffusible stimulant, most useful in cases of snake bite. Dose, twenty drops in a glass of water, frequently repeated. Externally it is occasionally used to produce a blister, and in combination with olive or camphor oil (one part of liq. ammon. to four parts of the oil) it forms an excellent liniment for sore throats, etc.

It forms the principal ingredient in eau-de-luce, and is used to increase the pungency of smelling salts.

Blistering Liquid

A convenient preparation for forming a blister quickly. The part to be blistered should be smeared or painted over with the liquid for a few minutes. and then covered with a layer of cotton wool. Blisters, if large or full, should be pricked with a clean needle, and a plantain (banana) leaf oiled, or lint soaked in salad oil, applied over them, or they may be covered with simple cerate spread on lint. Loose skin should not be cut away. The strangury, or difficulty in passing urine, frequently the result of a blister, may be remedied by copious drinks of rice or barley water, or linseed tea, and by hot fomentations over the bladder.

Calomel.

This medicine should not be given in regular or repeated doses, except under medical supervision. It is useful as an occasional purgative, and for this purpose the ordinary adult dose is four to six grains, alone, or combined with other purgatives, such as the compound extract of colocynth.

Calomel, in combination with an equal quantity of powdered camphor, destroys insects in foul festering sores; but even in these cases it must be used with caution.

* The doses specified are for adults. The proportionate doses for children may be ascertained by referring to the table, page 310.

CAMPHOR.

This medicine enters into the composition of several preparations (for internal and external use) in the Pharmacopœia, paregoric being the most important. It has been much extolled as a remedy for cholera if given early, thus :—Two drams of camphor dissolved in 1½ ounce of spirits of wine. Dose, two to four drops with rice water or syrup every five or ten minutes, till the purging or vomiting begin to abate.

Camphor julep or water is made by mixing a quarter of an ounce of camphor, in small pieces, with one pint of water. The bottle should be shaken occasionally for two days, and the liquid then filtered. A teaspoonful of sweet spirits of nitre added to the above causes a larger quantity of the camphor to be dissolved. Dose, half a wineglassful two or three times a day, as a gentle stimulant in cases of nervous depression, or when the stomach is irritable.

Camphor oil is made by dissolving, with the aid of gentle heat, a quarter of an ounce of camphor in two ounces of salad oil, forming a useful liniment to remove swelling after sprains, etc.; and when combined with strong liquor ammoniæ, in the proportion of four of camphor oil to one of ammonia, forms an excellent liniment for sore throat. Spirits of wine or brandy may be substituted for the salad oil in the above liniments.

PREPARED CHALK AND COMPOUND CHALK POWDER.

Antacid and astringent. Most useful for infantile diarrhœa, arising from teething or undigested milk; and may be either given alone in doses of four to five grains for a child under one year, or in the form of compound chalk powder or mixture.

Externally it is used in fine powder in the treatment of burns, and as a dusting powder in moist excoriations in children.

CHLORODYNE.

This deservedly popular medicine is most useful in many ailments. For diarrhœa, either simple or as the premonitory symptom of cholera; for colic, or pains in the stomach or bowels; for nausea and vomiting; for pains in the chest, or oppression in the breathing, as in asthma, etc.; for pains of a neuralgic character in the head, and for sleeplessness —this medicine, if judiciously administered, will be found most beneficial.

The only cautions to be observed are:—1. Not to repeat the dose at less intervals than two or three hours. 2. Not to give more than three or four doses during twenty-four hours without medical advice. 3. Not to give any at all if there is pain with a sense of fulness in the head, or if there is flushing of the face; and, 4. Not to continue the medicine if it disagrees with the patient, as it sometimes does.

Dose.—Twenty-five to thirty drops in half a wineglass of water; and for children, one drop for every year of age.

The following recipe will be found to answer all the purposes of the chlorodyne ordinarily sold as a patent medicine.

Take of	Chloroform	four drams.
	Sulphuric ether	two drams.
	Treacle	one dram.
	Mucilage of gum arabic . . .	one dram.
	Muriate of morphia	eight grains.
	Diluted hydrocyanic acid (2 p. c.) .	two drams.
	Oil of peppermint	four to six minims

Mix.

A still more easily prepared and convenient chlorodyne, and one quite as useful as the patent medicine, may be made thus:—

Take of	Chloroform	one dram.
	Essence of peppermint . . .	one dram.
	Sal volatile	one dram.
	Laudanum	one dram.
	Syrup of poppies or treacle . .	four drams

The dose of both these preparations is the same as that given. Chlorodyne should always be kept in *glass-stoppered* phials.

Carbolic Acid.

Used externally in the treatment of wounds, especially when there is much suppuration. It must be mixed with glycerine or with linseed oil, in the proportion of one part of the acid to twenty parts of the glycerine or oil. It is also used for skin eruptions, and proves beneficial in removing dandriff, or in allaying the irritation so often attendant upon cutaneous affections. For such cases it must be used in a very diluted form (one part of the acid to forty parts of oil or cerate). As a disinfectant it should be mixed with water (1 to 100), and is thus used for washing floors, utensils, and clothes, or indeed any place or thing in which foul matter exists.

Condy's Fluid.

This is chiefly used also as a disinfectant, and in the same manner as carbolic acid. It may be placed in saucers, sprinkled over the apartments, or cloths soaked in it may be hung up where contagious disease is present.

Two or three drops of the fluid, added to each gallon of water requiring purification, will render the water quite fit for drinking purposes.

Caustic (Lunar),

Chiefly used for external application to wounds unhealthy in appearance, or with redundant proud flesh (granulations). In wounds produced by the bite of a dog or cat or other animal, caustic should be immediately applied, pressing it well into the bitten part. Caustic is a remedy of great value in certain cases of persistent chronic dysentery, and also in some stages of purulent ophthalmia, but as a rule it ought in such cases to be used only under medical advice.

Castor Oil.

The simplest and safest of all purgatives for all ages. One or two teaspoonfuls are generally quite sufficient to relieve constipation. It may be taken alone or floating on water; or it may be rubbed up (for infants) with a little tepid water and sugar. It is a valuable remedy in those cases of diarrhœa or dysentery which are caused by constipation or by irritating substances in the bowels (see pages 257 and 268). Externally it soothes the irritation produced by skin eruptions, and allays the itching, stinging sensation caused by musquito bites.

Cream of Tartar.

An agreeable cooling purgative and diuretic. One teaspoonful of cream of tartar, one tablespoonful of sugar, and one lime or lemon cut up, mixed with a pint of water, forms the "imperial drink" so refreshing in hot climates and in fever. In combination with an equal part of sulphur, it is a most useful and safe gentle aperient for those affected with hæmorrhoids, or piles, the dose of the preparation being one teaspoonful in milk or water.

Dover's Powder.

A valuable sudorific or diaphoretic, anodyne and sedative; used in fever, diarrhœa, dysentery, cough, rheumatism, colic, and pain anywhere, except in the head. The adult dose is from five to ten grains, alone, or with four grains James' Powder, when the object is to promote perspiration. This dose taken at bedtime, along with a large draught of warm barley or rice water, will often prove effectual in cutting short a common cold or simple fever.

Emetic Tartar,

Chiefly used as an emetic in doses of one grain. It is generally combined with twenty grains of powdered ipecacuanha mixed with a glass of water, followed a few minutes afterwards by copious draughts of tepid water. If vomiting does not soon occur, it may be excited by tickling the throat with a feather, etc.

The above dose is recommended at the outset of fever or in the cold stage of ague, if the tongue is foul or coated; it may be also used to remove from the stomach any indigestible substance or poison, when no more speedy emetic is at hand.

ETHER (SULPHURIC OR CHLORIC).

Stimulant and antispasmodic; specially useful for relieving nervous headache, depression of spirits, hysterical symptoms, spasmodic asthma, colic, etc. Dose, half-dram to one dram in plain or peppermint water, and may be combined with sal volatile or camphor water.

EPSOM SALTS.

Purgative in large, and alterative in small doses. Dose, one dram to one ounce; seldom used as a purgative in India, and ought on no account to be taken as such during the prevalence of cholera.

As a simple tonic aperient, to act gently on the bowels and to assist in removing impurities from the blood, the following mixture is recommended:—

TONIC APERIENT.

Take of	Epsom salts	one ounce.
	Sulphate of iron . . .	half-dram.
	Sulphate of quinine . . .	one scruple.
	Diluted sulphuric acid . .	two drams.
	Water	eight ounces.

Mix, and take a tablespoonful two or three times a day.

GINGER (ESSENCE).

Aromatic and stimulant; dose fifteen to twenty drops in water, to relieve flatulency, colic, and to assist the action of such purgatives as magnesia, rhubarb, etc.

Gregory's Powder,

Composed of magnesia, one ounce; rhubarb, two drams; and ginger, one dram. One of the safest, simplest, and most efficacious of all purgatives, specially useful for children, where there is irritation in the bowels with acidity of the stomach. Dose for adults, two scruples to one dram, *shaken* with about half a glass of plain or peppermint water; for a child one or two years old—ten to fifteen grains.

Grey Powder.

A preparation of mercury with chalk; to be used cautiously and rarely, except under medical advice. Most commonly given to children for dysentery, diarrhœa (when the stools are clay-coloured), and fever. It is generally combined with Dover's powder, James' powder or carbonate of soda. Dose for a child five years old, three grains.

Ipecacuanha.

Emetic in large, and expectorant in small doses. As an emetic the adult dose is twenty grains, given alone, or with one grain tartar emetic. This dose may be taken at the commencement of fever, and those diseases generally where the tongue is coated, or foul, or where there are other indications of a foul stomach.

In tropical dysentery, no single remedy proves more frequently successful (see Dysentery, page 265).

As an expectorant, it is given in the more convenient form of ipecacuanha wine for catarrh, bronchitis, hooping cough, asthma, and those affections of the chest generally where it is desirable to "loosen the phlegm," so as to facilitate its expulsion or expectoration. The adult dose of ipecacuanha wine as an expectorant, is one to two drams, alone or combined with honey or syrup of squills. For the occasional dry cough of children it is especially useful, and for this purpose the following simple mixture is recommended :—

Cough Mixture.

Take of	Ipecacuanha wine . . .	half-ounce.
	Antimonial wine . . .	half-ounce.
	Syrup of squills or tolu . .	one ounce.

Mix : dose for a child five years old, a small teaspoonful in barley water two or three times a day.

Powdered ipecacuanha made into a paste with liq. ammoniæ or liq. potassæ applied externally, relieves the severe pain produced by the sting of scorpions, centipedes, etc.

Jalap.

An active purgative ; relieves constipation due to a torpid or loaded condition of the bowels ; best given in combination with other substances, as follows :—

Purgative Powder.

Take of	Magnesia	one dram.
	Rhubarb	fifteen grains.
	Jalap	fifteen grains.
	Ginger	four grains.

In the form of compound powder of jalap it is used for certain kinds of dropsy, the dose of this preparation being one to two drams.

James' Powder.

Sudorific, febrifuge, and sedative ; given in fever to promote perspiration, and to reduce the frequency of the pulse.

Dose, from four to six grains, alone or with Dover's powder, quinine, etc. It should be given with syrup, honey, or jelly, *not* with water.

Laudanum, or Tincture of Opium.

Narcotic and anodyne ; most useful in diarrhœa, dysentery, the first stage of cholera, colic, and for relieving pain generally wherever situated, for procuring rest, and allaying irritability of stomach.

It should not be given, without medical advice, to persons with tendency to determination of blood to the head, or to those suffering from congestive headache.

Dose for adults, fifteen to twenty drops; and for children, one drop for every year of age.

Externally, it is valuable in relieving pain, and may be applied by friction, or by laying a piece of lint or cloth soaked in it, over the part affected; or the laudanum may be combined with an equal quantity of chloroform, or three parts more of soap liniment or camphor oil.

Two or three drops locally applied often give relief to earache or toothache.

Laudanum is also used with great benefit, by injection into the bowels in cases of dysentery attended with great straining, the dose being the same as that internally.

MAGNESIA.

A safe and gentle purgative, especially for children, when there is irritation in the bowels with acidity of stomach. It is particularly useful in those cases of infantile diarrhœa, caused by undigested milk in the stomach and bowels, and for this purpose it is best given in the form of a carminative mixture, as follows:—

Take of	Magnesia	two drams
	Rhubarb	five grains.
	Sal volatile	twenty drops.
	Tincture of asafœtida . .	ten drops.
	Essence of aniseed . . .	ten drops.
	Dill or peppermint water . .	two ounces.

Dose, a small teaspoonful, two, three, or four times a day.

Magnesia in small doses sometimes proves beneficial in those eruptions of the skin (pimples) more especially about the nose, chin, and forehead, which are not unfrequently caused by acidity of stomach. Dose of magnesia for adults, one dram mixed with water or milk.

PAREGORIC.

A preparation containing opium and camphor, etc., one ounce of paregoric containing one grain of opium. Chiefly used for coughs or simple catarrh; most useful in allaying the tickling sensation in the windpipe which provokes cough and disturbs respiration.

Dose, one to two drams, with simple syrup or honey, or it may be combined with expectorant doses of ipecacuanha wine.

ESSENCE OF PEPPERMINT.

Cordial and carminative; relieves flatulency, puffiness of stomach, and griping. Dose, fifteen to twenty drops.

QUININE.

Tonic, febrifuge, and antiperiodic. As a tonic it is beneficial in all cases of debility, however produced; it promotes digestion and secretion, gives tone to the heart in constitutions enfeebled from disease or from climate, and the pulse becomes smaller but stronger under its use. It may be given with wine, or combined with iron if there is pallor of the features.

As a febrifuge it is a specific, and no remedy is equal to it in those fevers and other diseases, the attacks of which come on in paroxysms or at fixed intervals; even in fevers, where there is no distinct remission, it is often used with the greatest benefit.

The best time for its administration is during the remission or intermission, or when the fever has somewhat abated, when the skin is moist and the pulse soft. For ague it should then be given in full doses,—fifteen to twenty grains in a wineglassful of water, with half a dram diluted sulphuric acid, or the juice of one small lime; and this dose may be repeated two or three times during twenty-four hours, or until some degree of deafness or uneasiness in the head is complained of. As a rule, quinine should not be given when there is high fever, when the pulse is quick and full, or when the stomach is foul. The efficacy of quinine in fever is ensured by previously giving an emetic, or a simple purgative, or both, if there are any indications of disordered stomach and bowels. Quinine should not be continued if there is vomiting, severe headache, flushing of the face, or delirium.

For tic-douloureux and neuralgia, wherever situated, quinine is invaluable, and may be given in doses varying from two to five grains, alone or with five drops tincture of aconite.

Quinine is also believed to possess some value in preventing ague, and many persons living in malarious districts, take with their meals one grain of quinine to counteract the effects of the malaria.

In persons who are liable to be affected with crops of boils, so common in India, a full dose (ten grains) of quinine taken immediately on their threatening to appear will sometimes arrest their progress.

Dose of quinine as a tonic, one to three grains; as a febrifuge and antiperiodic, five to twenty grains.

RHUBARB.

A mild purgative in full doses and an astringent in small doses. When used alone as a purgative, the dose is twenty grains, but as such, it is generally combined with magnesia and ginger, forming Gregory's powder, or with jalap and carbonate of soda. In dyspepsia attended with flatulency and an irritable state of the bowels, five grains of rhubarb, with the same quantity of carbonate of soda and one or two grains of ginger, taken once a day, will be found very useful.

In doses of one or two grains, rhubarb acts as an astringent, and proves beneficial in obstinate cases of diarrhœa in children.

SAL VOLATILE.

A diffusible stimulant and antispasmodic; relieves nervous headache, giddiness, fainting, lowness of spirits, and hysterical symptoms generally, when produced by debility or any depressing cause. Dose, twenty-five to forty drops in half a glass of plain or camphor water. In cases of snake bite, or scorpion sting, it may be given in the above dose every fifteen or twenty minutes, to rouse the patient from extreme depression.

SALTPETRE OR NITRE.

Diuretic and febrifuge; given in doses of from five to ten grains it promotes the secretion of urine in dropsies, its action being improved by other diuretics, as cream of tartar, sweet spirits of nitre, etc. It is most useful in encouraging perspiration in fever, and, when combined with small doses (half dram) of Epsom salts, it has a beneficial effect in cutaneous eruptions (pimples) on the face.

Externally it is used with an equal quantity of sal ammoniac, dissolved in water, as a cooling lotion, for sprains attended with pain and swelling, and in the form of sal prunella balls it is an excellent remedy for hoarse sore throat.

SANTONINE.

One of the best of all remedies for removing round worms from the intestines. Dose for adults, five to seven grains, given at bedtime; the same quantity early next morning, followed one hour afterwards by a dessert-spoonful of castor oil. The dose for a child one year old is, one to one and a half grains, repeated as above.

It is also useful for removing the small thread worms which infest the lower part of the bowels of children, and for this purpose three grains, dissolved in half a wineglass ful of water, should be injected into the bowels.

Santonine frequently causes the urine to be stained of a deep reddish colour, and the vision is sometimes so affected as to make all objects appear of a greenish yellow tint.

SODA (CARBONATE OF).

Antacid. Arrests acidity of the stomach and the flatulence caused by it; most useful in heartburn and in those cases of dyspepsia which are attended with sour eructations and flatulency. Dose, from fifteen to twenty grains.

The ordinary effervescing draught is made by dissolving half a dram of carbonate of soda in half a tumbler of water, and adding twenty grains tartaric acid, or a dessert-spoonful of lime juice.

SUGAR OF LEAD.

Astringent and sedative; especially useful in obstinate diarrhœa and dysentery, and also for hæmorrhages from the stomach, bowels, or lungs. Dose, four to six grains, in a tablespoonful of water, with a teaspoonful of vinegar.

Externally, it is used as a lotion, for bruises and sprains, as well as a collyrium for the eye, in which latter case it must be used with caution.

SULPHATE OF ZINC.

A safe and speedy emetic, producing immediate vomiting, in doses of fifteen to twenty grains, and specially useful in cases of poisoning. As a safe lotion for simple ophthalmia, with discharge from the eyes, ten to twenty grains may be dissolved in six ounces of plain or rose water.

SWEET SPIRITS OF NITRE.

Diuretic, febrifuge, antispasmodic, and stimulant; promotes the flow of urine, encourages perspiration, and is useful in hysteria and in simple catarrh. It may be given alone in doses of one dram, or may be combined with other diuretics, as nitre, squill, etc., or with ipecacuanha wine and paregoric when used for children's coughs.

Tincture of Catechu.

The simplest and safest of all astringents for diarrhœa, resulting from a relaxed state of the system generally, from injudicious diet, from suppressed perspiration, or as the premonitory symptoms of cholera.

Dose, one dram, either alone or combined with aromatics, opiates, etc., as in the recipes pages 256 and 263.

As a safe and efficacious remedy for simple diarrhœa in young children, the following is recommended :—

Astringent Mixture.

Take of Tincture of catechu . . . . four drams.
Compound chalk mixture . . one ounce and a half.
Mix, and give one teaspoonful after each loose motion.

Laudanum or Chlorodyne (one drop for every year of age) may be added to each dose of the above, if diarrhœa persists.

SUPPLEMENT

ON THE

MANAGEMENT OF CHILDREN IN INDIA.

DURING the earlier years of life, that is till the age of seven or eight, European children, enjoy on the whole, as good health on the plains of India as they do in England They are less liable to severe attacks of such diseases as scarlatina, diphtheria, measles, hooping cough, etc., and when they do suffer from them, the attacks and the secondary effects are generally much less serious, while the mortality is much less also.

It is during the first year of life that the European child requires the greatest care and watchfulness; not merely such as are required in England, but specially with a view to guarding against the mischievous practices too often resorted to by native female servants,—amahs and ayahs,—practices which too often seriously damage the health of the child, and not unfrequently even sacrifice it altogether.

Taking the infant then from its birth, it may be laid down as a general rule, from which there are but rare exceptions, that it ought not to be nursed oftener than once every two hours during the first two months,—once every three hours during the next two months,—and once every four hours afterwards, until the teeth begin to appear, and it has become able to take more solid food. More children are unhealthy, weak, and ailing, from being irregularly fed, than from any other cause. They are fed sometimes every few minutes, awake or asleep, whenever they cry, or appear restless or uneasy, under the mistaken impression, that this will cause them to grow up robust and healthy. Nothing, however, can be more injurious, and the reason is so obvious, that it is surprising that mothers, otherwise intelligent, do not at once perceive it: the admission of fresh milk into the infant's stomach, while the previous milk is undergoing digestion, impeding, if it does not arrest, the digestive process altogether.

The half-digested milk, in the form of curd, is, under such circumstances, either vomited, or passes without further change into the bowel, causing in nine cases out of ten, griping, flatulence, diarrhœa, dysentery, and not unfrequently convulsions. The infant in fact, so far from being nourished, is simply being slowly poisoned. It is all important then, that the nursing should be so systematically arranged that the infant should have its food at fixed times, and only after the definite intervals, already *specified*, in accordance with its age.

If the infant wakes up and cries in the intervals, on no account let it then be nursed, but let it have some sweetened milkwarm water either from a feeding bottle or from a spoon.

The young mother must guard against the officious and mischievous practices of native nurses, who too often persist in feeding the baby whenever it cries, even within half an hour of the previous feeding; the poor little infant is often kept constantly at the breast at all hours of the day and night, the nurse, and perhaps even the mother, being quite oblivious of the fact, that the crying is as frequently an indication of repletion as of hunger. During the night, an infant should not be nursed as frequently as during the day. Twice or thrice in the course of the night are sufficient at first, but after the first month, twice is quite enough, that is, late at night and early in the morning. Frequent nursing during the night is most injurious to mother and child. It interferes also with sleep, doubly here "nature's sweet restorer," for it is during sleep that nature is busy at work in storing up the material for the benefit of the infant. In the above remarks, it is taken for granted that the infant is solely nursed by its mother; and every mother, if she is tolerably healthy in body and mind, ought to nurse her own child. It frequently happens, however, that from feeble health, or owing to an attack of illness or other causes, the mother is either entirely unable to nurse, or her supply of breast milk is insufficient in quantity or poor in quality. It is under such circumstances as these that the all important question arises: Shall a wet nurse be employed, or shall the infant be brought up by hand feeding?

If the mother is at all able to nurse her infant, however imperfectly, that is, if she is healthy and her milk is of good quality, though not sufficient in quantity, she certainly ought to continue to do so, even if she has no hope of being able to go on permanently. The breast milk can be supplemented by other food to be hereafter specified. The infant will generally thrive well under this method, while the mother will have the satisfaction of performing a duty which she naturally feels most reluctant to relegate to another.

If, however, the deficiency in the mother's milk is due to impaired health, or if there is a total inability to nurse, owing to the state of the breast, or any other cause likely to affect the infant's health, then the safest and wisest course unquestionably is to engage a wet nurse, and the earlier this is done the better.

In selecting an amah, or dhai (wet nurse), the family medical attendant ought to be consulted, if possible; but as there are many Anglo-Indian parents far beyond the reach of any doctor, a few rules and hints may be given here, which may assist in making a judicious selection.

1st. The age of the amah should as nearly as possible correspond with that of the mother, except where the mother is either very young or very mature, when the amah ought to be a few years older than the first, and some years younger than the second.

2nd. The amah's own child should be as nearly as possible the same age as the child for whom she is engaged.

3rd. The general appearance and proportions of the body of both mother and amah should resemble each other as closely as possible, except when there are in the former manifest indications of impaired health. An amah may, however, have all the appearance externally of robust health, and yet turn out to be quite unfit for her duties.

If she is moderately plump, has a fresh clear complexion, clear cheerful eyes, deep red coloured lips, well formed moderately firm breasts, with nipples free from soreness or eruption, she possesses all the external indications of a suitable amah. "Violence of temper, sluggish indolence, or extreme nervousness of disposition, intemperance, want of truthfulness, inattention to order and cleanliness, and other moral defects, are insuperable objections when they are conspicuous. Sound health, a robust constitution, freedom from any hereditary taint, cheerfulness and presence of mind, orderly, neat, and temperate habits, patient kindliness and good humour, and above all, spontaneous activity and innate liking for children are of the very first importance." But perhaps the best of all tests is the condition of the amah's own child. If it is robust, plump, active, bright and clean, with a spotless skin, the indications are decidedly favourable.

But in thus judging, be sure that the child produced is in reality the offspring of the amah. It is no uncommon thing for amahs to borrow children from their friends, in order to deceive the lady engaging them, or even the doctor appointed to examine them. I have known women present themselves as amahs, when in reality they were either pregnant themselves, or when their own child was upwards of a year old, and when they had little or no power to nurse a baby.

In all cases the amah should be made to draw off half a

wineglassful of her milk at her first examination *in the presence of the mistress*, every attention being at the time paid to the nature of the flow. The good quality of the milk may be judged of, by the absence of any odour, by its blueish white color, by its light cloudy appearance when dropped into water, and by its not sinking to the bottom in thick drops.

The amah, before entering upon her duties, should be ordered to have herself thoroughly washed with soap and water, she must be forbidden to chew betel, to smoke, or to drink toddy or arrack, or any other intoxicating beverage. The greatest care and watchfulness are required on the part of the mother, in order to ensure that her child shall receive not only its due amount of nourishment, but also that it receives it in the regular, definite and systematic manner already referred to.

In the absence of any other indication of a good flow of milk from the amah, the mother, when at all suspicious or doubtful, should occasionally judge for herself, by making the amah, in her presence, draw off some milk into a glass before commencing to nurse the child. I have known amahs persist in placing a child to the breast, when there was, not only no milk there, but when there was also no possibility of any being then there. Indeed, some of the worst cases of infantile wasting that I have seen in India, were discovered to be the result of simple starvation only. The infant was placed frequently to the breast by the amah, when its fruitless efforts to obtain nourishment soon exhausted it and lulled it into sleep; the amah well knowing that she was useless as such, but leading the mother all the time to believe that she had plenty of milk, and that the child's sleep was that of satiety.

But perhaps the most pernicious of all habits of these amahs, is that of administering narcotic drugs to infants with the object of inducing sleep, and thus relieving them of some part of their duty. The bazaars of India and even the gardens round European houses, offer facilities for obtaining any quantity of the most dangerous drugs, and it is astonishing how well their noxious qualities are known to natives generally. I have known instances, where the amah or the ayah for obvious reasons, has given narcotics, concealed under one of their finger nails, under the pretence that they were quieting the child by allowing it to suck her finger. Suspicion may fairly be excited, whenever the child becomes listless, apathetic, or disinclined to take the breast, without any apparent or obvious cause, and the correctness or otherwise of this suspicion, may be tested by removing the baby at once from the care of the amah or ayah, for one or two days, giving some simple milk and water in the meantime. If the suspicion prove to be well grounded, the amah must be dismissed forthwith, and another one substituted, or if the baby is healthy and not too young, recourse may be had to artificial or hand feeding.

HAND FEEDING.

Many children thrive uncommonly well when brought up even entirely by hand. The mother may be quite unfit to nurse, and a suitable substitute may not be procurable. Moreover, some mothers have a deep-rooted and unconquerable prejudice against entrusting their infants to native wet nurses.

In order to ensure success in hand feeding, two things are essential: 1st. A healthy condition of the infant; for if at all feeble and delicate, hand feeding will probably fail, and do more harm than good. 2nd. Unremitting care and attention, as well as some self denial, on the part of the mother, to see that her infant is regularly and systematically fed, that the food is in every respect properly prepared, and that the feeding bottles are kept scrupulously clean. Very few native servants can be entirely trusted with this duty, without the direct personal supervision of the mother, for they can never be made to bestow that attention to punctuality, cleanliness and exactness in quantity, which are essentially necessary to success. It is especially during the first two months, that there is the greatest difficulty and risk in hand feeding. If the mother, therefore, is at all able to nurse her infant during this early period, however imperfectly, she ought to do so, as before stated.

The great secret, if secret it can be called, in selecting the most suitable food for an infant, is to imitate nature as closely as possible. Human milk is of course the most perfect of all foods for infants, and there is no other food with precisely the same constituents. The nearest approach to it is found in the milk of the ass, and when procurable, it ought always to be given. Goat's milk stands next, and last of all the milk of the cow. In India there is seldom any difficulty in procuring either an ass or a goat in milk, and there is little or no trouble in keeping them. In either case, ass or goat, the milk should be given fresh drawn, and not after it has been allowed to cool, but neither the first nor the last drawn milk should be given. It should be mixed with an equal quantity of water for an infant under one month old, gradually diminishing the quantity of water as the child grows older. When neither ass' nor goat's milk is procurable, good cow's milk must be used, and if possible the milk of the same cow. If the infant is being nursed by the mother, but not sufficiently for its requirements, the cow's milk may be commenced by giving one teaspoonful with one or two wine-glassfuls of lukewarm water. This should be continued for two or three days, when the quantity of milk should be doubled, so increasing the proportion of milk every two or three days, till the proportion is one part (half a wine-glassful) of milk to three parts (one and a half wine-glassful) of water. The great mistake, and the almost invariable cause of failure, is commencing at once with such a large quantity of milk, that the delicate stomach is unable to digest it. The milk is probably condemned forthwith, instead of the injudicious system in giving it. By adopting the graduated or progressive plan above recommended, if the milk disagrees, it will in all likelihood do so at the very outset, by causing flatulence, diarrhœa, or vomiting, when it can at once be stopped. If, however, it causes neither of these symptoms, which are really the only indications of its unsuitableness, the proportion of milk to water above specified, viz., one to three should be continued till the end of the first month. Equal parts of milk and water may then be given during the second month, and the proportion of water may then be gradually diminished and replaced by milk till about the sixth month, when pure undiluted milk should be given and continued till the first teeth make their appearance.

As a rule milk fresh from the cow is best, though occasionally it will be found, that milk that has been simply scalded (or even boiled and skimmed after cooling) will agree better. As fresh milk during the hotter months of the year in India very soon turns sour, it is advisable to have that portion which is reserved for the night, scalded or boiled, and skimmed. Even although some slight diarrhœa or flatulence may come on while cow's milk is being given to an infant, the milk need not be too hastily condemned. A teaspoonful of lime water (made from lime shells) with each wineglassful of milk may often be of great benefit to remedy this. Occasionally constipation of an obstinate character occurs, but this is easily rectified by occasional doses of castor oil, or calcined magnesia, or by both combined, or by gentle friction over the centre of the abdomen with castor oil, or by a soap suppository. See page 349.

The milk should always be sweetened with good crystallized white sugar, or with the sugar of milk sold by chemists.

The condensed milk, Swiss or Aylesbury, is a very convenient substitute for fresh milk, when such cannot be procured at all, or in sufficient quantity, but it cannot be relied upon, as the sole article of food for any length of time.

No other food than milk, should be given until the child is about six months old, or till the first teeth appear. Farinaceous substances given during the early months, are positively injurious, and must therefore be religiously avoided; but after the age of six months they may be commenced, gradually at first, the food consisting of a mixture of some farinaceous substance with the milk, twice a day only. The quantity may be steadily increased until all the meals are prepared with it. Corn flour, Robinson's patent groats, baked wheat flour, "semola" and bread crumb, are about the safest and most nourishing farinaceous food that can be given. Arrowroot, sago, and tapioca, all contain such comparatively small proportions of genuine flesh-forming nutriment, that they should never be used constantly. A child fed exclusively on these last-named substances, will commonly get fat, but it certainly will not get strong and healthy. The mother is too often deceived by this obese condition of her infant; and no one is more eloquent in praise of these very substances as food, than the ayah, who will do all she can to persuade her mistress, that they are the very best foods for "baby."

Almost all the substances advertised as "Food for Infants" are neither more nor less than rice flour, arrowroot, potato starch, baked flour, etc., sweetened with sugar. Some of them are very good, but the objection to them is our want of knowledge of their exact constituents. It is much better therefore to give such food, the precise nature of which is perfectly well known. Baked flour, corn flour, crumb of bread, and Robinson's patent groats afford ample scope from which to select. Flour is baked by placing it in an oven, or on a clean dry frying pan over a fire, until it becomes of a light brown colour. It is then reduced to powder and kept in tins. Crumb of bread may be baked in the same way. Another good way of preparing the flour, is to tie up some ordinary wheat flour tightly in a cloth, and boil it for three or four hours in water; if then taken out, and the outer rind removed, the inside, which will be found dry, may be reduced to powder.

In preparing the food, mix one tablespoonful of either of the above substances, with as much cold water, as will bring it into the consistence of cream; then pour over it about three-quarters of a pint of boiling milk, or milk and water, and boil it for ten minutes, stirring all the time, then add about a dessert-spoonful of sugar. Food is made with rusks, by boiling them for an hour in water, after which they must be well beaten up, and mixed with the milk, sweetened with sugar. But perhaps the simplest, safest, and handiest of all farinaceous food for children is the ordinary stale bread crumb. Cut up the bread in pieces, free from crust, and pour boiled milk over this, keeping the vessel covered for about five minutes.

The food recommended by Liebig (and known by his name) as equivalent in nourishing property to that of human milk, is prepared as follows:—one tablespoonful of wheaten flour, one dessert-spoonful of malt flour, seven and a half grains bicarbonate of potash, and one ounce of water, are to be well mixed; five ounces, or two and a half wine-glassfuls of milk, are then added, and the whole put on a gentle fire. When the mixture begins to thicken, it is removed from the fire, stirred during five minutes, heated and stirred again, till it becomes quite fluid, and finally made to boil; when, after being passed through a sieve, it is ready for use. By boiling it a few minutes it loses all taste of the flour. When the food is properly prepared, it is as sweet as milk, and any further sweetening is unnecessary. After boiling, it will keep twenty-four hours without undergoing any change.

If constipation is troublesome, the baked flour may be mixed, previous to being baked, with oatmeal or Robinson's patent barley, double the quantity of flour to oatmeal being used. A teaspoonful of this compound, boiled with about two wine-glassfuls of milk or milk and water, and sweetened, forms a most excellent and nourishing food for infants.

If the bowels are relaxed, good arrowroot may then be given, and should be prepared as follows:—Mix a table-spoonful of arrowroot with sufficient cold water to make it of the consistence of cream, then pour over it boiling toast-water, till it becomes the thickness of a moderately firm jelly. Recently boiled milk should then be added in sufficient quantity to thin the food, according to the age of the child. Another simple food, when the bowels are inclined to be relaxed, is prepared by mixing a dessert-spoonful of fine flour with about two wine-glassfuls of water; this should be poured into the same quantity of milk, as soon as the latter begins to boil, stirred for a few minutes, and sweetened in the usual way.

In bringing up an infant by hand, the feeding bottle ought always, during the earlier months, to be used. It is the most natural, and satisfies and comforts the child in a way no other method will do. Moreover, the very action of sucking, causes the food to be taken more slowly and regularly, and is less likely to cause the troublesome flatulence, which is so frequently induced, when the food is given by the spoon or by "boat."

The best feeding bottle is that known as "Stocker's Patent Crystal Union," manufactured by Brooks & Co., London. It is distinguished from all others by an ingenious crystal union between the nipple and the top of the India rubber tube. The transparency of this union enables the nurse to see at once, whether or not the food is passing freely from the bottle, along the entire length of the tube, without removing the nipple from the child's mouth.

As the success of hand feeding depends to a great extent on these bottles and their tubes being kept scrupulously clean, they ought never to be entrusted entirely to native servants. Every time that they have been used the tubes should be immediately afterwards taken to pieces, the nipples detached, and the whole well cleaned, by passing fresh clean water through them, and using the little brush sold for this purpose. They should then be placed in a vessel (a finger-glass answers well) containing clean water, and allowed to remain there till again required. The bottle should be well washed out immediately after being used, (once a day with tea leaves), keeping the bottle full of water till again required. Too much care cannot be taken in this respect, for the least particle of milk, unremoved from the tubes or bottle may, and often does, cause the subsequent food to be refused, or, if taken, to disagree; and few native servants will ever pay the requisite attention to these details unless supervised by the mistress.

The proper quantity of food for an infant must be determined by its age and constitution. Some infants require considerably more than others of the same age; while the quantity which can be easily digested by an infant when in health, will disagree with it when sick. Above all things, over-feeding must be avoided. This is the most common cause of flatulence, vomiting, and diarrhœa, and it is, further, the most frequent cause of failure in hand-feeding. It is the safer course to give rather too little than too much, for the obvious reason that the little will be well digested, and afford more nourishment, than the quantity when given in excess. The infant will, as a general rule, take just what it wants, and then it will withdraw its mouth from the nipple. Be guided then by this indication, and do not force it to continue. Do not be afraid of its starving itself; the danger lies in the opposite direction.

As a summary to the preceding remarks, the following rules, (modified to suit the climate of India), drawn up by a committee of the Obstetrical Society of London, will be found of great value as a guide to management of infants.

WASHING.—Cleanliness is of the utmost importance to

the health of all children. Healthy infants should have a warm bath night and morning. The body should be cleansed from head to foot, with a sponge or flannel, and then quickly dried with a soft warm towel. After three or four months, the heat of the water should be gradually lowered, but it is not advisable to use quite cold water for very young children.

CLOTHING.—The clothing of infants should be light and soft, and arranged so as not to interfere with the free play of their limbs. All tight bandaging should be avoided.

VENTILATION.—Pure fresh air is of extreme importance to children. The rooms in which they sleep should be as large and airy as possible, and, when not occupied, the windows should be opened freely and frequently.

SLEEP.—Unless the weather be cold, or the child premature and feeble, it is desirable that it should, from an early period, sleep away from the mother or nurse, in a cradle or cot, care being taken that it is warmly covered. For the first few months, a healthy infant will naturally spend the greater part of its time in sleep. Up to three years of age, a midday sleep is beneficial. In sleeping, as in feeding, regularity is of the utmost importance, and the child should be put to bed at stated times. Infants should be put directly into their cot or cradle, after being fed, and not get into the habit of being nursed to sleep in the arms.

AIR AND EXERCISE.—In fine weather, the child should be taken out at least twice a day, care being taken to protect the head from the sun.

SUCKLING.—Nature provides breast milk as the proper food for infants, and suckling is by far the best way of feeding a child.

Provided the mother, or wet nurse, has plenty of milk and is in good health, the child requires, and should have no other food but the breast milk, until about the sixth month. The milk for the first few days acts as a laxative, and no other aperient is necessary. Should the formation of the milk be delayed, a little cow's milk, diluted with thrice the quantity of warm water and slightly sweetened, may be given until the mother is ready to nurse.

The child for the first six weeks should be put to the breast at regular intervals of two hours during the day; during the night it requires to be fed less often. As the child gets older, it does not require to be fed so frequently.

A child soon learns regular habits as to feeding. It is a great mistake, and bad both for the mother and child, to give the breast whenever the child cries, or to let it be always sucking, particularly at night. This is a common cause of wind, colic, and indigestion.

HOW A NURSING MOTHER, OR WET NURSE, SHOULD BE FED.—A nursing woman ought to live generously and well. She may take a little porter or ale in moderation with her meals. It is a common mistake for wet nurses to live too well, and this often causes deranged digestion in the child.

Should the nursing woman suffer from dizziness, dimness of sight, much palpitation and shortness of breath, or frequent night sweats, it is a sign that suckling disagrees with her, and that she should cease to nurse.

MIXED FEEDING WHEN THE MOTHER HAS NOT ENOUGH OF MILK. — When the mother has not enough milk to nourish her child, other food may be given, especially during the night. This should consist at first of the best milk, with two-thirds of warm water added.

The plan of combining breast-feeding with bottle-feeding is better than bringing up the child by hand alone.

WEANING.—The child should not be weaned suddenly but by degrees; and, as a rule, it should not be allowed to have the breast after the ninth month. After the child has cut its front teeth, it should have one or two meals a day of some light food, such as bread and milk or nursery biscuits, and these may be gradually increased until the child is weaned.

When the child is about from seven to ten months old, according to its strength, it may have one meal a day of broth or beef-tea, with crumbs of bread soaked in it, or it may have the yolk of an egg lightly boiled.

When it is about a year and a half old, it may have one meal a day of finely-minced meat; but even then, milk should form a large proportion of its diet.

Meat, potatoes, and food such as grown-up people eat, are often given to young infants. This kind of food, and all stimulants are entirely unsuitable, and are common causes of diarrhœa and other troubles.

HAND-FEEDING.—Milk, and milk only, should be used for this purpose. Cow's milk is generally used, but ass' or goat's milk is good. Two thirds pure and fresh milk, with one third the quantity of hot water added to it, the whole being slightly sweetened, should be used at first. A teaspoonful of lime-water may often with great advantage be added to each wine-glassful of the mixed milk and water, if there is flatulence or slight diarrhœa.

The milk should be given from a feeding bottle, which should be emptied and rinsed out after each meal, and the tube and cork and nipple kept in water when not in use. Perfect cleanliness is most important, otherwise the milk may turn sour, and disagree with the child.

The child should be fed regularly just as if it were suckled, and it is a bad habit to give it the bottle merely to keep it quiet. The milk diet only should, as a rule, be given until the child begins to cut its teeth, when other food may be gradually commenced as recommended under the head of "Suckling." Most of the mortality from hand-feeding arises from the use of arrowroot, corn-flour, and other unsuitable kinds of food, given during the earlier months of infancy. They consist almost entirely of starch, and should not be used as substitutes for milk.

CHILDHOOD.

The child having been brought through the period of infancy, and the foundation being laid for a sound physical constitution, the next important subject for attention is its moral and intellectual training. The responsibility of "training up a child in the way it should go" rests almost entirely upon the mother. In India, the father is generally so much occupied with his official duties, that he has not the requisite time, even if he had the inclination, to attend to the moral culture of his child. With the mother it is otherwise; she has ample time at command, but in too many instances, the ever ready plea of the enervating effects of a tropical climate, is put forward as an excuse for her neglect or indifference; or she postpones this all-important duty "till a more convenient season;" or she believes her child too young, to understand good precepts; thinking that little or no harm can come to it, during the first few years of its life, and that it is best not to interfere with its natural proclivities. Or she may delude herself with the idea that if her child has contracted any bad habits or tendencies, they will be thoroughly rubbed out by mingling with other European children when sent "home." This is a serious mistake.

Nothing can ever compensate for the want of good moral and intellectual training during the earliest years of life. "A child is governed by the well directed affection and kindness of its parents or guardians, and to wait for the development of its understanding, before we commence its moral training, is to wait till years of unregulated indulgence shall have cultivated and strengthened its more selfish and imperious appetites and passions,—is to wait in short till the mind shall have had time to grow and to ripen and shed its seed, before attempting to extirpate it from the soil which it has usurped."

Surrounded by native servants, and in too many instances,

almost entirely left to their mercy and control, the European child, unless carefully watched by the parents, cannot fail to be contaminated to a serious extent.

Few Hindoo servants will be found to exercise the same power and authority over a young child, as the European nurse. They allow the children to have their way in almost everything; they yield to their whims and fancies, however absurd and wrong they may be; and in the course of time the child becomes self-willed and, accustomed to the servant, ends by attempting the same thing with his parents.

The child becomes strongly attached to these servants, simply because every wish is conceded by them; indeed it is no uncommon thing to find children in India, preferring the society of their native servants to that of their parents. Here lies a danger which must be guarded against by every possible means.

The characteristic feature of child-life, is its imitative propensity. It will do what it is in the constant habit of seeing others do, it will repeat the same language, use the same expressions, and even imitate the same gestures, no matter how gross or improper the one or the other may be, that it is always hearing or seeing. The result of this tendency may be imagined, in cases, where the child's intimate associates during the greater part of the day are native servants only. Few Europeans have any idea of the ordinary habits and customs, or of the nature of the language, commonly used, in their intercourse with each other, by that class of Hindoos from which native servants are taken. Their private morals and their conversation generally, are of a very different character from those of European nurses. They are notoriously untruthful and deceitful, and the European child, if left entirely under their charge, can hardly fail to be so imbued with the same characteristics, that in course of time, his perception of the difference between right and wrong is seriously impaired, if not destroyed.

Exceptions there no doubt are to this character of servants, but they are so rare, that even with an apparently unquestionable testimonial from a former employer, the parent must not permit herself to be influenced entirely by it. She must judge for herself; she must keep a jealous and ever-watchful eye over her child, spending much of her time in intimate association with it, and taking every opportunity, by example and by precept, to instil into its young mind those high moral principles, which will enable it to resist the insidious and evil examples and teachings of the native servants. When parents are habitually on their guard, evil influences can be counteracted, and bad habits discovered, before it has become too late to eradicate them; the child may grow up untarnished, and free from those defects and vices which, in some schools in England, are considered necessarily characteristic of Anglo-Indian children.

The hygienic management of children is alluded to in another part of this work. Let me here briefly summarise what is essential to the maintenance of their health.

CLOTHING.—Should be light and loose; thin gauze, flannel, or merino banians, should be worn next the skin during the day, and the head protected from the sun's rays by a puggree over the bonnet or hat. Linen or cotton clothing next the body must not be used. During the night the best dress for children is a simple "overall" made of thin light flannel, to ensure its being kept over the body, to protect the skin from the morning chills, and to absorb perspiration. It is always advisable for children to sleep under the punkah during the hotter months.

EXERCISE.—Children should be sent out about sunrise, always giving them if possible a cup of warm milk first; they can have then one hour's exercise, running about before breakfast, or riding on ponies. Let them have as much out-of-door exercise as possible, during the morning and in the afternoon, taking care to protect them from exposure to the sun's rays.

SLEEP.—Up till three years of age, one or two hours' sleep should be indulged in, at least once during the day.

FOOD.—This should be simple, nutritious, and easily digestible. Variety of dishes at any one meal, should be avoided, and as a rule no wine, or beer, or other alcoholic beverage, need be given, unless under medical advice. At nine o'clock the breakfast should consist chiefly of milk and bread. At one p.m., dinner for those upwards of one year old, should chiefly consist of a little roast or boiled mutton, beef, or chicken, with potatoes or bread; some vegetables, as cauliflower or turnip, may also be used, followed by a light milk pudding or custard. For those who are younger, broth of either chicken, beef, or mutton (deprived of fat), and bread. Children are generally particularly fond of curries, which ought never to be made for them either too rich, or too highly seasoned, or too hot. At six or seven p.m., the child should have its last meal, consisting of the same articles as the breakfast. All fruits that are ripe and in good condition may be given in moderation. The plantain is about the safest of all fruits for children, and may be taken once or twice daily.

AGE FOR SENDING CHILDREN TO EUROPE.

As each hot season comes round, the important question of sending their children to England, is sure to present itself to the serious consideration of married Anglo-Indians. Painful as the step is, its expediency is never questioned by those whose means can afford it.

Uninterrupted residence of European children in a tropical climate, from birth upwards, is inimical to health, and antagonistic to the development of a sound, robust constitution. The child commonly grows up delicate, pale and flabby, comparatively feeble in mind and body; often timid and unstable, and but seldom able to compete on equal terms, either physically or mentally, with those who have been brought up in England, or even with the educated native. There are three obvious causes for this. 1st, The unquestionably enervating, and generally deteriorating effect of constant exposure to a high temperature. 2nd, The unavoidable association with native servants, or with those who have been brought up in constant intercourse with them. 3rd, The want of that training and that system of education, in its widest sense, which an English school or college can give, especially at the age when boys begin to think of their future career, and have a clear perception of the necessity of hard work in order to ensure success.

So far as the mere question of climate is concerned, European children might often with perfect safety be kept in India till the age of ten or twelve years; and as for elementary education, that is, mere book learning, they might remain in India till the same age, without any disadvantage. But mere book learning does not constitute the only, nor even the most important part of the education of a young child. It is that which he (or she) is always seeing and hearing—whatever impresses its susceptible mind and heart, what is picked up in fact on all sides from every one associated with it, that really makes or mars it for the future. "Education, meaning thereby the formation of character, and not merely intellectual instruction, necessarily commences with the very dawn of life. If this is delayed till the age of six or seven, nature will not remain idle till we are ready to begin. An unsystematic, irrational, and often hurtful education, namely, that arising out of the influences and circumstances by which every child is surrounded, and which never cease to act for good or for evil, for a single hour of its life, will have taken the precedence, and raised up obstacles which may then render our best efforts fruitless, for it is not in school alone that a child can be educated."* It is but a truism to say, that the disposition and character of the child, are to a large extent, influenced by the disposition and character, of those who are almost always in more or less close association with it.

Parents are anxious to send their children to Europe at an early age, not merely nor even primarily for the sake of a scholastic education, nor even to prevent their constitutions being impaired by the climate; but really, to remove them from the evil influences, inseparable from intimate association with native servants, and to place them at the most susceptible period of their lives, among those home influences, which are unattainable in what we call home in India. If a mother could be constantly with her children, and have them always under her immediate personal care, there would seldom be any necessity for her to send them "home" before the age mentioned. But it is utterly impossible to prevent children from mingling and associating, more or less intimately, with their native servants. Children long for variety in their associates, and finding in their servants, willing companions and ready playmates, they are much thrown together, and cannot fail to be influenced by all that they hear and see.

The best age, then, to remove children from India is between seven and eight years, that is, before the evil influences of native servants have had time to produce an ineradicable impression on the young mind, and before the climate has produced any injurious effect on its constitution.

But it is not all Europeans, who can afford to send their children "home," while there are many who, possessing means enough to do so, cannot make up their minds to part with them at all. The children of many such parents, under good management and care, do grow up with a fair measure of health and strength, and

---

* Combe.

seem to possess nearly all the requisites for worldly advancement and success. But they sooner or later find out that there is a certain something, however indefinable it may be, the want of which places them at a disadvantage in the battle of life.

The hill stations offer a convenient compromise or substitute for the change to Europe. They possess every climatic advantage that can be wished, and experience has proved beyond all doubt, that children who have passed the age of teething, do thrive remarkably well, and grow up as robust and as healthy (physically) as they would in England. Did these hill stations possess good schools, they would no doubt be taken advantage of, much more generally than they now are, if for no other reason than for the facilities they afford to parents, of frequently meeting their children, and thus avoiding that painful and distressing estrangement, so commonly experienced, when the latter are sent to England at an early age, and separated for many years from their parents.

On those hill stations, where good schools are established,*

* "The late Ootacamund Grammar School offered the nearest approach to what is wanted ; but as the Principal could not fill it with Europeans, he had to take boys who were not Europeans, and the charges mounted up one way and another until they equalled, or passed the sum that would be necessary for the education of a boy at home. The result was that the European element dwindled down, and parents made use of the school as a mere rest-house for their boys until they themselves could take them home. A school conducted by a European Principal, assisted by European assistants, and open to European boys only, of a certain class of society, would, we have no doubt, induce many an Anglo-Indian to defer his return home a year or two ; but would such a school pay? At the most the Principal could hardly calculate on having the charge of boys after they had passed their twelfth year ; and he could not be sure of having a succession of boys between eight and twelve, sufficient to keep the school open for several years together. And if his charges, as they could hardly fail to do, approximated very closely to the charges customary at the same age in England, the smallest thing would induce parents to send their boys home, in preference to accepting the compromise. The opening of the Suez Canal, by reducing the cost of a journey home, has placed another serious obstacle in the way of such a school as we have described."—*Madras Mail.*

and the discipline and general management are such as to prevent intimate association with native servants, no better plan could be adopted, than that of keeping children there till the age of fourteen or fifteen years. It is then, however, that the parent becomes fully alive to the necessity and importance of sending them to England. Girls are not so likely to acquire on the hills those accomplishments, nor that polish, to say nothing of that prestige, which the tuition, discipline, general training, and associations of a really good English school can give. Boys again, if destined for the civil, military, or medical service, or indeed for almost any professional career, have at present no alternative, but to proceed to England, for the obvious reason, that it is there only, that they can undergo the required competitive, or other examination; and as nearly all such examinations involve more or less special instruction, the boy is better able to obtain it at recognised schools or colleges in England, than on the hills.

Children, during the period of dentition, do not thrive on the hills so well as afterwards. They are then specially liable to attacks of diarrhœa and dysentery of a most obstinate character, often resisting all treatment, and not unfrequently ending fatally, unless removed in time to the plains.

AILMENTS OF CHILDREN.

The pernicious habit, to which too many are addicted, of constantly drugging their children, under the mistaken idea, that for every symptom, however trifling it may be, a medicine must be given, cannot be too strongly condemned; and without hesitation it may be asserted, that the mother or nurse who indulges in it, is utterly unfit for the duties imposed upon her. The human body, and especially that of a child, has within itself a wonderful power to recover from most of the slighter aberrations from health; and the injudicious administration of drugs, not only tends to interfere with this healing virtue of nature, or *vis medicatrix naturæ* as it is called, but also deranges the system, keeps the child ill, and aggravates the original ailment. A well known writer on the management of children has emphatically expressed his conviction that "a child can encounter few greater dangers, than that of being subjected to the rigorous discipline of a medicine-giving mother or nurse, and whenever a mother of a family is observed to be ready with the use of calomel, cordials, anodynes, and other noxious drugs, the chances are, that one-half of her children will be found to have passed to a better world."

In another part of this work, the symptoms and treatment of some of the more serious diseases that affect children are fully given. I will now give brief instructions regarding the management of some of the more common ailments of infants. But I would again repeat the advice given in the preface, that parents should never rely upon their own judgment, when medical aid is procurable. It is only when it cannot be had at all, or when not available before much valuable time is lost, that the treatment suggested should be adopted.

Flatulence and Griping.—This is most commonly caused by improper food, or irregular feeding. The obvious treatment, in the first instance, is to ascertain where the fault lies, and to act accordingly. If no cause can be discovered in the diet, or if the symptoms continue after modifying it, give to an infant from one week or upwards :—

One to three drops of essence of aniseed in a teaspoonful of water.

Or a teaspoonful of dill or omum water.

Or,

Mix a teaspoonful of sal volatile in a wineglassful of water, and of this, give a teaspoonful for a dose, two or three times a day, if necessary.

A teaspoonful of lime-water to each wineglassful of milk, if the child is being fed by hand, will often prevent flatulence.

If the bowels are confined, give a simple purgative (see Constipation) in addition to the above. Relief may also be given, by gentle friction with salad oil over the stomach, or by applying warm fomentations of hot flannel or bran, or even by warm bath. The carminative mixture recommended at pages 286 and 319 will be found convenient for such cases.

Constipation.—Some infants and young children are so habitually costive; that it is often most difficult to get the bowels to act without medicine. For an infant entirely fed at the breast, whose bowels are in this state, the safest drugs are castor oil and calcined magnesia, either alone or combined (in the proportion of a teaspoonful of the first to six to ten grains of the last). One to three drops of essence of aniseed, or a teaspoonful of dill water, may be added if there is flatulence or griping. The partial introduction into the bowel, of a soap suppository, is a simple, safe, and ready method of inducing the bowels to act. Take a piece of common bar soap, about two inches long, and pare it down at one end like a pastille or pencil point, smear it over with salad oil, and gently introduce about a quarter of its length into the bowel, allowing it to remain a few minutes there. The suppository will shortly afterwards be expelled, followed by a free action of the bowels. No other substance than soap should be thus used. Native servants, unless warned and watched, will use for the same purpose, tobacco leaves and other substances, which are certain to do harm. Gentle friction with castor oil round the navel, is often very beneficial. Gregory's Powder, and syrup of senna are also simple and safe purgatives, but the wiser course is to avoid drugs if possible. For those infants, who are not nursed entirely at the breast, a great deal may be done to avoid drugging them, by the judicious management of the food. Oatmeal, or Robinson's patent groats, alone or mixed with the corn-flour and milk, will often save the necessity of any purgative whatever.

Diarrhœa and Dysentery.—The treatment of these ailments has been already described at pages 255 and 265. In addition to the remedies there specified, I would recommend for those obstinate cases of diarrhœa, which seem to resist all treatment, the use of raw meat, minced very fine, given in doses of one teaspoonful two or three times a day, and if the child is very young, the expressed juice of the raw meat may be given instead. For those cases of diarrhœa, occurring in malarious districts, from half to one grain of quinine, will be found most beneficial. There are others again, where the frequency and urgency of the diarrhœa, irritability of stomach, and profuse perspiration threaten to overwhelm the little sufferer in a very short time. All treatment appears to do good at first, but fails afterwards, and the diarrhœa returns with unabated force. In such cases the treatment recommended by Dr. Thomas Chambers is most valuable, namely, by bismuth. The following is the best formula. Take of bismuth half a dram, syrup of poppies one dram, and water two ounces. Mix, and give one teaspoonful every three or four hours, for a child from two to six months old, and double the dose for twelve months.

The Swiss milk is often most valuable in troublesome infantile diarrhœa, and may safely be substituted *for a time* for the cow's milk. It now and then happens that even when every care is taken in preparing the infant's food, the cow's milk, which generally agreed with the child, will all of a sudden act upon it, as if it contained a violent purgative. It is in these cases that the Swiss milk should be tried, and it will generally be found to be retained when all other food was at once rejected.

But it must always be remembered, that in even the most obstinate cases of diarrhœa a judicious modification or a complete change of the ordinary food of the child, will prove more effectual than any amount of drugging. The wet nurse, if one is employed, may have to be substituted for another one, or even for the milk of the ass or the goat.

VACCINATION.

This ought to be done when the infant is between two and three months old, provided it is in good health and free from any eruption on its body. There is seldom any difficulty in having this operation performed, as native vaccinators are appointed by Government all over India; but as these men seldom exercise sufficient care in selecting a healthy child, from which to take the vaccine matter, it is necessary, in the absence of the doctor, that the parent should make the required investigation. The child brought, should have all the appearance of health, and be perfectly free from any eruption. Inquiries into the family history, as far as possible, should be made with especial reference to the present and past state of health of the parents and their other children; and unless perfectly satisfied on all these points, the vaccination had better be delayed till a more healthy child can be produced.

The only precaution to be observed, after the infant has been vaccinated, is to take care that the arm is not rubbed. The usual morning and evening bath may be continued, and the ordinary food and out of door exercise may remain undisturbed. There is no need to give any medicine whatever, even although the infant becomes feverish and restless, as it usually does on the eighth or ninth day; but if the bowels are then constipated, a teaspoonful of castor oil or a little calcined magnesia may be given. If the arm is much inflamed, as it sometimes is, after the seventh day of vaccination, apply a little salad oil or cold cream over the pustules, or a light bread and water poultice.

INDEX TO MEDICAL GUIDE.

FINIS.